TO

Albert S. Cook

WITH AFFECTION AND GRATITUDE

PREFACE.

THE present edition grew out of a doctoral thesis presented by me to the Philosophical Faculty of Yale University in June, 1895.

To the æsthetic student of literature, *The Seege of Troye* is of little interest, as its pretensions to intrinsic literary value are of the smallest; but its relation to the development of the Troy Cycle in mediæval literature, and particularly to the *Roman de Troie* of Benoît de Sainte-More, renders it of very considerable interest to the student of literary history. The linguistic scholar, also, will find in it suggestions of interesting problems relative to the Middle English dialects of the fourteenth century.

It should be borne in mind from the outset that this edition does not pretend to discuss the original poem, of which no copy is extant. There exist three manuscript poems on the same theme, evidently derived from a common ultimate source, and upon one of these, Ms. Harl. 525 of the British Museum, the discussion is based. The text is printed from an excellent facsimile of this manuscript. A diplomatic recension by Dr. A. Zietsch was published in *Herrig's Archiv* for 1884, but a careful comparison of it with the facsimile brought to light so many inaccuracies, that a new recension seemed necessary.

Nevertheless, to Dr. Zietsch, and to three other German scholars whose work will be mentioned in another place, I am indebted for the results upon which my own investigations are founded.   My contribution to the subject consists in a method of arranging their facts, and in an occasional new inference from them, rather than in the discovery of new data.

The critical apparatus does not pretend to be exhaustive in detail.   The discussion of Phonology, Inflection, and Prosody is chiefly valuable as an attempt at a logical presentation of the chief phenomena.   The Literary Notes are limited to considerations suggested by the Introduction; for example, the classical sources of the episodes, the relative accuracy of the L. I. and Harl. versions, the superiority in structure and picturesqueness of the latter to the former; whenever possible, I have tried to elucidate obscure Harl. readings by citations from the L. I. version; for the sake of fairness, I have also cited the most important passages of the L. I. version that tell against my conclusions.   The scholar will perhaps perceive many gaps and errors in the Bibliography, yet I trust it may be found complete enough to serve at least as a nucleus of the complete bibliography of the subject, which is so much needed.   The discussion of Sources will be found reasonably exhaustive, and, I trust, cogent.   The Glossary is a complete index to all important words, and registers the unusual forms of all unimportant ones.

In conclusion, I take pleasure in expressing my gratitude to Professor Albert S. Cook of Yale University, without whose encouragement this edition would hardly have been undertaken, and to whose wise suggestion it owes whatever merit it may possess.

KENYON COLLEGE, GAMBIER, OHIO,
March 15, 1899.

CONTENTS.

INTRODUCTION.

THE TROY CYCLE IN MEDIÆVAL LITERATURE.

THE literature of mediæval Europe is rich in reminiscences of the story of Troy. From the seventh to the sixteenth century, it was the subject of history, of poetical and prose romance, and of the drama. It is associated with the names of Benoît de Sainte-More, Boccaccio, Chaucer, Lydgate, and Shakespeare. It is therefore of the utmost interest to the student of literary history.

Its immense popularity, however, was not due solely to its literary interest. The new nations of Europe, desiring a national past as a basis for patriotism, sought a bond of connection with ancient Rome and Greece, and found it in the story of Troy. To the famous siege was traced the origin of the principal peoples of Europe, — the French, the Germans, the Britons, the Scandinavians, the Turks.

In the middle of the seventh century, Fredegarius Scholasticus, writing of the origin of the Franks, declares (*Chronicarum quæ dicuntur Fredegarii Scholastici*, Liber II, 4 *a*–6) that Priam was their first king ; that one part of them settled in Macedonia, where they founded the kingdom of Philip and Alexander; another part, under the leadership of their King Francio, who gave them their name, established themselves, after many wanderings through Asia and Europe, between the Rhine, the Danube, and the sea; while a third, halting on the bank of the Danube, between the ocean and Thrace, elected a king named Torquotus, from whom they were called Turks. This legend was long accepted, and forms a part of many mediæval chronicles and histories of France. As M. Joly points out (*Benoît de Sainte-More et le Roman de Troie*, IIe Partie, 1871, p. 615), the religious supremacy of Rome in the Middle Ages was an additional reason for believing and insisting upon this relationship, for it need hardly be said that Rome, too, through Æneas, claimed descent from Troy.

Before 1158, we find a German chronicler, Otto von Freysingen, claiming the same origin for his nation. During the Middle Ages, an attempt was also made to connect the legend with Scandinavian antiquities by identifying Odin with Priam, and Asgard, the seat of the gods, with Troy. On the authority of Dudo de Saint Quentin, who wrote in 1015, the Normans were descended from Antenor, and on their arrival in Britain in 1066 they found a people who claimed descent from Brutus, the grandson of Æneas, from whom they were named Britons. The earliest authority for this statement is the *Historia Britonum* ascribed to Nennius, of whom nothing is certainly known. The legend was much embellished by Geoffrey of Monmouth, who in 1135 wrote the *Historia Regum Britanniæ*. From this work, it may be said in passing, the legendary history of the Britons may be traced in unbroken descent through Wace, Crestien de Troyes, Malory, Spenser, and many others, to Tennyson.

In spite of the popularity of the Troy Legend, which I have merely indicated, the *Iliad* of Homer in the Middle Ages was practically unknown. The mediæval poets gained their knowledge of the events and heroes of the siege of Troy from Latin sources, — from Virgil, Ovid, Statius, among classical writers, and from Pindarus Thebanus, Dictys Cretensis, and Dares Phrygius, among the writers of the Latin decadence. Before proceeding, therefore, to an account of the mediæval poets of Troy, I shall briefly characterize those ' turbid sources,' to quote Ten Brink, from which the legend flowed down to mediæval times.

PINDARUS THEBANUS. — The *Epitome Iliados Homericæ*, a Latin poem of 1100 hexameter lines, was very popular in the Middle Ages. It is mentioned often in works of the period, and we are told that it was interpreted in the schools. It is ascribed by Lachmann (*Monatsbericht der Berliner Akademie*, January, 1841) and by Müller (*Über den Auszug aus der 'Ilias' des sogenannten Pindarus Thebanus*, p. 15) to the first century of our era. An editor of the sixteenth century informs us that Pindar reduced the *Iliad* to these modest proportions to render it more accessible to his son. The poem is of an acceptable Latin style ; the verse, correct and flowing. The author has followed the events of the *Iliad* so far as his narrow limits permitted ; but he has little sense of proportion, elaborating or abridging a recital arbitrarily, with no reference to its relative importance. The gods have lost their prominence in the narrative, their presence and activity being merely indicated. At times the author seems to translate from memory. He reproduces the error, become traditional since Virgil, that Achilles dragged the body of Hector thrice around the walls of Troy. In general he may be said to owe much more to Ovid and Virgil than to Homer. It is this *Iliad* that the Middle Ages knew.

DICTYS CRETENSIS. — The *Ephemeris Belli Trojani* professes to have been written by a participant in the siege. The prologue informs us that he was a Cretan of Gnossus, a companion of Idomeneus and Merion (cf. Homer, *Iliad*, II, 645–652), at whose request he wrote in the Phenician language the 'annals of the Trojan War.' We learn also from the prefatory letter and the prologue that this work of Dictys, enclosed in a tin chest, was discovered, during the thirteenth year of the reign of Nero, in the historian's tomb, which had been shattered by an earthquake. It was carried to the emperor, who ordered it transcribed in Greek characters and deposited in a library. It was afterwards translated into Latin by Lucius Septimius, who, in his prefatory letter, declares that he has followed closely the events of the first five books, but has condensed the last four into one.

During the Middle Ages, the history was considered authoritative, and the author's account of himself implicitly believed. The Greeks of the Lower Empire, from the seventh to the twelfth centuries, scholiasts, rhetoricians, grammarians, and historians, made constant use of him. Joannes Malalas, a Syrian monk, who flourished not later than the sixth century of our era (Krumbacher, *Geschichteder Byzantinischen Litteratur*, p. 112),[1] in his *Chronographia*, narrated with the utmost confidence the discovery of the *Ephemeris*.

The first mention of Dictys in literature is by Syrianus (fl. A.D. 380–450) : Ἡ γοῦν κατὰ Κάδμον καὶ Δαναὸν γραμματικὴ ἐπί τε τῶν Τρωικῶν ἠσκεῖτο, ὡς Δίκτυς ἐν ταῖς Ἐφημερίσι φησίν (quoted by Körting, *Dictys und Dares*, p. 12).

M. Joly (*op. cit.*, p. 677) maintains that the extant Latin version is the original one, and, on grounds of style and moral sentiment, assigns it to the close of the fourth century. His view of the independence of the Latin version is, however, no longer tenable, and it is now conceded that our version of the *Ephemeris* is probably a fourth-century translation from the Greek. The original was doubtless composed in the second century by a Greek who was perhaps Christian, and who certainly knew the works of the cyclic and tragic poets (cf. *Histoire de la Langue et de la Littérature Française, publiée sous la direction de L. Petit De Julleville*, I, p. 210). It is probable, too, that the prefatory letter of Septimius is correct in saying that the Latin version is an abridgment. Malalas and Tzetzes, the latter of whom flourished in the twelfth century, both refer to passages in the *Ephemeris* that are not contained in our version. The Greek original possibly contained a series of portraits similar to those of Dares.

DARES PHRYGIUS. — The Middle Ages were not entirely dependent upon a history of the Trojan War

[1] He is assigned to various periods, ranging from the sixth to the ninth century.

from the Greek point of view. In the *De Excidio
Troiæ* of Dares, they had the Trojan side presented
by a Phrygian priest, who was an eye-witness of the
events he described. A more critical age would have
suspected an imposture at once in such historical good-
fortune, but the authority of Dares in the Middle Ages
was no less firm and abiding than that of Dictys.

The name of Dares occurs in the *Iliad*, V, 9, 10 :

Ἦν δέ τις ἐν Τρώεσσι Δάρης ἀφνειὸς ἀμύμων, ἱρεὺς Ἡφαίστοιο·

'Now there was amid the Trojans one Dares, rich and noble,
priest of Hephaistos.'

A tradition was preserved in Greece that a Phrygian,
named Dares, had written a narrative of the siege of
Troy anterior to Homer, and Ælian (A.D. 170) speaks
of the 'Phrygian Iliad' of Dares (*Varia Historia*, XI,
2). The Latin recension that we possess purports to
be a translation from the Greek by Cornelius Nepos.
The prologue contains the following oft-quoted passage : 'Optimum ergo duxi ita ut fuit vere et simpli-
citer perscripta, sic eam ad verbum in latinitatem
transvertere, ut legentes cognoscere possent, quomodo
res gestæ essent: utrum verum magis esse existiment,
quod Dares Phrygius memoriæ commendavit, qui per id
ipsum tempus vixit et militavit, cum Græci Troianos
obpugnarent, anne Homero credendum, qui post mul-
tos annos natus est, quam bellum hoc gestum est. De
qua re Athenis iudicium fuit, cum pro insano habere-
tur, quod deos cum hominibus belligerasse scripserit.'

As the history of the Cretan Dictys was quoted and
copied by the Greeks of the Lower Empire, so was the
work of the Trojan Dares most acceptable to those

nations of the West that claimed descent from Troy. In France, the *De Excidio Troiæ* was considered a monument of national history. Manuscript copies of the work are almost numberless.

There can be little doubt, after the statement of Ælian, that there once existed a Greek or Phrygian history of the Trojan War, not contemporary with the events, but dating from an epoch when the work of the cyclic and tragic poets still existed intact. It is well known that these poets had popularized traditions quite different from those of the Homeric poems, and had filled up *lacunæ* in the Trojan legend.[1] This Greek Dares must have been translated into Latin about the first century of our era, and thus have given rise to the abridgment that we possess. Our version was probably made at the end of the sixth century, as it is cited by Isidore of Seville (570–640). Manuscripts are extant that belong to the ninth century.

The history is the merest bald outline of events, relieved only by the portraits of the heroes and heroines (Chapters XII and XIII). Ten Brink describes it (*History of English Literature*, Eng. trans., I, p. 168) as 'a wretched, barren, often self-contradictory piece of work, written in the worst of Latin.'

We have now to consider the most important of mediæval Troy Romances.

BENOÎT DE SAINTE-MORE. — The *Roman de Troie* of Benoît de Sainte-More offers, perhaps, the best point of departure for an investigation of the Troy Cycle in

---

[1] See De Julleville, *op. cit.*, I, p. 205. For an interesting account of the later accretions to the Troy Myth, see Lawton, *Art and Humanity in Homer*, Chap. 7.

the Middle Ages. His version was almost the first to give it a complete literary treatment, and from it we may 'look before and after,' not only upon the historical and literary tendencies which produced it, but also upon its results in the literature of all Europe.

In spite of its intrinsic value and historical significance, the work remained for many years obscured by the translation of an unscrupulous Italian, Guido delle Colonne, whose *Historia Destructionis Troiæ* professed to be a direct translation of Dares. From this imposture there resulted an immense injustice to Benoît, who was believed to be a translator of Guido. It was not until 1869 that Dr. Hermann Dunger (*Die Sage vom trojanischen Kriege in den Bearbeitungen des Mittelalters und ihren antiken Quellen*) and M. Joly (*op. cit.*) restored to Benoît his proper fame.[1]

The conclusions of Dunger and Joly with regard to Benoît's source, however, are no longer certain. The possibility that a more extended Dares than the one we possess once existed is now conceded, and it is therefore not necessary to hold with Dunger and Joly that Benoît's divergences from Dares are the fruit of his own invention. M. Léopold Constans, in De Julleville's *Histoire de la Langue et de la Littérature Française*, Paris, 1896, champions the cause of the extended Dares, ably espoused by Dr. Körting in his *Dictys und Dares*, Halle, 1874.

---

[1] As early as 1858, MM. Moland and D'Héricault (*Nouvelles Françoises du XIVe Siècle*, Introd., p. lxxx) spoke of Guido's *Historia* as 'une amplification de l'ouvrage de Darès, amplification non méprisable, mais aux mérites de laquelle Benoît de Saint-Maur n'as pas peu contribué.'

According to the investigations of Greif (*Die Mittelalterlichen Bearbeitungen der Trojanersage*, Marburg, 1886, p. 55), the sources of Benoît's *Roman* were, besides Dares,— Dictys, Ovid, Æthicus (*Cosmographia*, fourth century A.D.), and possibly Servius and Hyginus. The account of the Amazons was derived from a version of the Alexander Saga. All these materials were blended and transformed by the imagination of the poet. Little dependence can be placed upon his references to his sources; he felt no obligation to be accurate, for he was writing not the history but the romance of Troy.

The poem has been subjected to many recensions, manuscript copies abound, and translations have appeared in Latin, Greek, English, German, Dutch, Italian, and Spanish. The recension edited by M. Joly contains 30,108 lines. He considers the date of the poem to be about 1184, while M. Constans assigns it to 1160–1165. Benoît is almost certainly not the author of the *Roman de Thèbes* and *l'Eneas*, which have been attributed to him, and it is at least doubtful whether he can claim the authorship of the *Chronique des Ducs de Normandie*.

The *Roman de Troie* is of special importance in English literary history, as it is the ultimate extant source of the episode of Troilus and Cressida. The following lines of Joly's edition are devoted to it: 12931–12986, 13235–13830, 14211–14307, 14927–15112, 20057–20110, 20194–20330. The plot was later amplified by the addition of the *rôle* of Pandarus, and the character of the heroine underwent considerable modification, but the outline of the action was essentially complete when it left Benoît's hands.

GUIDO DELLE COLONNE.—The *Historia Destructionis Troiæ* was undertaken at the request of Mathæus de Porta, Archbishop of Salerno, and published in 1287. The author was a native of Messina, Sicily. He is known as one of the founders of Sicilian poetry. As I have already indicated, his work is a Latin prose translation of the *Roman de Troie*. According to Greif (pp. 59–62) and Dunger (p. 63), he made use also of the recension of Dares that we know. It is probable that he did not make use of Dictys.

The *Historia*, I believe, has not been published since 1494. There are in the British Museum seventeen manuscripts of the work, twelve in Latin, four in French, and one in South German (Ward, *Catalogue of Romances*, I, pp. 40–62). Besides these, versions exist in English, Italian, Spanish, German, Low Saxon, Dutch, Danish, Swedish, Icelandic, and Bohemian. In 1450, Jacques Milet dramatized it under the title, 'L'istoire de la destruction de Troye la Grant translatee de Latin en Francais mise par parsonnages et composee par Maistre Jacques Milet estudiant es loix en la ville d'Orleans' (mentioned by Sommer, *The Recuyell of the Historyes of Troye*, Introduction, p. xxxv).

The author was evidently a learned man. He knew Ovid and Virgil, and cited Ptolemæus Ægyptus, (Pseudo-) Dionysius the Areopagite, Justinian, Isidore, and Bede. He discussed, not always relevantly, questions of history, mythology, geography, natural science, and morality. He availed himself of the opportunity afforded him by the amours of Medea and Briseida to make considerable disgressions upon the perfidy of woman.

I quote the following interesting note from Warton's *History of English Poetry*, edited by W. C. Hazlitt, 1871, II, p. 128: 'Bale says, that Edward I, having met with our author in Sicily, in returning from Asia, invited him into England. This prince was interested in the Trojan story. . . . Our historians relate that he wintered in Sicily in the year 1270. A writer quoted by Hearne, supposed to be John Stow the chronicler, says that "Guido de Columpna arriving in England at the commaundement of King Edward the Firste, made scholies and annotations upon Dictys Cretensis and Dares Phrigius. Besides these, he writ at large the Battayle of Troye." Among his works is recited *Historia de Regibus Rebusque Angliæ*. It is quoted by many writers under the title of *Chronicum Britannorum*.' This tradition of a visit to England is, however, quite unsupported (cf. *Biographie Générale*, under Guido).

Among the most important of the versions of Guido mentioned above is the third book of the *Recueil des Hystoires Troyennes*, written by Raoul Lefèvre in 1464, at the command of Philip the Good, of Burgundy. 'It was about the same time (1468),' says Greif (p. 66), 'that the Order of the Golden Fleece was founded in Burgundy, in memory of the deeds of Jason.' In 1471 the *Recueil* was translated into English by William Caxton, and a little later, probably about 1474, was printed by him, thus becoming the first English printed book. It has been recently edited with great completeness by H. Oskar Sommer (*The Recuyell of the Historyes of Troye*, London, 1894). The introduction to this valuable edition (p. cxxxvii–clx) contains six citations of considerable length from Guido's *Historia*.

It was probably upon Benoît and Guido, both of whom were accessible in Italian translations, that Boccaccio based his *Filostrato*, which, it is well known, was the source of Chaucer's *Troilus and Cryseyde*. Shakespeare's *Troilus and Cressida* was probably inspired by Chaucer and by Caxton's *Recuyell*. He also knew Chapman's *Iliad* and possibly Lydgate's *Troy Book*. Brandes (*William Shakespeare*, II, p. 201) notices four plays based on the Troy legend between 1515 and 1599.

I have now to mention two Latin versions of the tale of Troy which slightly preceded Guido's *Historia*. They are perhaps a little aside from the main line of the discussion, but they deserve mention because of their intrinsic importance.

JOSEPHUS ISCANUS. — In 1187 or 1188, Joseph, a monk of Exeter (Isca Damnoniorum, from which his Latin name was derived), wrote his *De Bello Trojano*, a poem in six books and 3645 hexameter lines. According to Greif and Dunger, it is based upon Dares, Ovid, Statius, and possibly Virgil. Until 1620, when S. Dresemius assigned it to its actual author, it was believed to be the work of Cornelius Nepos. It is written in a somewhat elegant though artificial style. M. Joly says (*op. cit.*, IIe Partie, p. 860) he is 'plein de recherche, recherche dans les idées et dans les mots. Il aime les termes rares, singuliers. Il fait du bel esprit en latin; il aime les antithèses, les rapprochements forcés, et un romain de la bonne époque aurait peut-être parfois quelque peine à l'entendre.' He is believed to have written also an *Antiocheis*, and a poem entitled *De Institutione Cyri*.

ALBERTUS STADENSIS. — The *Troilus* of Albert, abbot

of the Monastery of Saint Mary of Stade, was published
in 1249. It is a Latin poem consisting of 5320 lines.
It is not, as its name might imply, the narrative of the
loves of *Troilus* and *Briseida*, but a treatment of the
whole Trojan story. The author says of the title,

> Troilus est Troilus Trojano principe natus,
> Et liber est Troilus ob Troica bella vocatus.

Of all the poets who have drawn from Dares, says Greif,
Albertus Stadensis is the most faithful to his original.
He has also made use of Pindarus Thebanus, Virgil,
Ovid, and Orosius.

THE GEST HYSTORIALE OF THE DESTRUCTION OF
TROY. — This poem, consisting of 14,044 alliterative
lines, is considered by Mr. Panton, one of its editors
for the Early English Text Society, as, in all probability, the very earliest version of Benoît and Guido
in our language. It belongs to the second half of the
fourteenth century. The dialect of the original poem
was almost certainly Northern or Scottish, though the
unique manuscript in which it has come down to us
(Hunterian Museum, University of Glasgow) was
written by a West Midland scribe. The authorship of
the poem was ascribed by Mr. Panton and his colleague,
Mr. Donaldson, to the poet Huchowne, author of the
Morte Arthure, the *Pystyl of Sweet Susane*, and *Sir
Gawane and the Green Knight*. This question, however, is not fully decided. The poem is pronounced by
Wilhelm Bock (*Zur Destruction of Troy*, Halle, 1883,
p. 6) to be a faithful translation of Guido's *Historia*.
M. Joly says (*op. cit.*, IIe Partie, p. 896): ' La traduc-
tion est des plus exactes ; on y retrouve la plupart des

embellissements que l'érudition de l'écrivain latin avait cru devoir joindre à l'œuvre de notre trouvère.'

Until its publication by the Early English Text Society, 1869–74, the poem was believed to be a translation of the *De Bello Trojano* of Joseph of Exeter. This misconception rested upon the following entry in the Catalogue of the Hunterian Museum (quoted by Mr. Panton): 'A Stately Poem called the *Destruction of Troy*, wrote by Joseph of Exeter, who lived in the reign of King Henry the Second, from 1154 to 1189.'

BARBOUR. — There was another important Scottish version of Guido's *Historia*, of which, however, but two fragments have come down to us. They were used to supply lacunæ in two copies of Lydgate's *Troy Book*, one in the Library of Cambridge University, the other in the Bodleian Library at Oxford. Together they consist of 3715 lines. By the scribe of the Cambridge MS. of the *Troy Book*, the lines there inserted are attributed to Barbour, in the following rubrics:

> Her endis the monk ande begynnis barbour,

and

> Her endis barbour and begynnis the monk.

Brandl says (*Paul's Grundriss der Germanischen Philologie*, II, 1, p. 665): 'Wenn die zwei Fragmente eines solchen (Trojanerkrieges), welche ein Kopist des XV. Jahrhunderts ihm zuschreibt, wirklich von ihm herrühren, hat er die lateinische Darstellung des Guido de Colonna treu und fliessend in kurze Reimpare übertragen, obwohl noch ohne poetischen Schwung.' As to the authorship, Körting says (*Grundriss der Geschichte der Englischen Literatur*, p. 117, note 1):

'Nach den Untersuchungen von Busse, Anglia IX
493, u. Köppel, E. St. X 373, ist dieser Barbour nicht
identisch mit dem Verf. des Bruce, sondern gehört dem
15. Jahrh. an.'

JOHN LYDGATE. — This poet, 'the most brilliant
disciple of Chaucer,' was born in Suffolk about 1371,
and lived as a friar in the Benedictine Abbey of Bury
St. Edmunds. He wrote his *Troy Book* probably between the years 1412 and 1420. It was completed
during the reign of Henry V, at whose instance it was
begun, and to whom the author presented it. An
elaborate manuscript of the poem in the Bodleian
Library at Oxford is probably the presentation copy.
It was printed for the first time in 1513, at the command of Henry VIII.

The poem, according to the author's own declaration,
is based upon Guido and a French original. The
French work is considered by M. Joly to have been
Benoît's *Roman*. 'Quant à Benoît,' he says (*op. cit.*, IIe
Partie, p. 895), 'on peut supposer que c'est de lui que
parle Lydgate lorsq'il nomme Darès, comme par
exemple dans la description du palais de Priam, que
Guido a écourtée et à laquelle Darès n'avait pas même
songé.'

The following passages (quoted by Ward, *Catalogue
of Romances*, I, pp. 76 and 78) refer to the poet's inspi-
ration and the source of his materials:

FOLIO 1 b.

And for to witen whom I wolde mene,
The eldest sone of the noble kyng,
Henri the Firthe, of knyȝthood welle and spryng,

In whom is schewed of what stok he grewe.
The rotys vertu thus can the frute renewe.
In euery part the parage is the same,
Lyche his fader of maneris and of name.
In sothefastnesse this no tale is,
Called Henry, ek the worthy Prynce of Walys,
To whom schal longe, by successioun,
For to gouerne Brutys Albyoun.
Whyche me comaunded the drery, pitus fate
Of hem of Troye, in Englysche to translate,
The sege also and the destruccioun,
Lyche as the Latyn maketh mencioun,
For to compyle and, after Guydo make,
So as I coude, and write it for his sake.

FOLIO 152, COL. 2.

I haue no more Latyn to translate,
After Dites, Dares, nor Guydo,
And me to adden any more ther to
Than myn auctours specefie and seyn,
The occupacioun sothly wer but veyn,
Lik a maner of presumpcioun.

The poem consists of 'five books, with a prologue and epilogue, and with a concluding address to Henry V in 13 seven-line stanzas, and an envoy in two eight-line stanzas; the whole amounting to upwards of 30,000 lines' (Ward, *Catalogue of Romances*, I, p. 75).

Of all the Troy Romances in English, Lydgate's is probably the most poetic. 'His feeling for nature,' says Ten Brink (*op. cit.*, II, p. 225), 'is often brilliantly expressed in charming descriptions and beautiful images. Psychological conditions and phenomena are sometimes vividly portrayed. He also shows a decided talent for graphic delineation in his elaborate descriptions of feasts, buildings, and the like, which gives his work a great archæological interest.'

In the Bodleian Library there is an unique manuscript (Laud 595) containing another metrical version of Guido's *Historia*, long ascribed to Lydgate. Of this version Warton says (*op. cit.*, III, pp. 93–95): 'It appears to me to be Lydgate's *Troy Book* divested of the octave-stanza and reduced into a measure which might more commodiously be sung to the harp. It is not likely that Lydgate is its author; that he should either thus transform his own composition, or write a new piece on the subject. . . . The language accords with Lydgate's age, and is of the reign of Henry VI; and to the same age I refer the handwriting, which is executed with remarkable elegance and beauty.' M. Joly, also, considers it anterior to the *Troy Book*, as its form is more archaic.

Sommer (p. xliv) refers to another version of Guido in the Bodleian Library, a prose adaptation contained in Rawlinson MS., misc., No. 82.

I shall now proceed to describe very briefly three Troy romances which have some importance in the discussion of the sources of *The Seege of Troye*.

KONRAD VON WÜRZBURG. — The poets of the Middle High German period, no less than those of the Middle English period, found in the story of Troy an attractive theme. Between 1184 and 1190, Heinrich von Veldeke wrote his *Eneit*, based upon the *Roman d'Eneas*. In the first years of the thirteenth century, Herbort von Fritslâr paraphrased the *Roman de Troie* under the title, *Liet von Troye*. The closing years of the same century witnessed the commencement

of the *Trojanischer Krieg* of Konrad von Würzburg.
The poem was begun in 1280 and left unfinished at the
poet's death in 1287. It was completed in quite a
different manner by an unknown writer who drew his
materials from Dictys. The whole work consists of
upwards of 50,000 lines, 40,000 of which, in round
numbers, are Konrad's.

As will appear in the succeeding discussion, Konrad
drew most of his materials from Benoît de Sainte-
More, though it is probable that the recension of the
Roman de Troie used by him was not the one that has
come down to us. Konrad certainly read Latin also,
and he extended his materials by the use of Ovid, Pindarus Thebanus, the *Ilias* of Simon Capra Aurea, and
possibly Statius and an unknown Latin life of Paris.

His work is rich in poetic detail, and displays much
originality of treatment. It is undoubtedly the best of
the German versions of the legend, and one of the best
in mediæval literature. The citations given below will
perhaps sufficiently exemplify its style.

TROJUMANNA SAGA. — The unknown author of this
prose version of the Troy Legend drew his materials
chiefly from Dares. He was conversant also with Ovid,
Pindarus Thebanus, Virgil, and probably the Latin life
of Paris already mentioned. The legend, however, became thoroughly mediævalized in his hands. Dunger
conjectures (*op. cit.*, p. 75) that it was this version which
supplied the materials for the preface and epilogue of
the Younger Edda, in which 'die Asen sind die
Asiamänner, welche unter Priamus, d. i. Odin, und
seiner Gemahlin Hecuba oder Frigg aus dem Tyrk-
lande nach dem Norden einwanderten; Priamus' Sohn

Hector ist Oeku-Thor, d. i. der Thor, welcher in einem
Wagen fährt, der trojanische Krieg ist das, was man
gewöhnlich Götterdämmerung nennt u.s.w.'

TROJANSKA PRICHA. — This Old Bulgarian prose
version of the legend, discussed at length by Greif (pp.
269–278), was in all probability drawn from Ovid, Pindarus Thebanus, and the unknown Latin life of Paris,
without reference to Dares or Dictys.

MANUSCRIPTS AND EDITIONS OF THE SEEGE OF TROYE.

We have now considered the principal mediæval versions of the story of Troy, and turn to one that has
perhaps for us more immediate interest than any of
them ; for besides being a monument of an interesting
period of our language, it supplies some valuable details
as to the cultural history of England in the fourteenth
century.   In the present discussion, however, it will be
considered chiefly in its relation to a version of the
Roman de Troie of Benoît de Sainte-More, of which, as
I shall try to show, it is little more than a condensed
paraphrase.

So far as our knowledge extends, there are but three
manuscripts of the poem in existence : one in the
British Museum, No. 525 of the Harley Manuscripts ;
a second in the Library of Lincoln's Inn, London, num-
bered 150 ; the third in the library of the Duke of
Sutherland, at Trentham.   The first two were edited
diplomatically by Dr. Zietsch, in Herrig's *Archiv für das
Studium der neueren Sprachen und Literaturen*, Band

72, 1884. The third, which is the shortest of the three, containing only 1828 lines, will probably be the basis of Professor Kölbing's edition of the poem, promised in 1884 (*Englische Studien*, VII, p. 193), but not yet published. An edition has also been promised by Wilhelm Fick, in his Breslau dissertation, *Zur mittelenglischen romanze Seege of Troye*, p. 14. To this work I am indebted for my information concerning the Sutherland and Lincoln's Inn MSS., neither of which is accessible to me. I present herewith a summary of his results.

Inasmuch as the Sutherland MS., in its contents and in its rimes, agrees with the Lincoln's Inn, and differs from the Harleian, it is evident that the three manuscripts fall into two classes, the one represented by the Harleian, the other by the Lincoln's Inn and Sutherland versions. The chief passages in which the two last named versions agree with each other and differ from the Harleian are as follows :

1. They omit the battle between Jason and Laomedon (Harl. 145–152).

2. They agree that Priam's messenger to the Greeks, to demand the restoration of Hesione, was Antenor, and not Hector (Harl. 313–315).

3. Their version of the judgment of Paris differs in many details from the Harleian (cf. the citation from the Lincoln's Inn version on p. lxxiii of this Introduction).

4. They fail to mention the falsehood which Paris told on his arrival in Greece (Harl. 501–506).

5. They represent Protesilaus (Prestolay, Portuflay), in his fight with Hector, as unhorsed, not killed (Harl. 935, 936).

6. They furnish details concerning the training of Achilles that are omitted by the Harleian version (cf. the citation from the Lincoln's Inn version on p. lxxxii of this Introduction).

7. They agree in many details of the fight between Achilles and Hector that differ from those of the Harleian version, 1239–1292. For example, they do not mention Achilles' wound in the thigh (Harl. 1254), thus avoiding inconsistency with the previous assertion (Harl. 1027–1029) that he was vulnerable only in the soles of his feet. They avoid a similar inconsistency in the description of Achilles' death :

L. I. 1657 (cf. Suth. 1633).

In mony steodis he ȝaf heom wounde.

HARL. 1630.

In sexe stedes þey yaf him a wounde.

In the description of Hector's death they fail to mention Syr Annys (Harl. 1273–1292).

8. They fail to mention the dialogue between Achilles and Troilus (Harl. 1509–1516), and they represent Achilles as smiting off Troilus' head, instead of piercing him to the heart (Harl. 1528).

That this agreement does not indicate the derivation of one manuscript from the other is proved by Fick in the same manner as I shall try to show (p. xxxiii) that the Harleian and Lincoln's Inn versions are independent of each other. Their agreement, then, indicates they are derived from a common original, designated as y. It is evident that the Harleian version is not y, as the latter contained much information which the former does not embody. It is improbable that this information was independently added by the transcriber of y, as in some cases we know it to have been contained in the source of the original poem. An example will be found on pp. xxxiii–iv. Fick's contention that y could not have been the original *Seege of Troye*, because the Harleian version contains matter not found in the other two versions, is hardly convincing. We have no right to assume that the Sutherland and Lincoln's Inn versions together reproduce y completely. It is of course probable that two independent versions of a short poem would not omit anything of great importance. Yet it is far from certain that the transcriber of the Harleian version did not derive from y matter that was omitted by the transcriber of the other versions. For example, the marriage of Peleus and Thetis, which is alluded to in the Harleian version, 403–4, was certainly contained in the source of *The Seege of Troye* (cf. p. xxxiv of this Introduction). It was, therefore, probably embodied in the original English poem. It is not impossible that y embodied it, and that the Harleian transcriber reproduced it from y, while the other transcribers omitted it. I am not sure, however, that the Sutherland version omits it, as I have not seen the manuscript. If, on the publication of the manuscript, it should be found that the allusion is contained therein, it would remove one objection to y as the version from which the Harleian may have been transcribed.

Again, there is other additional matter in the Harleian version that may have arisen from the transcriber's invention and his collateral reading. I cannot, therefore, positively assert that the Harleian version was not derived from *y*, and that *y* was not the original *Seege of Troye*.

In the remainder of this discussion, I shall be obliged to limit my comparisons to the Harleian and Lincoln's Inn versions, as I have merely the hints of Fick to guide me as to the contents of the Sutherland version.

The Harleian version is presented here. That a new edition is not superfluous, may be gathered from a comparison of the text with that of Zietsch. The latter's deviations from the readings of the manuscript are very numerous, and the critical apparatus, which he published the same year, leaves much to be desired in the direction of accuracy and completeness.

The two versions to which we have access are evidently related to each other through an ultimate English original. The very numerous passages that are virtually identical in phraseology preclude the possibility that we may have to do with independent versions of an Old French original. The original that they represent was, therefore, English. That one cannot be derived from the other may be easily proved. For example, at line 249 of the Lincoln's Inn version, we read that Paris was seven years old when he was entrusted by his mother to the swineherd. This exactness was not obtained from the Harleian version, which says, ll. 225–6:

> Whanne he was born she sent him
> Too an herd, to kepe swyn.

Now there is another narrative of the youth of Paris, drawn from the same ultimate source as this passage; it is the *Trojanska Pricha*, an Old Bulgarian prose

version, published, with a Latin translation, by Fr.
Miklosich, in 1871. (For the source, cf. Greif, *op. cit.*,
pp. 102, 103.) At p. 159, l. 29 of this version we read
the following: 'Et adolescebat valde cito. Et cum
esset septem annorum, pueri ambo ibant in campum
cum patre suo,' the two boys being Paris and the herdsman's own son. Taking this passage in conjunction
with the passage already quoted from the Lincoln's Inn
version, it is safe to infer that the latter here reproduces the original English poem. Other instances
might be adduced to strengthen the argument. We
therefore conclude that the Lincoln's Inn version was
not derived from the Harleian.

In a similar way it is proved that the Harleian was
not derived from the Lincoln's Inn version. In lines
403, 404 of the Harleian version, we find an evident
reference to the marriage of Peleus and Thetis. This
cannot come from the Lincoln's Inn version, which does
not mention the marriage even remotely. Konrad von
Würzburg, however, in his poem drawn from the same
source as *The Seege of Troye*, describes the marriage at
length. We may therefore conclude that at least a
hint of the marriage was to be found in the English
original. This one instance merely serves to indicate
the method of proof that the Harleian was not derived
from the Lincoln's Inn version.

But one conclusion remains, namely, that the two
poems are independent versions of an ultimate English
original. Both poets may have added to their materials
by making use of contemporary literature. For example, the proper names in ll. 529–50 of the Harleian
version, and particularly the reference to the Alexander

Saga in 'Neptanabus' and 'Olimpias,' are possibly an addition by the transcriber of that version, as the other does not mention them.

Professor Kölbing assigns MS. 150 of the Lincoln's Inn Library to the end of the fourteenth or the beginning of the fifteenth century. It contains, in addition to the *Batayle of Troye*, four other romances: part of *Sir Libeus*, the *History of Merlin*, the *Alisaunder*, and *Piers Plowman*. Of this manuscript, Hunter says: 'On examining the covers attentively, I discovered that there had been used in the binding a large piece of a document relating to the hospital of Saint John of Beverly; and connecting this with the fact that at Beverly there was, in the times when the manuscript was written, a noted fraternity of minstrels, a probability is raised that the contents of this book were originally transcribed for their use, and that the manuscript may, without much hazard of misleading, be called hereafter the *Book of the Minstrels of Beverly*.' — A Catalogue of the Manuscripts in the Library of the Honourable Society of Lincoln's Inn, London, 1838, p. 145 (quoted by Professor Kölbing).

Against this conjecture, Professor Kölbing admits (*Eng. Stud.*, VII, p. 194) that he has nothing to urge. In its favor, one may point out the fact that the monastery dedicated to St. John of Beverly was in Yorkshire, and that, according to Zietsch, the phonology of the *Batayle of Troye* gives many indications of a northern origin.

The Harley MS. 525 is attributed by Ward (*op. cit.*, I, p. 84) to the fifteenth century. The date is given a little more precisely by Horstmann (*Altenglische Le-*

genden, Neue Folge, p. 528) as the beginning of the fifteenth century. The manuscript is well preserved. Its contents are: *The Seege of Troye, King Robert of Sicily,* and *Speculum Gy de Warewyke heremite secundum Alquinum.* Zietsch considers the first two as transcribed by the same hand; the last by a later hand.

Zietsch, on p. 3 of his dissertation, quotes the following entry in the Harleian Catalogue:

HARL. 525:

A MS. Parcham., where in are cont. (as it seems) some Poems of John Lidgate Scil.:
1. The Seige of Troy.
2. A Tale of Rob. King of Sicily and how by miracle God abased his pride.
3. Speculum Gydonis de Warewyke secundum Alquinum Heremitanum (A theolog. Poem).

This improbable conjecture by the maker of the Harleian Catalogue, suggested of course by Lydgate's *Troy Book* and his *Guy of Warwick,* is, so far as I can ascertain, the only one that has ever been made as to the authorship of our poem.

The Seege of Troye occupies folios 1–34*b*. It is divided by illuminated capitals into twenty-four parts, which generally correspond to the natural divisions of the story. As will appear in another place, it is written in the Southern dialect of English.

I have already indicated that the two versions are not identical. Details appear in the one that are absent from the other. The Lincoln's Inn version contains sixty-six lines more than the Harleian. This

naturally suggests the question, which of the two
reproduces the original more exactly. Zietsch, and
after him Granz, declared for the Harleian. I shall
now try to show that the credit belongs to the Lincoln's
Inn version.

The poet of the latter is not so artistic in his methods
as the poet of the former version. He has not the same
regard for conciseness, for rigid exclusion of unimportant names and details, and, consequently, does not give
quite the same impression of having in view a definite
goal, to the attainment of which everything is deliberately subordinated. For this reason, we should expect him to be more accurate than the other. He was
not so strongly bent upon making an artistic poem, as
upon reproducing his original.

In the first place, the proper names of the Lincoln's
Inn version conform more closely than those of the
Harleian to the proper names of Benoît and Dares.
Examples are:

Ben. 703, Peléus; L. I. 22, Pelyas; Harl. 22, Pelles. In this case
the original form was possibly Dares' Pelias.
Ben. 989, Laomedon; L. I. 73, Leomadan; Harl. 63, Lamatan;
100, Lymadone; 146, Lymadown; etc.
Ben. 2916, Ecuba; L. I. 318, Ecuba; Harl. 278, Ekeuba.
Ben. 5614, Nestor; L. I. 839, Nestor, and so in every instance;
Harl. 723, Nectour, the form Nestor occurring but once out of
five instances.
Ben. 5613, Pile; L. I. 839, Pyle; Harl. 723, Pelye.
Ben. 5639, Protheselax; Dares XIV, Protesilaus; L. I. 927, Pres-
tolay; Harl. 753, Portislay; 913, Portuflay.
Ben. 5677, Patroclus; L. I. 1075, Patrode; Harl. 937, Padradod.
Standard form, Thetis; L. I. 1159, Tetes; Harl. 1021, Tytes.
Ben. 24373, Anthenor; L. I. 1802, Antynor; Harl. 1772, En-
temor.

In the second place, there are several questions of fact in which the Lincoln's Inn version is seen to be nearer than the Harleian to the source of *The Seege of Troye*.

Benoît, 709–16, makes it plain that Jason was the nephew of Peleus, the son of his brother 'Eson.' Harl. 26 calls Jason the 'cosyn' of Pelles, while L. I. 26 reads:

> And hadde a neuow þat hette Jasoun.

As I have indicated (p. xxxiv), it is probable that the source of *The Seege of Troye* represented the boy Paris, when he was banished from his father's house, as adopted by a poor herdsman, who reared him with his own son. Harl. 225–6 merely says:

> Whanne he was born she sent him
> Too an herd, to kepe swyn,

while L. I. 261–4 reads:

> þe qwene sende hire owne child
> Into a contray, wast and wilde,
> And made him kepe swyn þere,
> As he a pore monnes sone weore.

Benoît, 3029–3124, in his description of the rebuilding of Troy, describes at some length 'Ylion, de Troie le mestre danjon,' wherein was a chamber containing an altar and statue:

> L'image au Dé où mielz creieient
> Et où graignor fiance aveient,
> C'est Jupiter li dex poissanz.
> Cel fist faire li reis Prianz,
> Del meillor or qu'il onques ot,
> Ne que il onques trover pot.

Of this chamber and altar, the Harleian version makes no mention, while L. I. 303–8 reads:

> In Troye he made a tour,
> Of alle toures hit was flour.
> And in þe tour he made an auter
> Of þe false god sire Jubiter,
> A mawmet riche, for þe nones,
> Of gold, seoluer, and precious stones.

As I shall show (p. lxii), it is probable that the source of *The Seege of Troye* named Antenor as Priam's messenger to the Greeks, to demand the restoration of the captive princess Hesione.   Harl. 314, assigns the function to Hector, while the Lincoln's Inn version names Sire Antynor.

In relating the promise made by Venus to Paris, on condition that he shall award her the golden apple, *Trojanska Pricha*, p. 161, l. 35, says : 'Adjudica (mihi) hoc aureum malum et declara me pulcherrimam, in potestate enim habeo amorem et dabo tibi bonum amorem, te amabunt pulchrae dominae,' etc.   (Cf. p. xxxiii.)   This general promise does not appear in the Harleian version, while L. I. 560–8 reads:

> Knʒt, ʒef me þeo bal, for þy cortesy,
> And þou schalt haue loue and wolde.
> Alle folk þe schal, boþe ʒonge and olde;
> Alle wymmen þat þe seon wiþ syʒt
> Schole þe loue, wiþ al heore myʒt;
> Maydenes in chaumbre schal loue þe alle,
> Ladyes in boure, and wyues in halle;
> Alle wymmen schole beo in þy pouste,
> And alle schole þey loue þe.

L. I. 1562 represents Achilles as smiting off Troilus' head. In the Harleian version, 1528, Troilus is pierced to the heart. Benoît, 21416, says, 'Que cil li a chief lo colpé.'

It is somewhat suggestive that while Harl. 1832–3 speaks of Sir Neptalamus, Prince of Macendoyne, L. I. 1868–9 calls him Sir Pirrus, Prince of Murmydoun. Ben. 24059–60, reads: —

> Mirmidoneis ont remonté
> Pirrus lo nouvel adoubé.

In the third place, in the descriptions of places and events, the Lincoln's Inn version is closer than the Harleian to the source of the original poem.

As will appear in the discussion of sources, the Lincoln's Inn version is much richer in detail than the Harleian in the following descriptions: the training of Paris, the training of Achilles, and the scene of Paris' hunting. It will appear also that these details were not independently added by the translator of the Lincoln's Inn version, but that they probably were to be found in the sources of the original poem. Moreover, in the catalogue of ships, the Lincoln's Inn version mentions twelve more heroes than the Harleian, six of whom, at least, may be identified with names in Benoît's list.

I admit that it is quite possible that the above-mentioned deviations of the Lincoln's Inn version from the Harleian may be the work of the transcriber. I admit that we cannot know exactly what were the readings of the original *Seege of Troye*. But, as I have tried to show, these deviations in every case represent the readings of what we believe to be the sources of *The Seege of Troye*. It is, then, not unreasonable to assume that they are the readings of the original poem, and hence that the original poem is reproduced more exactly by the Lincoln's Inn version than by the Harleian.

It should be added that there is a small number of instances in which the reverse is true. They will appear in the course of the following discussion, but will not, I think, invalidate the argument already presented.

SOURCES.

It is not easy — perhaps impossible — to arrive at definite and complete knowledge of the sources of *The Seege of Troye*. It might be expected that the difficulty of the task would be proportionate to the length of the poem, but, on the contrary, the extreme compression of the work renders a return to its sources unusually difficult. The *Gest Hystoriale of the Destruction of Troy*, with its 14,044 lines, offers a much simpler task to the investigator of sources than the 1922 lines of our poem. The investigation is further complicated by the presence in the poem of episodes which cannot be traced to any work that has come down to us, and which were certainly not original with the poet.

We should naturally expect to find in the poem traces of the influence of Chaucer's *Troilus* and the *Gest Hystoriale*. Ten Brink affirms that 'there is no doubt but the popularity of the tale of Troy in England was largely due to Chaucer's *Troilus*.' There is, however, no indication that our poet made use of any

English Troy romance.   The poems of Barbour[1] and Lydgate on the same theme are probably later than The *Seege of Troye.*

The direct source of our poem is unquestionably the *Roman de Troie* of Benoît de Sainte-More, and its only relation to the other English versions of the Troy story is through the Old French romance, which was the ultimate source of them all.   But Lydgate, Barbour, and the author of the *Gest Hystoriale* drew their materials directly from the *Historia Destructionis Troiae* of Guido delle Colonne, the translator of Benoît into Latin, and for many years the appropriator of his fame.   Chaucer, however, supplemented the materials derived from Boccaccio's *Filostrato,* which, according to Mr. Rossetti's calculation, constitute less than one-third of the *Troilus and Criseyde,* by copious borrowings, possibly from Guido, certainly from Benoit (Skeat, *Oxford Chaucer,* II, pp. liii-lxii; Broatch, *Jour. Germ. Philol.,* II, 1, pp. 14-28).

The episodes already mentioned furnish conclusive evidence of our poet's independence of the other English versions.   These episodes, in the form in which they appear in *The Seege of Troye,* are entirely absent from those versions, and, as a consequence, from that recension of the *Roman de Troie* which Guido translated.

As I shall try to prove, there can be little doubt that a recension of the *Roman de Troie* was the direct source of our poem.   This proposition is susceptible of more

---

[1] If the poem alluded to is correctly ascribed to the author of the *Bruce,* it would be nearly contemporary with *The Seege of Troye,* as Barbour died in 1395. (Cf. *Paul's Grundriss der Germanischen Philologie,* II 1, p. 665.) According to Busse (*Anglia,* IX, 493) and Köppel (*Englische Studien,* X, 373), however, it is the work of a poet of the same name belonging to the fifteenth century.

convincing demonstration than is to be found in the poet's own assertions. The following passages,

> Harl. 1522, 'Soo it is in Frenshe fownde,'
>
> L. I. 197, 'þeo romaunce me doþ to vndurstande,'

to be sure, point to a direct use of Benoît; but it was so common a practice with mediæval writers to make such references, that the lines must serve merely as an indication, not as a proof. The mediæval poet frequently sacrificed literary veracity for the sake of lending to his work the weight of a standard authority. Thus, Guido delle Colonne names Dares Phrygius as the source of his *Historia*, deliberately neglecting to mention Benoît, whose poem he translates. Benoît himself, while following the outline given by Dares, ascribes to the *De Excidio Troiæ* much that is undoubtedly his own invention. Our own poet, lines 13–20, professes to be a translator of Dares, but, as we shall see, his debt to the Latin historian is inconsiderable. In one of the instances under discussion, line 1522, the event that is attributed to the French original was probably not found there. But the assertion, taken in connection with the great number of correspondences between *The Seege of Troye* and Benoît's *Roman*, may be received as generally, if not specifically, true.

Three German scholars have investigated the sources of this poem, A. Zietsch, W. Greif, and E. T. Granz. The first, in his dissertation, *Ueber Quelle und Sprache des mittelenglischen Gedichtes Seege oder Batayle of Troye*, published in 1884, pronounced in favour of Dares as its chief source. He attributed little importance to its references to a French original; the correspondences

between the poem and the *Roman de Troie* he ascribed to
a common use of Dares; and he even considered the
brevity of the poem an argument against the use of
Benoît, forgetting that the old Italian poem, *L'Intelligenza*,[1] contained a paraphrase of the *Roman de Troie* in
414 lines. In his view the chief episodes could be
accounted for by the author's acquaintance with the
Alexander Saga and the *Achilleis* of Statius.

In 1886, W. Greif published *Die mittelalterlichen
Bearbeitungen der Trojanersage*, in which he affirmed
that while Dares was the chief source, traces of Benoît,
at least in the beginning, are numerous and unmistakable. He believed the author to have used Statius merely
from memory, and to have derived the episode of the
birth and youth of Paris from an unknown Latin source,
common also to three other mediæval versions of the
legend. He supported the last contention by many
convincing parallelisms. Greif's opinion, it should be
noted in passing, is espoused by H. Oskar Sommer, in
the introduction to his edition of *The Recuyell of the
Historyes of Troye*, translated from *Raoul Lefèvre* by
William Caxton.

In 1888, Emil Theodor Granz published his Leipzig
dissertation, *Ueber die Quellengemeinschaft des mittelenglischen Gedichtes Seege oder Batayle of Troye und
des mittelhochdeutschen Gedichtes vom trojanischen Kriege
des Konrad von Würzburg*. There, from a long and
careful comparison of *The Seege of Troye* and Konrad's

---

[1] P. Gellrich, *Die Intelligenza, ein altitalienisches Gedicht, nach
Vergleichung mit den beiden Handschriften herausgegeben*, Breslau,
1883; and A. Mussafia in *Literaturblatt*, 1884, columns 153–58.

poem with the *Roman de Troie*, together with a consideration of those passages in which the Middle English and Middle High German poems differ from the old French romance, he concluded that the source common to both was a recension of the *Roman de Troie*, embodying the episodes ascribed by Greif to the influence of Statius and the Latin life of Paris. He assigned to Dares a sure but inconsiderable place among the sources.

Although this extended form of the *Roman de Troie* has not come down to us, there is no inherent improbability that it once existed. Manuscript G of the *Roman de Troie*, in the Bibliothèque Impériale of Paris, is a version by Jehan Malkaraume, who has made use of Ovid to fill gaps in Benoît's story, notably as to the dream of Hecuba and the loves of Paris and Œnone. Malkaraume's version, however, is not the one we seek. It is certain that many versions of the *Roman de Troie* were made during the Middle Ages in France, Italy, Spain, and Germany, nor is it improbable that some poet, conversant with Ovid, Statius, and other Latin writers, went even further than Malkaraume in extending Benoît's romance. Possibly, too, like Malkaraume, he failed to mention Benoît's name, and arrogated to himself the authorship of the poem.

It is the hypothesis of Granz that will be presented in these pages, not, however, in all respects with quite the certainty evinced by its author. One perceives in the German student of sources a desire to find a single solution for a complex problem, and such an inclination to account for every difficulty as leads him, it may be, to strain his hypothesis, and to deny to the poet any possible originality. It is not, then, wholly without reserves that we are to accept Granz's theory of the source of our poem.

Moreover, it is constantly to be borne in mind that if our poet was not pre-eminently an artist, he had an artistic conception of brevity and simplicity, and that this conception reacted powerfully upon his treatment of his materials. He everywhere shows a tendency to avoid multiplying characters and incidents, and to limit the action of the poem to a few important persons. This tendency explains several divergences from his model for which otherwise a new source must be conjectured. For example, he assigns the golden fleece to Troy (Harl. 34, 62, 177), though both Dares and Benoît mention Colchis as the scene of the quest. He makes no reference either to Medea and her arts or to Argus, thus indicating that while he felt the necessity, shared by all mediæval poets, of beginning at the logical commencement of the action, he realized that he was to narrate the siege of Troy, and must not delay unduly upon the introduction, nor embarrass the action by introducing unnecessary names and events. Yet it is clear that at this stage of his narrative he was strongly influenced by Benoît. We must not, therefore, fail to credit him with considerable originality in the treatment of his materials.

I shall now proceed to indicate as briefly as possible the grounds for believing that *The Seege of Troye*, from beginning to end, is little more than an epitome of the *Roman de Troie*. It shows traces of the influence of Benoît, first in passages practically translated from him, secondly in episodes condensed and transformed.

It is true that verbal correspondences with the

Roman de Troie are more numerous at the beginning
of the English poem than at the middle and end. It
was this fact, no doubt, that led Greif to limit Benoît's
influence to the first quarter of the poem. The explanation is that, owing to the simpler construction of
the episodes that are contained in the first 4752 lines
of the *Roman de Troie*, namely, the expedition of the
Argonauts, the first destruction of Troy, and the ravishing of Helen, which serve as introduction to the
English poem, the author was able to follow his original with comparative fidelity; but in describing the
events of the siege, the limits of his poem forced him
to condense and transform Benoît's narrative, so that
the traces of the latter's influence are much less distinct.
Nevertheless, that influence is to be found in the last
lines as in the first. I have chosen the more striking
correspondences. There are innumerable minor ones
no less convincing, the importance of which becomes
manifest, however, only in such a consecutive and
detailed comparison of the two works as that instituted
by Granz.

The account of the first destruction of Troy is nearly
a literal rendering of Benoît, as the following comparison will show:

BEN. 2373.

En la vile est li criz levez,
Li plus séurs est effréez.

2376.

Quant il [*Laomedon*] oï conter et dire,
Que li Griu erent retorné,
Pol lui destruire et son regné,

Isnelement arme son cors,
De la ville s'en issi fors,
O tant de geut com il i ot.

2389.

Et dès qu'il vindrent as espées,
Molt s'entredonent grant colées.
La ot maint hialme decerclé,
Et maint chevalier decolpé.

2388.

. . . maint abatu et ocis.

HARL. 119.

Thorowout the cite the cry arose,
That eche man of hem aferd was.
The kyng of Troye hathe vndertakyn
That folke o Grece bene icomyn
With a grete ost stought and grym,
And thenke þey wull besegen him.
Himsilf armith him aryght,
And all his meyne well idyght,
And bene igadered vpp and down,
And sued þe kyng out of town.
Sone þey be togeder mette,
There was strokes well isette;
There myght men see shaftis shake,
And many krounes all tocrake;
Many nobill men vnder sheld
Sone were slayn in þat feld.

The description of Priam and of his grief at the ruin
of his country is plainly from Benoît :

BEN. 2851.

Laomedon un filz aveit,
Riches, sages et prouz esteit.

Et esteit appelez Prianz.
De sa femme avoit oit enfanz.
En ost esteit loiug del païs.

2858.

Et quant ço li fu annoncié,
Que Troie et tote la contrée
Estoit destruite, arse et robée,
Et sis pere ocis et sa mere,
Et ses serors et tuit si frere,
Fors une sole, la plus sage,
Qui en fu menée en servage.

HARL. 186.

He had a sone left in þat reaulme;
His name Sir Priamus he hitt,
He was a prince of myche myght;
In Fygry he dwelled tho,
His wyf and his chyldryn also.
Of the discomfeture wist he nought,
How the Troyens were down brought.
Whan he vndirstode bothe all and summe,
His fader was slayn, Sir Lymadon,
And his thre bredryn him by,
And also his systryn lad away, —

Priam's reply to the Greek messengers who demanded
the return of Helen strongly suggests Benoît:

BEN. 6355.

Ço sachent li Grezeis de veir
Que gie lor ferai à saveir,
Quel cuer gie ai, et quels amis.
Assez ai gent en cest païs.

HARL. 823.

For I have here, I vndirstond,
All þe power of my lond,
For to defende . . .
Troye . . .

In the description of the battle that followed, our
poet has evidently drawn his simile from the French
source :

BEN. 7117.

Car pluie, ne gresle par vent
Ne chaï plus espessement
Que font saietes barbelées,
Darz et engeignes enpenées.

HARL. 846.

And shett men with dartis and arblast,
And sharpe quarell, and eke floon,
As þyke as ony hayle ston.

Achilles' threat against Hector almost literally translates Benoît :

BEN. 10298.

Bien sache Hector, si gie le truis,
Qu'il ocirra mei, ou gie lui.

HARL. 1152.

The first batayle þat he cometh inne,
He shall me slee, or I will him

In the following passages also, the French and English poems closely correspond :

BEN. 10574.

Parmi les escuz à peinture,

10577.

Et parmi les broines safrées
Sont les lances enastelées,
Qu'andui chaïrent en l'erbei.

10583.

hialmes vert gemez
I ot senpres escartelez,
Si qu'à mainz perent les cerveles,
Et que morz trebuchent des seles.
Par grant ire se sont requis,
Assez i en ot des ocis.

HARL. 1182.

Good knyghtis be her styroppis hyng;
Many an helme þere was ofwevyd,
And many a basnett þere was cleved,
Many a spere and many a sheld
Fley abowte into þe feld;

1195.

Many a doughty man in þe feld
Layne þere slayne vnder shelde.

The story of Hecuba's plot against Achilles in the
English poem differs from the French version chiefly
in the employment of more direct discourse; and in
general we find a strong tendency on the part of the
English poet toward the dramatic form. I may observe
in passing that this tendency is perceptible in most of
the poets of the Middle English period. It appears
to be a trait of the English genius. It is so strongly
marked even in Genesis B of the Junian MS., and in
Cynewulf, that Mr. Stopford Brooke (*The History of
Early English Literature*, p. 298) is inclined to think
that the drama might have been developed much sooner

ı England, had it not been for the influence of long-winded story-telling' introduced from France.

BEN. 21804.

Un jor comença à penser,
Com seroient si fil vengié
Del traïtor, del reneié,
Qui les a si morz et toleiz.

21814.

Paris a fait à sei mander.

21828.

Mès preier te voil une rien :

21885.

Filz, fai le desirrier ta mere,
Si que soient vengié ti frere.

HARL. 1543.

' Achilles, þat tretour, that thef,
Hath slayne my sones þat were me soo leef.
Myne hole herte woll tobreke
But I of him be awreke,
Alisaunder, sone, come too me.
For my love, I prey now the,
On my blessyng, doo after my rede,
Awreke þy brodren þat ben dede.'

Priam's lament over the final destruction of his ‹ inds a close parallel in Benoît:

BEN. 25094.

Eschif me sont tuit et salvage.
N'a onquor pas treis anz passez,

Se cist consalz me fust donez,
Ainz qu' Ector mis filz fust ocis,
Troylus li prouz et Paris,
Qu'il me fust grant profit de faire.

HARL. 1761.

. . . 'were Ectour on lyve,
He wold our fomen all todryve;
Or his broder, Alisaunder Parys—
Litill durst we dowt our enmys.'

The description of the havoc wrought by the Greeks points conclusively to Benoît:

BEN. 25962.

Del ocise li palès seingnent;
Tuit decorent li pavement,
De sanc sont vermeil et sanglent:
N'i a ne rue, ne sentier,
Ou n'ateigne jusqu'al braier.

HARL. 1865.

There was shed soo moche blode
þat man and hors to þe knees yode.

The word *braier*, modern French *braies*, from Latin *bracæ*, meaning breeches, undoubtedly suggested the phrase 'to the knees,' which finds no parallel in Dares. And indeed a reference to the sections in Dares corresponding to the passages above quoted, will prove conclusively that they were not drawn from the Latin historian. While the order of events is in general the same, in every case there are significant details that point unmistakably to the *Roman de Troie*.

Two instances will sufficiently exemplify the manner in which the English poet condenses and transforms

the narrative of Benoît. Such transformations probably
arise, not, as Granz suggests, from the poet's misinter-
pretation of the French romance, but from his constant
effort to simplify and abbreviate the narrative. He
declined to complicate the story by the introduction of
unimportant characters, and therefore attributed to his
heroes deeds of valour that were not their own. Moreover, appreciating the monotony of Benoît's long battle
scenes, he chose only such as had interest and significance for himself, condensing and combining them to
a form almost unrecognizable. His omissions appear
neither ill-judged nor arbitrary, though, to an unde-
veloped critical faculty like his, the great mass of
material must have presented extreme difficulty of
choice. In general, we may say that the poet's aim
was to describe the siege and final destruction of Troy
with the utmost brevity consistent with interest. For
this reason, he passes briefly over the two causes of the
war, namely, the expedition of the Argonauts and the
ravishing of Helen, omitting everything not strictly
pertinent, — Pelias' hatred for Jason, the loves of Jason
and Medea, the magical winning of the fleece, — and
hurries on to his main theme. He neglects Calchas, the
sacrifice of the Greeks at Aulis, Palamedes' rebellion
against Agamemnon, the loves of Troilus and Briseida,
the description of the Amazons, the wooden horse, and
the ultimate fortunes of the Greek chiefs, with a description of which Benoît closes his narrative. The prowess
of his favourite heroes, Hector, Paris, Troilus, the fortunes of Priam, the love and valour of Achilles, the treason of Antenor and Æneas, are his themes. To these
everything is subordinated. Crude as is the language

and versification, *The Seege of Troye*, as an epitome of Benoît's poem, may justly be called artistic.

The best example of the transformation to which our poet has subjected his materials is found in the story of the first destruction of Troy, lines 121–64. Benoît's version is briefly as follows: When the Greeks land before Troy, part of the army under Hercules, Telamon, and Peleus lies in ambush near the city, while the remainder, under Castor, Pollux, and Nestor, guards the ships. The arrival of the enemy is announced to Laomedon, and he hurries out of town with his force to meet them. In a combat with Nestor, he is unhorsed. A young Trojan, Cedar, hastens to the assistance of his king. Nestor deals him a blow in the breast with such force 'que la lance en clices vola' (cf. Harl. 147, 148), but is finally unhorsed by the youth. They then engage in a combat of swords (Harl. 149, 150), and at last are separated by the Greeks. Meanwhile, Castor, hurrying to the assistance of Nestor, meets the Trojan, Seguradan, cousin of Cedar, and grievously wounds him. Cedar turns to avenge his kinsman with his lance, unhorses Castor, and makes him prisoner. Pollux, with the help of seven hundred Greeks, rescues him, and mounts him upon his steed again. At last Laomedon, hearing of the havoc which the other detachment of the Greeks is working in the city, hastens back, meets Hercules, and is slain by him (Ben. 2373–2742).

We have here six episodes, which are condensed by the English poet to three. Like Benoît, he represents the battles as taking place without the city, but says nothing of the occupation of Troy by the Greeks until

after the death of the king.   In other words, he assigns
one locality to the battle instead of two.   The version
of the Lincoln's Inn MS., following Benoît, as usual,
more literally, omits all mention of the battles at the
ships, and merely narrates the death of Laomedon at
the hands of Hercules.

The first combat, namely, that between Laomedon
and Nestor, is represented by the first combat between
Laomedon and Hercules (Harl. 139–44); but Laomedon represents Benoît's Nestor, and Hercules Benoît's
Laomedon.   In the second combat, Cedar is represented by Jason, and Laomedon still represents Benoît's
Nestor.   As in Benoît, they engage first with lances
and then with swords.   Benoît's third combat is not
specially represented in the English poem.   His fourth
combat, however, the unhorsing and capture of Castor
by Cedar, shows its influence in the fight between
Laomedon and Hercules already described, Laomedon
representing Benoît's Cedar, and Hercules Benoît's
Castor.   The fifth episode, the rescue of Castor by
Pollux and seven hundred knights, is of course represented by Harl. 154–56.

The final combat between Laomedon and Hercules
now takes place.

It must be agreed that the manner in which the
English poet has condensed Benoît's narrative of 367
lines to one of 40 lines, omitting nothing of importance, yet assigning the entire action, for which Benoît
makes use of six combatants, to three, thus avoiding
the introduction of new characters, is most ingenious.
Our appreciation of his art is increased by a comparison of his method with that of the poet of the Lin-

coln's Inn version. The latter mechanically omits the battles at the ships, thus losing the dramatic effect of the Harleian version.

Nor can the artistic credit of this transformation be denied our poet. He evidently could not have derived his version from Dares, who says: 'Laomedonti regi nuntiatum est classem Græcorum ad Sigeum accessisse, et ipse cum equestri copia ad mare venit et cœpit prœliari. Hercules ad Ilium ierat et inprudentes qui erant in oppido urgere cœpit. Quod ubi Laomedonti nuntiatum est urgeri ab hostibus Ilium, ilico revertitur et in itinere obvius Græcis factus ab Hercule occiditur'.(Chap. III).

It is equally certain that this condensation was not derived from the extended and altered Benoît, which was probably used by our English poet, and which we are soon to discuss. For Konrad von Würzburg, who made use of the same source, follows with sufficient closeness the narrative as we have seen it in the recension of Benoît that we possess. We are compelled therefore to attribute it to the originality of the English poet.

The second example of condensation is simpler, and arises from the author's effort to avoid Benoît's prolixity in the description of battles. In 141 lines (829–970), the English poet narrates the events of the first three years of the siege. Of the first year, the description is general, no hero being mentioned. The second year, the prowess of Hector and Paris is related. The third year, however, contains the slaying of Protesilaus (Portuflay) and Patroclus (Padradod) at the hand of Hector, the wounding of Hector by Menestheus (Monastew), and the wounding of Menelaus by Paris. Of these four events, the death of Protesilaus occurs in Benoît on the first day of the first campaign, the death of Patroclus and the wounding of Hector on the second day, and the wounding of Menelaus by Paris in the fourth campaign.

Evidently the English poet chose the events of the first four campaigns that he considered most significant for his heroes, and massed them in the third year for the sake of simplicity. The details of the battles are often wholly at variance with Benoît. It is here that our poet permitted himself the greatest freedom. In his view, it was important merely that he should relate events that aggrandized his heroes or pointed to their fall. For details, he relied wholly upon his imagination and general reminiscences of his French original. Again we must concede that if a choice was to be made out of the immense storehouse of events furnished by Benoît, he has chosen with no little judgment.

From this point, Achilles becomes the central figure. The story of his youth is introduced by the assertion that he alone can vanquish Hector. Until that end is accomplished, no other hero is allowed to appear. Syr Annys, l. 1275, is merely the immediate instrument of Hector's destruction. Andromache's dream and the combat between Hector and Achilles occupy the narrator exclusively. Hector dead, the instrument of his slayer's destruction appears in Polyxena. Troilus comes upon the stage only, by his death, to hasten Achilles' end. Hecuba's grief at the loss of her two sons and her thirst for revenge result in her conspiracy. Achilles meets his death in the temple at the hands of

Paris. Now the end of the siege approaches. Paris is removed from the stage by Ajax. The last Trojan hero gone, the city is betrayed by Antenor and Æneas; Neoptolemus, son of Achilles, is fittingly introduced as the instrument of vengeance upon the treacherous family of Priam, and the story ends. The credit for the artistic development of this plot does not belong, of course, to our poet. It is to be found baldly outlined in Dares, and almost wholly obscured by irrelevant details in Benoît. The merit of our poet consists in discovering this development and freeing it from the obscurity into which Benoît had cast it, employing only such details as would give life to the narrative, and at the same time point inevitably to its end.

We have already indicated two of the methods by which our poet diverges from Benoît : by omitting what he considered unessential, and by condensing what was too long and complex for his purpose. Examples might be multiplied, but additional ones must be assigned to the Notes.

We have now to consider those divergences that arise from the use of a source other than the *Roman de Troie* in its present form. The first of these is evidently Dares. The following list of instances will serve to show that in all probability the English poet was familiar with that version of Dares known as MS. G, now in the monastery of St. Gall.

In Harl. 25, we read that Pelles was king of Pelpeson. Benoît does not mention the Peloponnesus, while Dares G (Chap. I) reads : 'Pelias rex fuit in Pelopenenso et Æsonem fratrem habuit.'

Harl. 162, 197, and L. I. 160, 217, mention the three

sons of Laomedon, who were slain by Hercules. Benoît's only reference to them is in l. 2861-2 :

> Et sis pere ocis et sa mere,
> Et ses serors et tuit si frere ;

Dares G (Chap. III) reads : 'Laomedontis filii qui cum
eo fuerant occiduntur, Hypsipilus, Uolcontis, Ampitus.'

Harl. 191, and L. I. 213, name respectively Fygry and
Fryse as the residence of Priam at the time of the first
destruction of Troy. Benoît does not speak of Phrygia,
but Dares (Chap. III) says : 'Priamus in Phrygia erat.'

Harl. 297, applies the adjective 'rede' to Menelaus'
head and hair. No such description of him is given by
Benoît, and the poet is evidently dependent upon
Dares' 'rufum' (Chap. XIII).

Archeley, Harl. 729, is more easily derived from the
Archelaus of Dares G (Chap. XIV) than from Benoît's
Archelax.

Finally, the English poet has evidently been influenced by Dares in assigning so important a function to
Neoptolemus in the closing events of the siege. Benoît
calls the youth Pyrrhus, and does not allow him such
prominence.

It may reasonably be objected, to be sure, that the
author of the extended *Roman de Troie*, of which we
are now to speak, may very well have incorporated
these additions of Dares into his own narrative, and
that the English poet obtained them from him. At
any rate, the ultimate source of them is almost certainly
Dares G. As I have remarked before, too much importance must not be attributed to the poet's assertion,
Harl. 13-20, that Dares was his original, for the lines
are probably a translation of Ben. 87-124.

We now proceed to a consideration of Granz's hypothesis that there existed a version of the *Roman de Troie* differing materially from our present one, and that this version was the common source of *The Seege of Troye* and *Der Trojanische Krieg* of Konrad von Würzburg. We have seen how important are the grounds for believing that Benoît's poem is the source of *The Seege of Troye*. Dunger, Greif, and others, have shown conclusively that Benoît was as certainly the chief source used by Konrad. But a comparison of the Middle English and Middle High German poems reveals the fact that they contain several common divergences from the *Roman de Troie* that we know. It is not unreasonable, therefore, to suppose that these divergent passages were contained in the version of the *Roman de Troie* used by them. Indeed, we are forced, by the similarity of these divergences in the two poets, to conclude that they were drawn from a common source. What more natural, then, than to assume that common source to be an extended *Roman de Troie*, especially as we have already shown that such extensions of the poem actually existed? The whole matter, to be sure, is one of conjecture. There may have been materials accessible to the English poet and to Konrad of which we know nothing; but so far as our knowledge extends, Granz's conjecture seems most weighty. Nor is it possible that the English poet drew from Konrad, for, besides the improbability that he knew Middle High German, in several instances he furnishes a detail which we can prove to have been in the conjectured original, but which Konrad does not contain. An excellent example will be found on p. xxxiii.

There are five principal episodes, in the development of which, by the Middle English and Middle High German poets, we trace the influence of an extended *Roman de Troie*. They are : Priam's effort to regain Hesione, the dream of Hecuba, the judgment of Paris, Paris' residence in Greece, and the youth of Achilles.

First, Priam's effort to regain Hesione (Harl. 285–348). According to the narrative of the *Roman de Troie* that we possess, Priam, after the rebuilding of the city, calls a parliament, and proposes a war of retaliation against the Greeks, but professes himself willing to maintain peace and forget his other wrongs if they will restore to him Hesione. The parliament agreeing, the king sends Antenor as a messenger to Greece. He visits Peleus, Telamon, Castor, Pollux, and Nestor, at their several homes, and lays before them Priam's demand. He obtains from them, however, only an insulting refusal. Upon hearing the report of his embassy, Priam and his council decide upon war. (Ben. 3183–3704.)

It is evident that the English version differs from this narrative in two respects. In the first place, Priam speaks unconditionally for war ; the parliament, however, is unanimous for peace in case the Greeks will restore Hesione. In the second place, the messenger, instead of visiting the Greek chiefs severally, meets them all together at a place not named. Moreover, in the list of chiefs, Hercules is substituted for Peleus.

The Harleian version represents Hector as the ambassador, instead of Antenor, but as the Lincoln's Inn and Sutherland versions agree with Benoît in this respect, I conclude that this divergence is due entirely to

the author of the Harleian version. I have already
tried to show that he is less faithful to his original than
the author of the version represented by the other two
manuscripts, and it is evident that he assigns the embassy to Hector in order to avoid the introduction of a
new name.

Now, Konrad's version agrees with the English poem
in the two divergences from Benoît above mentioned.
He represents Priam as speaking for war, and the parliament for peace on condition of the restoration of
Hesione. Moreover, instead of sending the messenger
on a round of visits to the Greek princes, he makes him
meet them together in one place. This method avoids
the wearisome repetitions of our version of Benoît, and
we might readily conclude, were it not for Konrad's
agreement, that the English poet adopted it independently, in his effort after compression, especially as he
has pursued the same method before. Harl. 83–107
relate how Hercules and Jason find Telamon, Nestor,
Castor, and Pollux, together, rouse them to vengeance
against Laomedon, and receive their promise to make
war upon him. Our version of the *Roman de Troie*
occupies 79 lines (2083–2162), in describing Hercules'
visits to the princes individually, his appeals to them,
and their replies. In this case, Konrad follows Benoît
exactly. We are, therefore, driven to the conclusion
that the English poet's compression is original. Granz
conjectures that he may have received this suggestion
from the method of compression adopted by the author
of the extended *Roman de Troie* in his description of
the embassy of Priam's messenger to Greece. This
may very well be true, but in general we may say that

the English poet needed no such suggestion.   His effort
after condensation was original.

　　The following correspondences between *The Seege of
Troye* and Konrad's poem certainly indicate a common
source :

Kon. 18026.

. . . 'ir herren tugenthaft,
der werde künic rîche
von Troye, Priamus genant,
der hât ze boten mich gesant
vür iuwer angesiht dâ her.'

18035.

er hiez iuch vrâgen alle,
wan iu daz wol gevalle,
daz ir büezent im den schaden,
dâ mite er von iu wart geladen
bî sînes vater zîte,
den ir an eime strîte
ze tôde sluogent âne schult.

18088.

. . . ir widersenden
geruochent im die swester sîn.

18066.

daz man die frouwen hôchgeborn
hât anders, denne ir schône stê
daz tuot im alsô rehte wê.   .

18078.

(er) heizet iuch gelîche
und algemeine biten hie,
daz ir geruochent eteswie
ze buoze sîner hende stân
der dinge, der im sî getân.

HARL. 323.

'Lordyngis,' he seyde, 'I am now here,
Com from Troye as a mesenger;
The king Pryamus me hedur send,
And asketh howe ye will be demened
Of that ye comyn ayens his pees,
And slouwe his fader gyltles.
And wheche of you haue his suster hend,
I rede þat ye ayen her send,
For sekerly it is nought right
A kyngis doughter to serue a knyght;
I rede þat ye to him gone,
And in his grace put you anone.'

Secondly, the dream of Hecuba (Harl. 209–38). The present form of the *Roman de Troie* contains no mention of this episode. It appears, however, in Malkaraume's version, MS. G. Paris has related to his father and brothers the story of his awarding the golden apple to Venus, and her consequent promise to bestow upon him the most beautiful woman in Greece. Upon this promise he bases his claim to lead the expedition then planning against the Greeks. His brother, Helenus, foretells the disaster that will result if Paris' claim is allowed, and his warning is emphasized by Hecuba, who narrates the premonitory dream that visited her before Paris' birth. In the English poem, this episode is connected with the mention of Paris in the account of Priam's family, and therefore is related before the story of Paris' judgment. Konrad introduces it at the very beginning of his poem.

Malkaraume founded his version of the episode upon Ovid, *Heroides*, V and XVI, and therefore relates, not only the dream of Hecuba, but the loves of Paris and

Œnone. He omits, however, all other description of
Paris' life in the fields, which plays so important a part
in the English and German poems. This circumstance,
together with the position in which the episode is found
in MS. G, renders it highly improbable that this was the
version used by Konrad and the English poet. The
version is important in this connection merely because
it indicates the possibility of another recension of
Benoît which better suits our theory. For similar
reasons, it is improbable that Konrad and the English
poet made use of Ovid directly for this episode.
Ovid does not account for all the facts. Moreover,
it is impossible that those facts should have been
independently added by the two poets, for there is a
striking agreement between them in many particulars.
We owe to Greif conclusive evidence for this view.
By careful comparison, he has shown that, in the episodes relating to the birth and youth of Paris, no less
than four distinct versions are in substantial agreement; namely, Konrad's *Der trojanische Krieg*, *The
Seege of Troye*, the *Trojumanna Saga*, and a prose re-
daction in the Old Bulgarian tongue. From the forms
of the proper names, Greif (*op. cit.*, pp. 102, 103)
conjectures a Latin life of Paris as the common source
of these works; moreover, Pipin has declared for a
Latin original of the Old Bulgarian version, and Meister (*Daretis Phrygii de Excidio Troiæ Historia*, Præfatio, p. XLII), comparing the Bulgarian version with
Konrad's, says: 'Quæ modo attulimus quamvis eius-
modi sint, ut inde suspicari liceat auctorem e fonte
quodam fortasse latine scripto hausisse, cuius auctor
non ignarus fuit litterarum Romanarum, ex aliis facile

comprobari potest eum posteriore tempore vixisse atque seri huius temporis fabulas, quibus tum homines delectabantur, adhibuisse.'

This Latin work, as Granz suggests, was evidently well known, and not improbably may have been used by the author of the extended *Roman de Troie*, in which case the English poet probably knew it only through the French. This conjecture is, in my view, extremely probable, though we must not fail to note in passing a valid objection. It may well be that the English poet used this Latin life of Paris directly, in addition to the extended *Roman de Troie*, which very possibly did not contain the episode at all. If it be suggested that Konrad, who in general follows the *Roman de Troie*, relates the episode, the reply is at hand: it is certain that Konrad in this very episode drew some of his details from the *Ilias* of Simon Capra Aurea (fl. circa 1150), and it is no less possible that he turned directly to another Latin work for the rest.

Yet when all objections have been made, there remain two considerations which render it not unlikely that the English poet, in this, as in other parts of his work, drew solely from the extended *Roman de Troie*. In the first place, he is seen to have followed his French original so closely in all other respects, that there is a strong presumption in favour of his having done so here. In the second place, we find that Konrad, the author of the *Trojumanna Saga*, and the author of the Old Bulgarian prose version, introduce the dream of Hecuba at the beginning of their narratives. This agreement would imply that the episode occupied a similar posi-

tion in the source common to them all.   If the English
poet made use of that source directly, why did he
change the order?   We have seen that he is independent in some respects, yet that in general he follows
the order of events in his original.   It is, on the other
hand, quite conceivable that the author of the extended
Roman de Troie, having the elaborate poem of Benoît
ready to his hand, and desirous of filling what appeared
to him gaps in the narrative, may have inserted the episode of the dream of Hecuba, drawn from the conjectured Latin original, in the place that seemed to him
most artistic, namely, in the description of Priam's
family.

No explanation is entirely satisfactory.   We can but
state presumptions in favor of one or another of many
possibilities.   In general, three main solutions present
themselves : (1) that in this particular episode, Konrad and the English poet followed a recension of the
Roman de Troie that had been extended by the use of
a Latin life of Paris; (2) that, temporarily abandon-
ing the *Roman de Troie*, they made independent use of
that Latin life; (3) that Konrad used the Latin life
directly, in addition to the *Roman de Troie*, thus altering
the place of the episode, while the English poet knew
the Latin life only through the French.   While I am
inclined to the view last mentioned, I can pronounce
positively for none of them.   In any case, a Latin life
of Paris, now lost, for the suggestion of which we are
indebted to Greif, was the ultimate source of this and
the succeeding episode in *The Seege of Troye*.   The
author of that life summed up the scattered references
of Ovid, Hyginus, Apollodorus, and Euripides, and

)ossibly made some original contributions to the
:tory.

A few correspondences between *The Seege of Troye*
ind the other versions of this episode will indicate how
:trong is the presumption in favor of an ultimate com-
non source.

The dream of Hecuba:

HARL. 209–12.

That nyght that Alisaunder was begeteth,
A mervelous dreme his moder dremeth,
That out of her body sprong a brond
That brent Troye and all þe lond.

KON. 350.

und dô si [Hecuba] swanger worden was,
dô viel ûf si der sorgen soum,
wande ir kom ein leider troum
in ir slâfe nahtes für
. . . von ir herzen lûhte
ein vackel, des geloubent mir,
diu gewahsen wære ûz ir
und alsô vaste wære enzunt,
daz si Troye unz an den grunt
mit ir fiure brande.

The age of Paris when he was sent into the fields:

L. I. 249–51; 257, 258.

And whan þe child was seoue ȝer old,
He was fair and of speche bold.
His modir þouȝte on hire dremyng,

*   *   *   *   *   *

And made him to þeo feld to gon,
To kepe swyn, wiþ staf and ston.

TROJANSKA PRICHA, p. 159, l. 29.

Et adolescebat valde cito.   Et cum esset septem annorum, pueri
. ambo ibant in campum cum patre suo.

His life in the fields :

L. I. 267–74.

Bote when þe child sawȝ fyȝte bole or bor,
Or any oþir best, lasse or more,
He hadde gret ioye heom to byholde,
Whiche of heom oþir ouercome scholde.
þeo child wolde do ilke best to fyȝt,
And hade gret ioye of þat syȝt;
Wilke best wolde fyȝte and stande,
He wolde him coroune wiþ a garlande.

KON. 646.

swaz dâ gesigte bî der stunt .
ez wære ein ohse, ez wære ein wider,
daz reht einleit er dô niht nider,
wan er im eine crône
sazt ûf sin houbet schône.

TROJANSKA PRICHA, p. 159, l. 31.

Pariz committebat duos boves et pungebant inter se et uter
vincebat, ei nectabat coronam e floribus.

TROJUMANNA SAGA, p. 20, l. 6.

Ok á nokkorum degi, er hann gætti feárins, kom til hans griðúngr einn mikill, er hann hafði eigi fyrr sét, ok barðist við einn af
hans griðúngum, ok varð sá sigraðr er Alexandr átti, þa setti þórr
kórónu af dyrlegum blómum yfir höfuð hans; ok annan dag kom
griðúngr, ok fór sem hinn fyrra dag; ok hinn þriðja dag kom hinn
sami griðúngr, ok mátti sá minna fyrst, er Alexandr átti, ok þá
batt hann brodd einn mikinn í enni honum, ok mátti sá þá ekki
við, er til var kominn, ok undi þá Alexandr vel við, ok því setti
hann kórónu á höfuð honum, ok tiguaði hann þá svá fyri sigr sinn.

The name Paris :

L. I. 275, 276.

Of alle dedis þe the child was wis,
Forþy he was called child Parys.

Kon. 662, 663, 673.

Daz er geheizen Pâris
wart dur sin gelîchez reht.
Dô wart er Pâris dô genant.

Thirdly, the judgment of Paris (Harl. 400–70). As in Benoît, this episode in the English poem is part of Paris' address to Priam, urging that the command of the expedition to Greece be entrusted to himself instead of to Hector. In Konrad, however, its place is different. The story of the dream of Hecuba is followed by the loves of Paris and Œnone, and the marriage of Peleus and Thetis. This serves to introduce the episode of the judgment of Paris, which, as in the English poem, is not a dream, but an actual occurrence. Later in the poem, when Konrad wishes to introduce it into Paris' address to Priam, to avoid repetition he makes Paris relate how, in a dream, Mercury had brought him a letter from Venus assuring him that now she would keep her promise and help him to win Helen from the Greeks. This is manifestly an original detail of Konrad's, invented to bring the episode into relation with his main theme. We may see here additional proof that the place of the episode in the Latin life of Paris was at the beginning, and that the author of the extended *Roman de Troie*, more clever than Konrad, allowed it to stand where Benoît had placed it, in the most artistic position possible. It was natural for

the author of a life of Paris to place the episode at
the beginning of his hero's career, but Konrad had
not sufficient penetration to allow for the difference
in theme between the Latin work and his own, and
so was obliged to resort to the artifice above described.

The Latin life of Paris probably contained the Œnone
episode and the marriage of Peleus and Thetis, as these
are to be found in Konrad and the Old Bulgarian version.   In *The Seege of Troye* there is no mention of the
former whatever, though Granz conceives lines 243, 244
to be a reference to it; but the context and the corresponding lines of the Lincoln's Inn version 281, 282,

> His qwene, his sone, wiþ him he nam,
> And hastely to Troye he cam,

indicate clearly that the reference is to Priam.   A
reference to the nuptials of Peleus is to be found in
lines 403, 404, but neither incident was of sufficient
importance for the English poet to linger over it.   It
is possible also, though not probable, that the Latin
life contained no mention of Œnone, in which case
there would be an excellent reason why she should not
be mentioned in the English poem.   Greif contends
that Konrad and the author of the Old Bulgarian version derived the story independently from Ovid.

Benoît's narrative offered abundant opportunity to
the interpolator.   The source from which the engraved
apple came is not intimated; this suggested to the
interpolator the description of the nuptials of Peleus,
which is treated at length by Konrad, the *Trojumanna
Saga*, and the Old Bulgarian version, and suggested
by *The Seege of Troye*.   Benoît merely indicates the

strife between the goddesses, and simply describes their promise to Paris, Venus' promise alone being expressly stated. Konrad, the *Trojumanna Saga*, the Old Bulgarian version, and *The Seege of Troye*, all dramatize the occurrences, and relate the conversations with varying degrees of completeness. If their agreement were not so striking, we might conceive that the direct discourse of the English poet arose from his dramatic tendency, to which allusion has been made. Under the circumstances, we must conclude that he found the dramatic form in the extended *Roman de Troie* which lay before him.

The Lincoln's Inn version follows Benoît closely in the description of the scene of Paris' hunt, as will be evident from the following comparison. The Harleian version omits it, probably for the sake of brevity.

BEN. 3842–54.

L'autrier ès kalendes de Mai,
Chaçoe en Inde la major
Un cerf, onques ne vi graignor.
Le jor le chacièrent mi chien,
Azzez corui, onc ne pris rien.
Molt fist grant chalt d'estrange guise;
Le jor ne venta gaires bise.
Mes veneors et toz mes chiens
Perdi; el vals de Tariens
Lez la fontaine où nus n'aboivre,
Très desoz l'onbre d'un geneivre
M'estut dormir, nel poi muer
Anceis qu'avant poïsse aler.

L. I. 457–76.

þis endurday ich wende into þeo forest,
To hunte and take som wilde beste

Y tok þeo honte and houndis tene,
To witen how þey wolde renne.
We haden mukil gomen and gleo,
Of venesoun we haden gret plente.
þo wente we ilkon oure way fer,
To honte for þeo wilde deor.
Y prikide and rod forþ good pas;
þeo weder chaunged, gret myst þer was,
So þat Y loste my felawes ilkon,
Of alle heom no saw Y neur on;
And in þeo forest Y rod so longe,
þat my ryȝte way Y loste and tok þeo wronge;
So in wiþ a litel while,
Y passede into þeo forest two myle.
Anon aslep me tok,
þat Y no myȝte ryde no loke;
Y alyȝte adoun apou þe grounde,
And lay and slepte a litel stounde.

The Lincoln's Inn version makes great confusion in the names of the divinities who visit Paris. They are Venus, Jupiter, Saturnus (Juno), Mercurius (Pallas). They are evidently conceived of as goddesses, as is indicated by l. 480,

> 'Foure ladies of eluene land.'

Whence this singular blunder is derived cannot be determined. The number four instead of three may possibly arise, Greif conceives, from a misunderstanding of Benoît 3855-8:

> . . . . . . en avison
> Vi devant moi Mercurion;
> Juno, Venus, et Minerva,
> Vindrent o lui,

though it is hardly likely. But Greif's further conjecture that the names show the influence of the Latin
life of Paris, in which Jupiter, and, according to the
Old Bulgarian version, Phœbus, direct the striving
goddesses to Paris for the award, seems to me most
improbable.

Fourthly, Paris' residence in Greece. Harl. 497–
623. The versions of Konrad and the English poet
differ from Benoît's in two important respects. According to Benoît, 4203–4582, Paris on his way to
Greece meets Menelaus who is sailing for ' Pirre' to
visit Nestor, though the poet distinctly assures us, l.
4208, that he does not know the object of the visit :

Mès gie ne sé dire por quei.

Arrived at 'Citherea' where a religious feast is cele-
brating, Paris joins in the ceremony, and when asked
by the Trojans who he is, frankly admits that he is the
son of Priam, seeking Castor and Pollux to obtain of
them the restoration of his aunt, Hesione. Helen,
learning that Paris has arrived in the island, goes to
the temple to sacrifice, and there meets the Trojan
prince. The poet does not expressly state that the
object of her going to the temple was to see Paris, but
he certainly implies it. From this point, the English
poet agrees sufficiently with Benoît. There are minor
divergences, but they arise from his tendency toward
compression.

It is evident, however, that he has made two important changes in the earlier part of the story. Menelaus
is present in the island throughout Paris' stay, but
apparently does not meet him. Moreover, when asked

who they are, Paris and his party answer that they are
merchants from the Ottoman Sea.

We find in Konrad a partial, though significant, agreement with the English version. Menelaus is present
with Helen when Paris enters the temple, and invites
him to his home. A few days later, Menelaus departs
to the aid of Castor and Pollux in war, and entrusts
his guests to Helen and the servants. Moreover, on
Paris' arrival in the island, he declares that he is from
the city of Karthage in Libya.

KON. 20466.

güetliche wart der clâre
gevrâget dâ der mære,
von welhem land er wære.
Des antwurt in dô Pâris
als ein bescheiden herre wîs,

20476.

'ich wart erzogen ze Lybiâ,

20478.

geheizen ist Karthâge
ein stat, von der ich bin geborn.'

HARL. 501-6.

Eueri man come hem to behold,
And curteysley asked hem what þey wold.
Sir Allsaunder seyd, and al his,
And answerd hem with wordis wyse:
'Marchauntis,' þey seyd, 'þat we be;
Out of the See Octaman comen wee.'

As to the first partial agreement, it may serve as an indication, no more, that the author of the extended *Roman*

de Troie represented Menelaus as present throughout Paris' stay. To do this, he had merely to omit the unexplained journey to Nestor and the meeting of Paris and Menelaus on the sea, as Menelaus has no further part in Benoît's narrative. Konrad extended the story by the free use of Ovid, *Heroides*, XVI.

As to the second, and much more significant agreement, it is almost certain that, in the extended *Roman de Troie*, Paris did not make a truthful answer to the inquiries of the Greeks. It was hardly likely that he would do so, considering the treatment that Antenor, on a similar errand had already received. The author of the extended *Roman de Troie* perceived the improbability, and made Paris declare himself a Carthaginian, and possibly a merchant. He forgot, however, that Benoît immediately allows it to come to the ears of Helen that Paris has arrived in the island, and so we have this inconsistency remaining in the Harleian version of *The Seege of Troye*. The Lincoln's Inn version, 607–10, avoids it by a general statement :

> Mukil folk com heom to byholde,
> And hendly axed what þey wolde.
> Alisaunder Paris and alle his
> Answerde þo wiþ wordis wis.

Konrad, too, avoids the inconsistency by letting Menelaus remain ignorant of Paris' identity.

Fifthly, the youth of Achilles (Harl. 999–1126). Of this episode, the ancient source is plainly the *Achilleis* of Statius. The question is whether Konrad and the English poet used Statius directly, or whether they adopted the version of his poem interpolated into the extended *Roman de Troie*. The poem of Benoît, with which we are familiar, makes no mention of Achilles' youth. The hero is introduced at line 5645, in the description of the Greek fleet, and his first part in the action of the poem is his mission to the oracle of Delphi.

We are led to conclude that Konrad and the English poet had not direct access to the *Achilleis* by several divergences from it, common to them both. Statius, l. 447, represents the Greeks as at Aulis when Achilles is needed, and his whereabouts learned by Calchas. Konrad introduces him in the first campaign after the death of Protesilaus, while in the English poem he appears at the end of the third campaign, after the death of Protesilaus and Patroclus. But, as we have already seen, p. lvii, the English poet treats Benoît's battles with great freedom, and the third campaign of *The Seege of Troye* is really a combination of the first and fourth campaigns as described by Benoît. However, the English poet agrees with Konrad in introducing Achilles immediately after the death of Protesilaus.

In the second place, the search for Achilles, according to Statius, arises from the fame that has gone abroad of his rigorous training by Chiron, and of his bath in the Styx, and from the hope that he, at any rate, is Hector's peer. Both Konrad and the English poet represent the Greeks as reminded of Achilles by severe defeat at the hand of Hector and the loss of some of their heroes. The circumstances of his introduction, therefore, by the English and German poets, are quite different from those of Statius. In fact, Protesilaus, who in the *Achilleis* incites Calchas to the discovery of Achilles' hiding-place, is the very hero whose death, in the English and German poems, rouses the Greeks to send for the young avenger.

In the third place, Statius represents the fame of the young hero's prowess and invulnerability as the ultimate cause of his summons. According to Konrad, that cause is the prophecy of Proteus, who foretells that Troy can be subdued only through Achilles' might. In the English poem it is Palamedes (Palmydes) who reads the prophecy ' in a planete.' Though the English and German poets differ as to details, as to the essential thing they agree with each other and differ from Statius.

In the fourth place, Konrad affirms that it was Thetis' recollection of Proteus' prophecy that her son should fall before Troy, which led her, on the return of Paris from Sparta, to conceal him at Scyros. In *The Seege of Troye*, Thetis reads this prophecy in 'the furmament.' Statius, however, does not expressly say that Thetis was led to her act by the prophecy, but merely by her fears arising from the growing fame of the youth. In the relation existing here between the English poem and Konrad's there is a strong resemblance to that existing between them in the third instance under this head.

Following are instances of rather close verbal correspondences between Konrad's poem and *The Seege of Troye:*

As to the music played at Lycomedes' feast :

HARL. 1074–76.

Diuerse melodye for to shewe
Of trumpes, tabours, and nakeres —
Pypers, sarsynners, and symbaleris;

KON. 28204.

Man hôrte lûten under in
Tambûren, schellen, phifen.

As to Achilles' appearance 'in maydens wede':

KON. 27752.

sin starker lîp,
der schœne was und ûfreht.
nû daz den wunneclichen kneht
die boten heten an gesehen
und si begunden bêde spehen,
daz er unvröuweclichen tete.

HARL. 1082.

Achelles was long and grete withall,
Brode brest and stought vysage.
*   *   *   *   *   *

All þe knyghtis þat þere was
Behelden euermore on Achelles,
*   *   *   *   *   *

And inwardly behylden him,
And seyd it was neuer woman,
So large. . . .

For parallel passages from Statius, see Literary Notes.
After the ruse of the messengers has succeeded, there
is, in Achilles' speech, as told by Konrad and the English poet, a tone of regret for his idle life among the
maidens, which is quite absent from Statius' version.

ACHILLEIS, II, 178.

At ferus Æacides. . . .
. . . conspicit hastam;
Infremuit torsitque genas et fronte relicta
Surrexere comæ; nusquam mandata parentis,
Nusquam occultus amor, totoque in pectore Troia est.

Kon. 28356.

halsperge, lanzen unde swert,
helm unde liehte schilte
besach der knappe milte
mit flizeclichen ougen.

28375.

Gedâhte in sinem muote des:
'bin ich der küene Achilles,
den Schŷron erzogen hât,
wes trage ich denne wibes wât?

Harl. 1111.

Achilles beheld aryght
The fayre armur þat was so bryght;

1117.

And to þe kyng he seyd thenne:
' Wenyst þow, sir, I were woman?
I am Achilles, soo mote I the,
Strenger thanne ony of þy men.'

There are, to be sure, many divergences of detail
between Konrad's poem and *The Seege of Troye*. For
example, Konrad has introduced the story of Achilles'
youth piecemeal. The first part, describing Achilles'
life with Chiron, is connected with the marriage of
Peleus and Thetis, and directly follows it. The second
part, his residence at Scyros, follows, as we have seen,
the rebuilding of Troy. Moreover, Konrad fails to
make it quite clear that the bath in the Styx was an
actual occurrence, and not a pretence on the part of
Thetis.

The English poet, unlike Konrad, confuses the Centaur Chiron with Peleus, the father of Achilles (Harl.

1017, 1018; L. I. 1155, 1156; 1173–80). This arises
probably, not from a misunderstanding of the original,
but from the poet's desire for simplicity. The names
of Achilles' parents were probably followed, in the extended *Roman de Troie*, by the mention of Chiron, and
the discipline to which he subjected his ward. The
English poet, to avoid the introduction of a new name,
attributed to Achilles' father the nature and work of
the Centaur. This transformation certainly appeared
in the original English poem, for both versions to which
we have access reproduce it. As the following lines
will show, the Lincoln's Inn version briefly describes
the training of Achilles:

L. I. 1171–82.

When Achilles was seoue ȝeir old,
He was wys and of speche bold,
And þus was his fadir wone
For til gere his ȝonge sone
To waden in þeo deope see feor yn,
And made him stonde vp to þe chyn,
To fyȝte aȝen þe wawes grete;
And ȝef he feolle, he wolde him bete.
And ȝet he made þeo child more do,
To take þeo lyounes wheolpes hire fro,
And for he was so hard of skyn,
þey no myȝte no damage do him.

A similar description occurs in the Sutherland MS.,
1151–62. It is natural to suppose that this passage
was found in the original English poem, but was omitted
by the maker of the Harleian version for the sake of
brevity. A similar omission of details that appear in
the Lincoln's Inn version occurs in the Harleian account

of the youth of Paris. Granz (*op. cit.*, p. 82), declares that, for the additional details of the story of Achilles, we are indebted to the transcriber of the Lincoln's Inn version, and not to the original poet. It seems, however, hardly reasonable to suppose that a copyist would revert to the source of his original, as Granz conceives, for the sake of adding unimportant details to his version. To this complex explanation of a simple phenomenon, Granz is forced by his primary conception, adopted from Zietsch, that the Harleian is the more accurate of the two versions of *The Seege of Troye*. As I have already tried to show, p. xxxvii–xli, the contrary is the fact.

If we had to deal with either Konrad or the English poet alone, we might believe, with Greif, that he used Statius from memory; but their agreement in divergence from Statius forces us to conclude that they used a common original, and that original was probably the version of the episode found in the extended *Roman de Troie*.

As to the point of the old French poem, at which the interpolation was probably made, Konrad furnishes us some light. He tells us that Achilles, on his arrival in the camp of the Greeks, was received by his friend Patroclus with a hearty welcome, and moreover he describes later Achilles' lament over his dead friend. This excludes the notion that his arrival followed Patroclus' death, as in *The Seege of Troye*. Since both agree to make his arrival follow the death of Protesilaus, we may conclude that the description of the youth of Achilles in the extended *Roman de Troie* occurred after the death of Protesilaus in the first campaign.

The introduction of the hero at this point necessi-
tated some changes in the earlier part of Benoît's poem.
Achilles' name was stricken from the catalogue of
ships, and we find his place taken in the Harleian version of *The Seege of Troye* by Ulysses (Suth. and L. I.
MSS. — Daries), the portrait of whom, however, is evidently drawn from Benoît's description of Achilles.
Moreover, he is called (l. 718) lord of Parpachy,
which is the very land (l. 1006) in which Achilles was
said to have been born.

In the Harleian version of *The Seege of Troye*,
Ulysses (Suth. and L. I. MSS. — Daries) consults the
oracle of Delphi, a function assigned by Benoît to
Achilles. Konrad omits the episode altogether. The
journey of Achilles and Telephus to Mysia was also
probably omitted in the extended *Roman de Troie*.

I have already shown, p. lxv, that Malkaraume's
version of the *Roman de Troie* is not the one used by
the poet of *The Seege of Troye*. Even in the passage
that reminds us most strongly of the English poem,
namely, the story of Hecuba's dream, Malkaraume does
not account for all the facts, and we have seen, by comparison with Konrad von Würzburg, that these additional facts are not to be ascribed to the originality
of our poet. We have in Malkaraume's account of the
visit of Ulysses to the court of Lycomedes, another
proof that we have not yet found the version we seek,
for he makes Neoptolemus, or Pyrrhus, the object of
Ulysses' mission.

I have now, adopting the theory and method of
Granz, tried to render probable the conjecture that a
version of the *Roman de Troie*, in part abridged and in

part extended, was the chief source of *The Seege of Troye;* that in fact the English poem is little more than an extremely condensed paraphrase of this original. It is in the method alone, not in the substance, that the English poet's originality is found, but in the method it was allowed the freest play. When Granz (*op. cit.,* pp. 86, 87) attempts to draw from the poem of Konrad and *The Seege of Troye* a definite notion of the contents of their common original, I believe he carries his theory too far, and loses sight of the originality of the two poets. Because neither Konrad nor the English poet mentions certain passages in Benoît, we have absolutely no ground for believing that the author of the extended *Roman de Troie* also omitted them. Our two poets merely chose from the materials at hand what suited their purpose. Because the last great event of the English poem is the death of Polyxena, it does not at all follow that the revised *Roman de Troie* did not contain Benoît's *Odyssey.* The English poet's object was to narrate the siege of Troy. We have seen how carefully his materials were shaped to that end. When the siege was over, his task was done, and he was quite capable of employing a formula, lines 1910–16, to sum up Benoît's additional 4000 lines.

I have tried to show that the immediate source of *The Seege of Troye* was a recension of the *Roman de Troie*, which, in respect to certain details, was more extended than the one we possess. Those details were derived, we have seen, from various Latin sources, — Statius, Dares, and, probably, an unknown life of Paris. In conclusion, I desire to add a word respecting the ultimate classical sources of those details.

As I shall indicate by references in the Notes, besides Homer, a large number of Greek and Latin writers were put under contribution in order to expand the Troy Legend to the complex form in which it appears in our poem. Among the tragic poets of Greece, Euripides appears to have contained the most abundant materials. The *Bibliotheca* of Apollodorus, a Greek grammarian of Athens (fl. B.C. 140), may be considered an ultimate source, for most of the works from which he derived his information are now lost (Smith, *Dictionary of Greek and Roman Biography and Mythology*). Ovid, of course, supplied much material, and Hyginus (*Fabularum Liber*), though hardly a classical writer, was probably the channel through which considerable information flowed. These are the chief names with which we associate those details of the Middle English version of the legend in which it diverges most strikingly from its Homeric origin.

DIALECT.

PHONOLOGY. — In spite of the labours of Zietsch and Fick, the phonology of our three versions of *The Seege of Troye* has yet to be thoroughly investigated. While their work must be the basis of all succeeding investigation, the examples cited by them are not sufficiently numerous nor classified rigidly enough to justify a sound induction. The present discussion, however, will have to do with the phonology of the Harleian version alone, and with that only so far as it throws light upon the dialect in which the version is written.

Both Zietsch and Fick are clear that it is the work of a Southern scribe. Zietsch further concludes that the original poem was written in that dialect, while Fick, having access to the Sutherland MS., is able to show that no such conclusion can be drawn. The most decisive phonological test of Southern English is the persistence of y and $\bar{y}$, representing the i-umlaut of O.E. u and $\bar{u}$; the most decisive test of Northern English is the persistence of O.E. $\bar{a}$. It should also be borne in mind that in the chaotic state of Middle English orthography, no trustworthy conclusions can be drawn from phonological examples that are not certified by rimes. Now Fick declares (*op. cit.*, p. 30) that 'not one rime in y, $\bar{y}$, or $\bar{a}$ can be found in which all the manuscripts agree.' It is, therefore, evident that we have no decisive phonological data for determining the dialect of the original poem.

While our chief concern is with the Harleian version, it should be said in passing that both the Lincoln's Inn and Sutherland MSS. give so many unmistakable indications of a Northern origin as to force us to conclude that they represent a version (cf. pp. xxx, xxxi) in the Northern dialect of English.

Besides the agreement of Zietsch and Fick as to the Southern origin of the Harleian version, we have the testimony of two other scholars. Brandl (*Paul's Grundriss*, II, 1, p. 658) says : 'Auf dem Gebiet des höfischen Epos finden wir im südlicheren England . . . eine Belagerung von Troja (Arch. LXXII, 11).' Karl Bülbring (*Geschichte der Ablaute der starken Zeitwörter innerhalb der Südenglischen*, Strassburg, 1889, p. 34) says : '*Seege of Troye* . . . Handschr. H. zeigt den südlichen Dialekt reiner. Zietsch . . . vermag als Heimat der Gedichtes nur allgemein den Süden anzugeben. Mir scheint es wegen folgender Reime und Formen in die Heimat Chestres zu gehören, nach Kent oder eine unmittelbar angrenzende Landschaft.' Fick does not admit the possibility of localizing the version so precisely. He says (*op. cit.*, p. 22 f.): 'Wenn Bülbring die hs. H. nach dem südosten von England versetzt, so ist dazu zu bemerken, dass, von belegen im versinnern abgesehen, wenigstens das verhalten von ae. *y* und *ŷ* in dieser beziehung nichts entscheidet. *y* erscheint als *e* nur in dem worte *dynt*, sonst zweimal als *i*, *ŷ* gar als *u*. Das verhalten von ae. *á*, das nur als *o* vorkommt, sowie die mehrfach gesicherten singular- und pluralform des präsens auf *th*, weisen nur auf den süden im allgemeinen hin.'

Without entering into an exhaustive discussion of the subject, a few of the principal examples may be cited upon which Bülbring bases his argument :

      y, representing O.E. $y < u + i$, riming with *e* :
Harl. 143. dynt : pament.
    1011. verement : dynte.
    1291. fundament : dynt.

      e, within the verse, representing O.E. $y < u + i$:
    1311. beryed (O.E. byrgan $<$ W. Germ. *burgjan).

      e, representing O.E. *ŷ* (= O.E. *ío*), riming with *e* :
    513. here (O.E. hȳran, hieran) : were.

      y, representing O.E. *i*, riming with *e* :
    1199. rynne (O.E. rinnan) : yerne (O.E. georn. A peculiarity of Kentish [Sweet, *History of English Sounds*, p. 406] is that it represents O.E. *eo* by *ye*, while, in the Southern dialect in general, O.E. *eo* persists).

e, within the verse, representing O.E. unstable *y*:
365. meri (O.E. myrge).

Brandl (*op. cit.*, p. 611) says: 'In den Reimen
verrät sich ein Kenter gegenüber andern Südländern
besonders dadurch, dass er nicht bloss mit ziemlicher
Consequenz *y* (aus. germ. *u*+*i*), sondern auch oft *y̆*
mit *e* bindet.'

While the above examples of *y* : *e* rimes are not sufficient to prove a Kentish origin, yet the additional
examples of *e* within the verse, as the representative
of O.E. *y*, certainly lend some weight to the conjecture. The question suggests an interesting field for
investigation.

I shall now proceed to enumerate the chief arguments
that prove the Southern origin of the Harleian version.

Vowels.

It may be broadly asserted that the representative of
O.E. *a* before *n* or *m*, with or without a following consonant, is, in the Southern dialect *o*, in the Northern
dialect *a* (cf. Wissmann, *King Horn*, Strassburg, 1876,
pp. 7-9; Schleich, *Beitraege zum mittelenglischen Roland*,
Anglia, IV, p. 307; Sweet, *op. cit.*, p. 406), though the
rule has many exceptions.

The following examples certified by rimes show that
O.E. *a* before *n*, with or without a following consonant,
d or *g*, is generally represented by *o* :

vndirstond : lond, 33; lond : fond, 115; brond : lond, 211; wrong :
strong, 339; etc. Sixteen instances.

But one rime occurs of *a* followed by *n*+consonant, namely:

wande : hande, 915.

There are eight occurrences of *a* : *o*, *ou*+*n* rimes, showing that the sounds must have approached each other rather closely :

became : vppon, 1027; wonde : onderstande, 925; man : Agamy-
non, 797 (L. I. 973, man : Agaman); Agamanoun : man, 705
(L. I. 819, Agaman : man); Agamenoun : man, 675 (L. I. 783,
Agaman : man); leman : vppon, 451; man : vppon, 425;
Jason : kanne, 41.

There are seven instances of *a* before *n* or *nne*:

þanne : man, 125; beganne : Lymadan, 151; man : Limadan, 1489;
etc.

A second means of distinguishing the Northern from the Southern dialect is to be found in the general principle that, in the former, O.E. *ā* persists, while in the latter it is represented by *ō*.

Examples are exceedingly numerous to prove that in the Harleian version, O.E. *ā* is uniformly represented by *ō*, frequently written *oo* :

wote : wrote, 19; nones : bones, 27; also : þoo, 73; goo : thoo, 83;
cloth : gothe, 179; woo : soo, 223; gone : foone, 373; soo : moo,
389 (L. I. 443, swa : ma); more : ore, 755 (L. I. 929, mare :
ore); etc.

This *ō*, representing O.E. *ā*, is frequently made to rime with original *ō*, which leaves no doubt as to its quantity.   Examples are :

anone : kyndom (O.E. dōm), 247; þerto (O.E. tō) : go, 311; kyndom : echon, 351; so : þerto, 453; also : too, 567; also : to, 699;

þertoo : go, 905; þoo : doo, 1149; to : go, 1349; moo : doo, 1399; tho : þerto, 1405; to : forgoo, 1652; woo : to, 1674; also : too, 1682.

For evidence that such rimes occur in Southern English at the end of the fourteenth century, see Schleich, *op. cit.*, p. 307–8.

The *ō*, representing O.E. *ā*, is also frequently rimed with *ē*, of various origin :

were (O.E. *æ*) : more, 541; there (O.E. *æ*) : soore, 1403; sleth (O.E. *ie*) : gooth, 1885; wote : fete (O.E. *ē*, umlaut of *ō*), 1617; goth : deth (O.E. *ēa*), 1167; slowe : drewe (O.E. *ō*), 815; ibore (O.E. *ŏ*) : eueriwhere (O.E. *æ*), 1013.

In *King Horn*, which, according to Wissmann (*op. cit.*) is Southwestern in origin, we find a similar rime: more : ȝere, 95. Examples are likewise to be found in the Middle English *Roland*, which Schleich ascribes to a district between the Southern and West Midland regions (*op. cit.*, p. 309).

It should be noted at this point that the vowels of O.E. *slēan* and *flēan* both became, in Southern English *e*, in Northern *o* (Wissmann, *op. cit.*, p. 29). A large number of instances may be cited to show that in the Harleian version the vowel is regularly *e*:

flees : Achilles, 1465; seeth : fleeth, 1219; seth : fleeth, 1295; with : sleeth, 1531; sleen (inf.), 1774; sle (inf.), 1818; sle (imp.), 1845; sleyn (ppt.), 1371; slayn (*ay*, as is shown by such rimes as batayle : dele, 15; mayn : ageyn, 67, is practically equivalent to *e*), 1780; etc.

The only forms in *o* are:

sloo, 1566; slow (pret.), 1656; slowgh (pret.), 1898; slowyn (ppt.), 1261.

Wissmann (*op. cit.*, p. 17) and Schleich (*op. cit.*, p. 308) prove by numerous examples that O.E. *i* frequently became *e* in Southern English. Following are a few of the instances of such change in the Harleian version:

> sethenne (O.E. siððan), 1500; shepp (O.E. scip), 50; leppis (O.E. lippa), 1417; þeren (O.E. þǣr+in), 1581; hedur (O.E. hider), 325; mekyl (O.E. micil), 746; wheche (O.E. hwilc), 84; thedyr (O.E. þider), 302; geve (O.E. giefan, gifan), 1093, 1094.

The following rimes will show that the *i*-sound, whether represented by *i* or *y*, approached the *e*-sound. Though *e*, in the examples, is not of O.E. origin, yet there can be little doubt of its quantity. Examples:

> siker (O.E. sicor) : beker (of uncertain origin), 1745 (cf. also seker : beker, 883; sekerly, 421); hyeng : kyng, 1664; yeng : kyng, 1437; hit (O.N. hitta) : smette, 1285; hitt : slette, 1205; rynne : yerne, 1199; hynde : wende, 1173; etc.

The change of O.E. *eo* to *e* is regarded by Wissmann (*op. cit.*, p. 19) and Sweet (*op. cit.*, p. 406) as a mark of Kentish origin. Examples of this change are:

> selke (O.E. seolc) : mylke (O.E. meolc), 1338 (cf. preceding list of examples); shorte (O.E. sceort) : herte (O.E. heorte), 1603; þenne (O.E. ðonan) : henne (O.E. heonan), 1801; smerte (O.E. smeortan) : herte, 1527; clerke : werke (O.E. weorc), 543; yerne (O.E. georn), 1200; erles (O.E. eorlas), 670; swerd (O.E. sweord), 1115; lerne (O.E. leornian), 228; ferre (O.E. feor), 1755; heven (O.E. heofon), 2; etc.

Wissmann (*op. cit.*, p. 22) declares that *y* as the equivalent of O.E. *i*-umlaut of *u* is represented in Kentish by *e* (cf. Sweet, *op. cit.*, p. 406), in Northeast

Midland English by *i*, in the West by *u*. Schleich (*op. cit.*, p. 309), on the other hand, proves by numerous examples that *i* as the representative of O.E. *y* (*i*-umlaut of *u*) is found in Southwestern English.

The following examples in our poem are perhaps not numerous enough to point conclusively to any single region as its home, yet on the whole they indicate a Southern origin:

y, representing O.E. *y* (*i*-umlaut of *u*), riming with *e* :
dynt : pament, 143; verement : dynte, 1011; fundament : dynt, 1291. Cf. p. lxxxviii.

y, representing O.E. *y* (*i*-umlaut of *u*), riming with *y*, representing O.E. *i* :
will : fylle (< full), 561; kynde (< *cundi) : fynde (O.E. findan), 1481. Within the line, gilden (O.E. gylden < * gulþins), 1492; fist (O.E. fȳst < * fuh [?]), 1896.

y, representing O.E. *y* (*i*-umlaut of *u*), riming with *y* (of same origin) :
dynt : stynt (O.E. styntan < adj. stunt), 953, 1231; mankyn (< Germ. *kun-jo) : syn (< Germ. *sunði).

CONSONANTS.

The representative of O.E. palatal *c* in Middle English is, in the Northern dialect, *k*, in the Southern, *ch* (cf. *Paul's Grundriss*, I, p. 839). While the Southern *ch* is unquestionably predominant in the Harleian version, the probable late date of the poem renders it not surprising that many instances of the Northern *k* are to be found as well.

EXAMPLES : O.E. micel is represented by myche, 188, moche, 370, 456, etc., 16 occurrences; a form with *k* occurs but

twice in the whole poem, mekyl, 746, 768. The Lincoln's
Inn version, on the other hand, has usually *k*, — mukil, 210,
etc., — and occasionally *ch*, muche, 546, etc.

dyche (O.E. dic), 257, 263; dyches, 268; lyche (O.E. gelīc), 258,
1200; liche, 708; ryche (O.E. rice), 493, 653, 656, 707, etc.;
reche, 1826; rycher, 1499; manlyche (O.E. -lice), 484; stowtelyche, 483; stoughtlyche, 814; sertenlych, 928; certenlyche,
1213.

Sweet (*op. cit.*, p. 196) indicates that -*ly*, as the rep
resentative of the O.E. adjectival suffix -*lic*, probably
had its origin in the Northern dialect, and Ten Brink
(*Chaucer's Sprache und Verskunst*, p. 134) conjectures
that it was derived from the Old Norse -*ligr*, -*liga*.
The following forms of the Harleian version are therefore of Northern origin :

sekerly, 421, 1040, 1055; rychely, 1065, 1493; manly, 45, 92, 97,
103; stoughtly, 98.

leche (O.E. lǣce), 969; techith (O.E. tǣcean), 1638; arechith
(O.E. rǣcean), 1639; fetche (O.E. feccean), 1755; fecheth,
1900 [fette, 254, and fett, 1309, are from O.E. fetian, perhaps
influenced by Old Norse feta, and hence, probably, Northern
forms (cf. Sievers-Cook, *Old English Grammar*, 196. 3)];
beseche (O.E. sēcean), 777; cheses (O.E. cēosan), 765; wachyn
(O.E. wæcc(e)an), 1816.

fishe (O.E. fisc), 1020; shappe (O.E. gesceap), 1090; washe (O.E.
wascan), 1728; shepp (O.E. scip), 50; shypp, 51; shall (O.E.
sceal), uniformly [the Northern form is sal (cf. *Paul's
Grundriss*, I, p. 841)]; shuld (O.E. sceolde), uniformly [North-
ern, suld]; Englishe (O.E. Englisc), 20

k as the representative of O.E. palatal *c*, occurs in
the following instance :

sekyn (O.E. sēcean), 1059

The following examples indicate the form assumed by O.E. final *lc* :

soche (O.E. swilc), normally; sweche, 274; eche (O.E. ǣlc), normally; iche, 1677; echon, 588, 807; euerichon (O.E. ǣfre + ǣlc + ān), uniformly.

A single Northern form with *k* :

ilkone, 420.

It should be noted incidentally that *can (kan)*, *conne (konne)* representing *gan*, *gunne*, are characteristic of Northern English. (Cf. Wülker, *Anglia*, I, p. 436, *anm.* 2. Also *The New English Dictionary, Can,* v. 2.) The Harleian version contains not a single instance of this characteristic Northern form, while the Lincoln's Inn version contains several.

Harl. gann, 1648; gan, 1735; ganne, 1115, 1199, 1849; etc.
L. I. kan, 1673; con, 1755, 1237, 1326; conne, 1889; etc.

The representative of O.E. initial palatal *g* in Middle English is, in the Northern dialect, stopped *g*, in the Southern, *y* or ȝ, though the rule has many exceptions. (Cf. Sweet, *op. cit.*, pp. 196, 197.)

The following examples will show that in the majority of instances of the verb *to give*, the Harleian version has *y* :

yeve (O.E. giefan), 296, 450, 1125, 1391, 1783, 1919; yeue, 1360; yef, 435, 1121; yaf, 1107, 1129, 1600, 1619, 1630; yave, 462, 1131; yeveth, 283; yiftis (O.E. gift), 655; yeftis, 1600; etc.

The following are the only instances with *g* :

geve, 295, 1093, 1094, 1918; gave, 150, 918, 931, 1108.

The verb *to get* (O.E. gietan):

foryete, 5; foryettet, 52; gete, 586, 1794; gotyn, 1022; begeteth,
    209.

This variation between Northern and Southern forms
is Chaucerian. Sweet (*loc. cit.*) says: 'Ch., as usual,
hesitates between Northern and Southern; yiven but
geten.'   •

yelde (O.E. gieldan), 1785; yeld, 1622; iyold, 40; yolde, 1894;
    yold, 1825.
ying (O.E. geong), 1044; yong, 30, 683, 1427, 1467, 1509, 1611,
    1858; yonger, 282, 376.
yit (O.E. giet), 25; yett, 850; yet, 1403, 1483; etc.
yere (O.E. gēar), 865, 867, 869, 898, 906, 907, 984, 1756; etc.
yate (O.E. geat), 1312, 1839, 1840; yatis, 259.
yerne (O.E. georn), 1200.

Of the O.E. 'front' or palatal group *og* (cf. Sweet,
op. cit., p. 147), represented in the Northern dialect
by stopped *g*, in the Southern by palatal *gg* (cf. Sweet,
op. cit., p. 196), there is no decisive case, as the qual-
ity of the *g* (*gg*) in the two examples *bryg* (O.E.
brycg) 260, *brygge*, 1840, is not certified by rimes.

The following examples illustrate the occurrence of
d as the representative of O.E. þ. Sweet (*op. cit.*,
p. 267) says: 'The first Modern change of (ð) into
(*d*) takes place mainly after *r* . . . or before *r* where
ð and *d* were confused.' Although in the case of *broder*,
anoder, *oder*, *toder*, *edere*, *wheder*, þ did not immediately precede or follow *r*, yet the change to *d* may come
under Sweet's general principle.

anoder (O.E. -ōðer), 24, 57, 383, 422, 711, 1207, 1262, 1512, 1531,
    1642, 1734, 1776; anodir, 340, 1644; anoþer, 378.

oder, 150, 300, 552, 575, 577, 794, 869, 918, 938, 1177, 1427; other,
576, 673 (the latter instance rimes with brodir).
toder, 85, 874, 906.

Kluge (*Paul's Grundriss*, I, p. 852) says: 'Innerhalb der me. Zeit begegnen vereinzelte *d* für ð, *th*:
dieser sekundäre Wandel dürfte vorliegen in mkent.
aider eider "jeder" ae. *æghwæþer*, Ayenb. *hwader* aus
ae. *hwæþer.* . . . Me. *coude* für *couthe* ae. *cūþe* beruht
auf Angleichung an die herrschenden Präterita auf
-de.'

edere (O.E. ǣgþer), 918; ether, 150, 576, 577, 1177, 1803, 1902;
eþer, 575.
wheder (O.E. hwæþer), 924, 1223, 1266, 1484.
cowd (O.E. cūþe), 1046, 1584; cowde, 923, 1579; koud, 544; koude,
542.

The New English Dictionary, under *Brother*, says:
'In M.E., esp. in north. dial. and Sc., the *th* was often
written *d*, perhaps after *fader, moder.*'

broder (O.E. brōþor), 200, 384, 705, 793, 802, 881, 955, 1328, 1437,
1452, 1470, 1552, 1655, 1733, 1763; brodir, 674, 708; bredryn
(O.E. brēþer), 197, 473; brodren, 1550.

In the absence of any definitely formulated criteria
by which a precise distinction may be drawn between
the Northern and Southern English of so late a period
as that at which *The Seege of Troye* must have had its
origin, the foregoing may serve as an incomplete presentation of the grounds for ascribing the Harleian version to the Southern dialect. Incomplete though it is,
it will at least show how strong is the presumption in
favor of such a view. The Northern forms, though
relatively few, seem to indicate a Northern original in

the hands of a Southern scribe, a conjecture supported
by the conclusion of Fick that the Lincoln's Inn and
Sutherland versions are undoubtedly of Northern
origin.

INFLECTION. — The Southern dialect of Middle English
abounded in plurals in -en. (Cf. *New English Dictionary*, under -en.)

The following instances of plurals in -en, -n, occur in
the Harleian version :

brodren, 1550; bredryn, 197, 473; chyldren, 243, 1784; chyldryn,
192, 1796; foon, 1774; foone, 374; eyen, 1049; sistryn, 198.

In Southern English, the nominative plural of the
third personal pronoun was *heo*, the dative and accusative, *heom*, and the corresponding possessive pronoun
was *here*. The corresponding forms of Northern English were *þei, þeim, þeire*, which show Scandinavian influence. (Cf. Sweet, *A New English Grammar*, p. 337.)

The Harleian version has always the Northern form,
þey, þei, or *þay*, in the nominative. In the oblique
cases, it has regularly Southern *hem;* occasionally *them*.
The plural possessive pronoun is regularly *her, here*,
or *hir;* occasionally *ther, þere*, or *þeyr*. For examples,
see Glossary.

The Southern form, *ich*, of the first personal pronoun
singular does not once occur. The pronoun is uniformly written *I* or *Y*, which is a derivative from the
Northern *ic* (*Paul's Grundriss*, I, p. 901). Moreover,
the Northern form of the third personal pronoun neuter,
it, regularly occurs instead of the Southern *hit*.

The following distinctions between Northern and
Southern English in the inflection of the verb are

derived from Sweet's *New English Grammar*, sections 1215–1238.

Northern English has *es* in all persons of the singular, present indicative; Southern English has *-e, -est, -eth.*

Harleian version: 1st person, vndirstonde, 1431; vnderstonde, 1709; rede, 333; hope, 763, 1770; beseche, 777; lyve, 1880; etc.

There are many forms of the first person singular without inflectional ending, but none with *es.*

2d person: wuldest, 37; þynkest, 343; spekest, 395; wenest, 398; wenyst, 1118; seyst, 421, 424; jugest, 444; holdest, 960; mystest, 1565; shuldest, 1566; fyndest, 1846; etc. Flees, 1465, and goth, 380, are probably singular.

3d person: loveth, 35; hereth, 47; clepeth, 48; foryettet(h), 52; taketh, 54, 55, 372, 615; comondeth, 67; armith, 127; cometh, 160; comyth, 375; dremeth, 210; yeveth, 283; etc., regularly.

Occasional forms of the third person singular in *s*:

dryves, 61; drives, 113; listis (certified by rime: his), 102; takes, 279, 481; takys, 583; makes, 280, 284, 482; metis, 575; gretis, 576; etc.

In Southern English, all forms of the plural present indicative end in *-eth*; in Northern English they end in *-es.*

1st person: no form occurs in *-eth.* Several forms occur without inflectional ending: desyr, 301; dwell, 509; fyght, 993; etc.

Occasional Midland forms of the first person plural in *-en* appear (cf. *Paul's Grundriss*, I, p. 904):

comen, 506; shuldyn, 1148; bene, 1476, 1747; arn, 1778; defenden, 1779; etc.

2d person: wote, 291; send, 330; gone, 333; put, 334; se, 991;
shull, 1770; besege, 1792; mowe, 1007; gete, 1794; etc.

3d person: arerith, 60; beth, 65; entreth, 66; goth, 167, 1912;
gothe, 180; robbeth, 167; hathe, 168; sleeth, 608; soroweth,
1306; berith, 1703; doth, 1912; etc.

aryves, 62, 496; ariues, 114; dryves, 147; drives, 495; toreves, 148;
fyghtes, 153; reves, 621; beleves, 622; hyes, 912; takes, 1907;
etc.

Weakened forms from the Midland plural in -en:

bene, 122; thenke, 124; begynne, 600; robyn, 621; flyng, 803;
make, 806; sene, 827; have, 828; turne, 828; turnne, 1310;
etc.

In Southern English, the preterite of weak verbs is
inflected, -ede, -edest, -ede, -eden.   In Northern English
there is no inflectional ending.

Regularly the Harleian version has no inflectional
endings:

turned (3d sing.), 18, (3d plur.), 80; loved (3d plur.), 30; cleped
(3d sing.), 31; stoffed (3d plur.), 109; etc.

Occasional inflected forms:

dyedist (2d sing.), 1727; answerdyn (3d plur.), 97; leyden (3d
plur.), 1621, 1854; broughten (3d plur.), 1901; stoftden (3d
plur.), 1911; ferden (3d plur.), 1917; etc.

In Southern English, the infinitive retained the final
-en or -e.   In Northern English the infinitive had no
such termination.

The Southern form appears generally in the Harleian version:

sayne, 923; leven, 1226; gnawyn, 1663; slene, 812, 994, 1012, 1749;
sleen, 1774; comen, 99; comon, 392; comyn, 685; done, 102;
doone, 762; don, 1793; herkyn, 116; besegen, 124; werryn,

367, 389; tellyn, 383, 540; beleven, 387; makyn, 404; meynten, 486; diskryvyn, 545; nombryn, 971; etc.

In Southern English the present participle ends regularly in *-inde*, *-ing*. In Northern English it ends in *-and*, *-ande*.

The Southern is the regular form in the Harleian version :

rydyng, 145, 1461; cryyng, 831; cryng, 1163; blowyng, 831; bekeryng, 831; cursyng, 962; wepyng, 1163; welteryng, 1442; dryvyng, 1713, 1721.

The following unmistakable Northern forms occur :

rustland, 136; rydant, 160; seyland, 488.

In Southern English, the past participle retained the prefix *i-* or *y-*, while in Northern English it was usually dropped. In Southern English, the final *-en* of strong past participles is often represented by *-e* ; in Northern English the final *-en* is usually retained.

Of the past participles occurring in the Harleian version, of which there are upwards of 220, but 23 have the prefix *i-* or *y-*. It must be remembered, however, that a very considerable part of the whole number would not take the prefix in any case. For example :

foryete, 5; vndertakyn, 121; ashamed, 76; agreved, 75, 1519; etc.

The following have the prefix :

ibought, 89; icomyn, 122; idyght, 128, 713; igadered, 129; iarmed, 156; islawe, 382; icomen, 440; icleped, 1018; iseyd, 565; iseyde, 790; islayn, 610; ifalle, 610; ywrought, 720; ibore, 1013; ifounde, 1003; idrawe, 1071; isette, 132, 1240, 1280; icome, 1467; imordred, 1673; iyold, 40.

Of the 125 strong past participles, a little more than

half have the termination *-en,* or its equivalent, while about a third have the termination *-e.*   Examples:

comyn, 74, 805, 1058; icomen, 440; vndertakyn, 121, 1201 ; taken,
      439; takon, 614; loryn, 171; lorn, 1222; slayne, 185; slayn,
      138; sleyn, 1371; slaynne, 1892; slowyn, 1261; born, 225;
      borne, 851; sene, 312; don, 336; done, 1827; knowyn, 411;
      fallyn, 519; gon, 785; wrekyn, 862; gotyn, 1022 ; etyn, 1077 ;
      hewyn, 1356; drawyn, 1372; toryven, 1443; etc.
befalle, 3, 1874; foryete, 5; nome, 81 ; come, 82; slauwe, 199;
      mette, 131; ouerþrouwe, 381; islawe, 382; totore, 385 ; forlore,
      386; begraue, 405; take, 1739; gete, 586; ibore, 1013; wonne,
      272; wone, 998; ifounde, 1003; fownde, 1522; idrawe, 1071;
      begunne, 1500; agryse, 1506; awreke, 1546; yolde, 1894; etc.

Like the discussion of phonology, the foregoing serves merely to indicate how strong on inflectional grounds is the presumption that our version is in the Southern dialect. The frequent occurrence of Northern forms, and the occasional appearance of a Midland form, indicate that dialectal distinctions were vanishing, and that English was becoming one speech.   Yet when all the facts, inflectional and phonological, are considered, the Harleian version is seen to bear distinct traces of a Southern origin.

PROSODY.

METRE. — The poem is written in the short riming couplet, each verse containing four stressed syllables. This metrical form is thus characterized by Dr. Morris (quoted by Schipper, *Englische Metrik*, I, pp. 269–70): ‘The chief rule is that every line shall contain four accents, the two principal types being afforded (1) by the eight-syllable and nine-syllable lines:

(*a*) For hém ne yéde góld ne fé, 44 [Havelok] ;
(*b*) It wás a kíng bi áre dáwes, 27 ;

and (2) by the seven-syllable and eight-syllable lines :

(*c*) Hérknet tó me góde mén, 1 ;
(*d*) Álle thát he mícthe fynde, 42.

To one of these four forms every line can be reduced,
by the use of that slighter utterance of less important
syllables which is so very common in English poetry.
It is not the number of syllables but of accents that
is essential.'

The short riming couplet is of French origin (Schipper, *op. cit.*, p. 107). The following example is taken
from the *Roman de Troie*, 1–6 :

> Salemons nos enseigne et dit,
> Et si lit len en son escrit,
> Que nul ne deit son sen celer,
> Ainz le deit len si demostrer
> Que len i ait prou et enor ;
> Car si firent li ancessor.

The first example in English is the paraphrase of
the Paternoster belonging to the middle of the twelfth
century. The following lines will exemplify this early
form of the measure (quoted by Schipper, *op. cit.*,
p. 112):

> Ure feder þet in heouene is,
> þet is al soð ful iwis !
> Weo moten to þeos weordes iseon,
> þet to liue and to saule gode beon,
> þet weo beon swa his sunes iborene,
> þet he beo feder and we him icorene,
> þet we don alle his ibeden
> and his wille for to reden.

From the middle of the twelfth century until the age
of Chaucer, this measure was extremely popular.   In
it were composed poems of a moralizing strain, like
The Owl and the Nightingale, and, especially in the
North, poems of a religious cast — homilies, legends,
Biblical paraphrases.   Everywhere it was adopted in
the development of Sagas from Romance sources.

In the North, it was strongly influenced by the alliterative long line which was there very popular.   The
latter measure, requiring of the poet merely two or
three alliterative syllables in the line, and demanding
no further attention to the metre, reacted upon the short
riming couplet in the direction of freedom and irregularity.   The anacrusis was frequently omitted, and was
sometimes even dissyllabic ; the thesis, or unstressed
interval between two stressed syllables, was sometimes
polysyllabic, sometimes omitted altogether ; when, by
the omission of the thesis, two stressed syllables were
brought into juxtaposition, the cæsura resulted, a phenomenon foreign to this measure in its normal form ;
finally, as might be expected, alliteration frequently
occurred.

Early in the fourteenth century, however, there was
a reaction in favour of a more precise treatment of the
measure, induced by the French system of versification.
A regular number of syllables was required of the line,
which henceforth approximated the octosyllabic iambic
measure.   Of this reaction, the *Cursor Mundi* is an
excellent example.   In this and similar poems, we find
the fundamental principle of Germanic stress — that
the stem-syllable shall always receive the ictus — frequently strained to conform to the French demand for

a regular succession of stressed and unstressed syllables.
This is most evident in the management of the present
participle in -*and* (Northern) and -*ing* (Southern), as
in the following examples from the *Cursor Mundi*:

> But for-þi þat na werk may stand
> Wit-outen grundwall to be lastand, 125;

> Of all þis werld mad adam king,
> Euer to last wit-outen ending, 670.

The Southern and Midland poets followed a middle
course between the excessive irregularity of the early
Northern poets and the strained precision of the later
ones. We discover, however, a tendency toward freedom in the earlier poets of the South and Midland,
and toward exactness in the later ones, caused by the
Romance influence, which entered the South after 1250.
Even in the later examples, however, there are traces
of the same licences that we have noted in the North.
The altered stress on present participles gives evidence
of Romance influence. Gower uses the measure with
the utmost regularity, as might be expected from his
French tendencies and training. Chaucer has employed
it in *The Book of the Duchesse* and *The Hous of Fame*.

In *The Seege of Troye* the verse is for the most
part regular, though we shall find examples of all the
licences already noted. The following lines will exemplify the normal forms:

With anacrusis, masculine ending,

> Sithýn that Gód this wórlde wróught, 1;

without anacrusis,

> Néuer ís nor néuer wás, 8;

with anacrusis, feminine ending,

> In Gréu he wrót it eúeri déle, 16;

without anacrusis,

> Mánye wóndris háve befálle, 3.

The number of verses in which more than four stressed syllables occur is not considerable. Examples are :

> Agéyn þe kýng of Tróye þat wás so grým, 11;
> He sáwe þe eńde and þe órder of þát batáyle, 15;
> But anóder þer wás ouer hím of gréter dignité, 24 ;
> The fáyrest I ám of þát is in óny lónd, 412;
> And ýf þou mýstest with súm wile cóm þertó, 1565.

It is clear how easily the line of five stressed syllables arose from the regular measure. We see here the origin of the metre of *The Canterbury Tales* and of many later poems.

Examples of lines containing fewer than four stressed syllables :

> They thérfore wére full wóo, 223;
> That wére in hís kyndóm, 248;
> That nó man éntere ne máy, 269.

Lines containing more than four unstressed syllables are very numerous. In this class I consider lines whose superfluous syllables cannot be eliminated by elision. Examples :

> That his sóne of the láwe wás so wýse, 240;
> And whánne the sée is hýe at the fúll, 261 ;
> Soo séker it wás it myght néuer be wónne, 272;
> An érldom he yéveth hím in hónde, 283.

All of the lines cited above contain examples of slurring (*Verschleifung*), which consists in the pro-

nunciation of two or more unstressed syllables in the
time of one; it does not include elision, which is the
suppression of a final vowel before a succeeding vowel, or
the blending of it with a succeeding vowel so as to form
a single syllable. Both slurring and elision are of frequent occurrence. Following are examples of the latter:

> Thát forsóthe amónge them álle, 2;
> The batáyle of Tróy that wás so stóught, 6;
> So séyde a knýght þat þér wás, 13.

Examples of lines containing fewer than four unstressed syllables, irrespective of feminine endings and
omitted anacruses:

> Of áll dómes hé was wýse, 237;
> Télle me nów I séy thé, 397;
> That hé so stróng a mán ís, 1479;
> In Tróye wás no mýrth thóo, 1757.

I have already referred (p. civ) to the deviations
from the Germanic principle of stress, which indicate
French influence upon the English versification of the
fourteenth century. *The Seege of Troye* contains a considerable number of such deviations. Usually the altered
stress is demanded by the necessities of rime. Examples
are:

> And whanne she waked of here dremeng,
> She sent for clerkys in grete hastyng, 214;
>
> That shall Troy to shame bryng
> Thorough his folly, withought lesyng, 222;
>
> There he was, out of knowyng,
> Yeres fyftene, without lesyng, 230;
>
> After masons he sent anone,
> That were in his kyndom, 248.

Romance words, when they occur in rimes, receive their natural stress, but within the verse they usually receive Germanic stress.   Examples :

> But game he hadde, and grete *solace,*
> Whereso he sawe in ony place, 232;

> But if it be with grete *tresoun.*
> In all this world was non sweche a town, 274;

> This *batayle* lastid, withoutyn misse, 1702;

> I may not to *batayle* gone, 1766;

> These to *traytours* plyte her trouthe, 1809.

ALLITERATION. — Alliteration is of frequent occurrence.   Two, three, and even four words in the verse may begin with the same letter.   There are several instances of double alliteration, though not enough to justify the elaborate analysis to which Ziotsch (*op. cit.*, p. 73) subjects them.   Fick's classification of alliterative words (*op. cit.*, pp. 32–35) is based upon their syntactical and lexical relations.   For a full list of examples, I must refer the reader to his dissertation.   Following are examples of the chief varieties of alliteration : .

Double alliteration :

> Fayrer formed was neuer none, 537;
> Here rode rede as blosom on the brere, 1416.

Two alliterative words :

> Soore he seyeth, and his full woo, 582;
> Toward his ost he gynneth gone, 587;
> For Alisaunder hir lordis love, 596.

Three alliterative words :

> They wrought þe walles wonder hye, 255;
> And goth to Greke in grete bost, 380;
> Wachyn wele his ward aryght, 1816;
> Of reche rentis and of rede gold, 1826.

Four alliterative words :

> The more myrthe þat eche man makes, 657.

RIMES.— The poem contains 957 rimes. A line has fallen out after l. 1627, as a comparison with the Lincoln's Inn version shows (cf. *Literary Notes*). Another line has probably fallen out after l. 1710. A scribal error is probable in l. 1831, where *strong* is made to rime with *eyre* (l. 1832); the Lincoln's Inn version has *feyr*. Line 436 is corrupt, which makes a fourth defective rime.

Of the 957 rimes, 264 are impure. Under the term impure rimes I include assonance, and the so-called perfect rimes (*rührende Reime*), which consist in identity of sound with difference of meaning (Schipper, *op. cit.*, I, p. 34; Gummere, *Handbook of Poetics*, p. 156). There are also numerous instances of identity or similarity of consonants with difference of vowels.

Feminine rimes are of frequent occurrence, though there is no pure example. I shall include under a separate treatment feminine rimes formed by final inflectional *e*, *es* (*ys*), *ed*.

Perfect rimes :

> was : was, 7; þou : þou, 395; ryt : ryght, 317.

The first two examples are, however, not pure specimens of perfect rime, as the riming words have identity of meaning as well as identity of sound.

Assonance:

him : swyn, 225; strong : garlond, 235; him : in, 243; anone : kyndom, 247; kyndom : echon, 351; drof : wroth, 507; Capharnoum : town, 525; becom : takon, 613; other : brodir, 673;
vysage : large, 1083; euerichon : come, 1133; ouercome : sone,
1449; ryve : blythe, 1525; fast : barst, 1636; engynne : him,
1660; bakke : hatte, 1696; next : best, 1799; fader : cradell,
1857, etc.

Other impure rimes :

e : *a* rimes — was : Pelles, 21, 1017; Castor : Nestor, 85, 95, 321, 335;
Ercules : was, 155, 319; thenne : Lymadan, 159; lees : was, 415;
Euluxes : was, 677; les : was, 971; Achilles : was, 1059, 1085,
1459, 1519, 1891; hadde : ledde, 1105; thenne : woman, 1117;
passe : lesse, 1851.

a : *o*, *ou* rimes (cf. p. xc) — Jason : kanne, 41; arose : was, 119;
ouerþrouwe : islawe, 381; man : vppon, 425; leman : vppon,
451; Agamenoun : man, 675, 705; man : Agamynon, 797;
became : vppon, 1027; woman : bone, 1089; smotte : satte,
1243.

a : *au* rime (probably scribal error) — cormerant : fesaunt, 1069.

aw : *ay* rime — idrawe : playe, 1071.

e : *o* rimes — In addition to the examples to be found on p. xci, the
following occur — herd : word, 563; shorte : herte, 1603; hert :
short, 1723.

e : *i* (*y*) rimes — In addition to the examples to be found on pp.
xcii, xciii, the following occur — dremeng : hastyng, 213; stopeth : comyth, 1289; selke : mylke, 1337; misse : witnesse, 1702;
mantille : welle, 1607; cete : pyte, 1853.

ē : *e* rimes — fete : sett, 1029; the : men, 1119.

e : *ey* (*ay*) rimes — ende : iseyde, 789; gayn : ayen, 827; þenne :
ageynne, 947; ayen : ongayn, 1721.

e (*ay*) : *eau* rimes — slayne : reaulme, 185; wene : reaume, 252.

i, *i* (*y*) : *ey*, *ay*, *ē* rimes — awey : sory, 175; by : away, 198; time :
sene, 349; awey : lady, 579; cry : awey, 617; Grece : iwis, 695;
prey : hye, 721; awey : twenti, 803; sey : hye, 957; dye : sey,
961; Monaly : þey, 1057; hye : fleye, 1257; fyre : chere, 1217;

weryn : ween, 1241 ; fyght : heyght, 1471 ; with : sleeth, 1531 ;
heyes : ascryes, 1680 ; day : Monaly, 1827.

o : *ou* rimes — stounde : fonde, 399 ; stounde : gronde, 477 ; adown :
akton, 929 ; down : lyon, 951 ; town : pavilion, 981 ; champyon :
renown, 1273 ; town : pavilion, 1299 ; barouns : pauelyons, 1455 ;
downe : treson, 1557 ; treson : conspiracoun, 1601 ; treson :
adown, 1615 ; baron : town, 1672 ; euermore : youre, 1797 ;
treson : town, 1869.

o : *ō* rime — word : mode, 215.

ou : *u* rime — town : summe, 1779.

ou : *y* rime — armour : fyre, 1457.

u : *o* rimes — sure : armore, 109 ; summe : Lymadon, 195 ; kun :
wone, 997 ; cunne : wonne, 1903.

u : *i, y* rimes — full : will, 53 ; insure : fyre, 1247 ; nyle : wulle, 1623.

y : *e* rime — dryves : toreves, 147.

y : *o* rimes — become : takyn, 593 ; lyf : goth, 611 ; aroos : agryse,
1505 ; toryven : toclovyn, 1443.

Feminine rimes :

Castor : Nestor, 85 ; togederc : faderc, 233 ; other : brodir, 673 ; hundrid : wonderid, 703 ; siker : beker, 1745 ; fader : cradell, 1857.

Anomalous rimes :

agreved : ashamed, 75 ; destroyed : avenged, 293.

Extended rime (*der erweiterte Reim*) occurs when
the riming words or syllables are preceded by unstressed words or syllables that rime perfectly with
each other. (Cf. *Paul's Grundriss*, II, 1, p. 1057 ;
Schipper, *op. cit.*, p. 303.) The following instances of
extended rime occur :

þis londe : his hond, 1143 ; him slow : him drow, 1656 ; to wend :
to shend, 471 ; and bold : and old, 29 ; eþer oder metis : ether
other gretis, 575 ; þe yate onto : þe yate ondo, 1839.

Of the pronunciation of final *e, es* (*is, ys*), *ed*, inflectional or not, the only safe criterion is to be found in

the rimes.   Of rimes impure in this respect 125 instances occur, which is about one-fourth of the whole
number of feminine rimes in *e, es, ed.*   Examples are:

ende : shend, 27 ; þanne : man, 125 ; owte : brought, 163 ; cloth :
    gothe, 179 ; honde : lond, 283 ; stronge : long, 489 ; mode : good,
    551 ; will : fylle, 561 ; men : fenne, 602 ; feld : yelde, 875, etc.
nons : bones, 27 ; enmyes : pryce, 367 ; nons : stonys, 655, 833, 1279 ;
    ryngs : noþyngis, 1107 ; Grece : pecis, 1662.
send : demened, 325 ; iseyd : payed, 565 ; voward : spared, 1686.

Out of thirty-five instances in which one of the riming syllables is *y*, or its equivalent *i, ey, ay*, there are
but eight occurrences of *y* : *ye* rimes, a fact that may
be regarded as a corroboration of Horstmann's conjecture (cf. pp. xxxv, xxxvi) that the Harleian version origi-
nated about the beginning of the fifteenth century.
Chaucer invariably rimes *yĕ* with *yĕ* (Ten Brink, *Chaucer's Sprache und Verskunst*, pp. 125, 193), and the
change from his usage was completed before the middle
of the fifteenth century (cf. Triggs' edition of Lydgate's
Assembly of Gods, p. xxxii).   The eight instances are :

squyery : hye, 112; prey : hye, 722; hye : chyualry, 738; sey : hye,
    958 ; dye : sey, 962 ; party : lye, 984 ; Lybye : vtterly, 1010 ; by :
    crye, 1659.

ANALYSIS.

Introduction. Importance of theme and indication of source, 1-20.

I. First destruction of Troy, 21-184.
  a. The quest of the Golden Fleece, 21-62.
  b. Lamatan warns the Greeks out of his dominions, 63-80.
  c. They prepare to avenge the insult, 81-114.
  d. Troy is destroyed and the king slain, 115-184.

II. Rebuilding of Troy by Priamus, 185-274.
  a. Priamus and his lamentation, 185-204.
  b. His family, and the dream of Ekeuba before the birth of Alisaunder, 205-246.
  c. He rebuilds the city, 247-274.

III. The parliament of the Trojans, and the unsuccessful embassy of Ector to Greece to demand the restoration of Isyon, 275-348.

IV. The ravishing of Elyn by Alisaunder, 349-660.
  a. The Trojans prepare for war, 349-374.
  b. Alisaunder relates the story of his 'judgement' as a guarantee that he will be successful in taking vengeance upon the Greeks, 375-486.
  c. Alisaunder arrives in Greece, and deceives the Greeks as to his object, 487-518.
  d. King Monaly and his beautiful queen, Elyn, 519-550.
  e. The meeting of Alisaunder and Elyn, 551-586.
  f. The battle with the Greeks, and the ravishing of Elyn, 587-620.
  g. Return of Alisaunder to Troy, and the lamentation of Elyn, 621-660.

THE SEEGE OF TROYE.

Sithyn that God this worlde wrought,
Heven and erthe all of nought,
Manye wondris have befalle;
That, forsothe, amongs them alle,
5 It maye nought bene foryete out,
The batayle of Troy that was so stought.
For soche a werre as it was
Neuer is nor neuer was;
Too and thurtty wyntyr, without fayle,
10 Men of Grece helde batayle
Ageyn þe kyng of Troye þat was so grym,
And at the laste þey ouercome him.
So seyde a knyght þat þer was,
He was cleped Sir Darras;
15 He sawe þe ende and þe order of þat batayle;
In Greu he wrot it eueri dele.
A mayster þat was full konyng syþyn
From Grewe it turned into Latyn,
And now from Latyn, God it wote,
20 A clerke into Englishe it wrote.
Lordyngis, somtime in Grece þer was
A kyng þat was called Sir Pelles.
He was not no kyng of hy degre,

But anoder þer was ouer him of greter digni
25 But yit he was kyng of Pelpeson,
And had a cosyn þat hit Jason.
Sir Jason was, for þe nons,
Fayre man of body and bones,
Curteys, hende, hardy, and bold,
30 Him loved boþe yong and old.
The kyng cleped this Jason,
And aresond him anon:
'Jason,' he seyd, 'I vndirstond
þe kyng of Troye hathe in his lond
35 A wonder þyng þat he loveth wele,
That is a gyldyn weders felle.
And wuldest þou, with summe gynne,
That wonder fell from him wynne,
And bryng me that fell of gold,
40 Thy whyle shuld bene well iyold.'
'Parfay,' seyd þenne Sir Jason,
'I wulle do þat I kanne.
Among the Troyeaunce I woll gonne
Mervayles to here, and that anoonne.
45 And if I may, manly and well,
Bryng I wull þe gylden fell.'
The kyng hereth þat he wull gone,
And clepeth his carpenters euerichon,
And bad hem þat þey shuld timber take,
50 A nobill shepp for Jaso to make.
And whanne þe shypp was redy wrought,
Sir Jasonne foryettet nought;
Of tresour he fellyd it full,
And taketh with him whom he will.
55 He taketh with him Sir Ercules,

A stalworth knyght, hardy and fers;
And many anoder, hardy and hende,
With him to Troye for to wende.
To the Crekkyshe See þey come anone,
60 Arerith seyle, and gyneth gonne.
Ouer þe se the wynde hem dryves,
And att the havon of Troye aryves.
The kyng of Troye, Sir Lamatan,
He was a wonder wyse man.
65 He herd telle that men of Greke beth
Into hys lond com and þerin entreth;
And comondeth with myght and mayn
That þei shuld seyle swythe ageyn;
And swore, so mote he thryve,
70 There shall none alyve fro thens ryve.
He bad hem thens swythe gone,
Or þey shuld dye euerichon.
Sir Ercules and Jason also
Into that lond were comyn þoo;
75 Of the kyng they were sore agreved,
And of his wordis sore ashamed,
To be so rebuked of a kyng,
So as þey mysdedon nothyng.
To dwell lenger it vaileth nought,
80 They turned her shep and cast abought.
So long thei have her wey nome,
Ayen to Grece they ben come.
Four barons ther gunne goo,
Wheche were gret lordis thoo:
85 The ton hit Pollex, þe toder Castor,
The therde Talamon, the fourthe Nestor;
And seyd: 'Lordyns, all thus atte ende,

The kyng of Troye thus gan vs shend
But these wordis bene ibought,
90 Eche of vs shull be told for nought.
And therefor helpith with socour,
And meynten manly our anour,
Or els the Troyens, þat bene so fers,
Woll vs holde for losengers.'
95 Sir Pollex and Sir Castor,
Sir Talamon and Sir Nector,
Answerdyn ryght manly,
And seyd they wold stoughtly
Among the Troyens comen and gone,
100 Magre þe kyng Sir Lymadone, —
'And magreth him and all his,
We well done that vs listis.
Nowe go we manly abought,
And gader we vs a noble rought.
105 Vppon his lond we will vp ryve,
And loke who will vs ayen dryve.'
They did do ordeyn for hemself
Good new sheppis twelfe,
And stoffed hem well and sure
110 With vitayl and good armore.
They gedered hem nobil squyery,
And went to shep all in hye.
Ouer the see þe wynde hem drives,
And the havon of Troye þey ariues.
115 They armed hem well and went to lo:
Auntres to herkyn and to fond.
The Troyens were myspayed,
And of her comyng evel afrayed;
Thorowout the cite the crye arose,

120 That eche man of hem aferd was.
     The kyng of Troye hathe vndertakyn
     That folke o Grece bene icomyn
     With a grete ost stought and grym,
     And thenke þey wull besegen him.
125 He lete make a crye ouer all þanne,
     'To hors and armes, eueri man.'
     Himsilf armith him aryght,
     And all his meyne well idyght,
     And bene igadered vpp and down,
130 And sued þe kyng out of town.
     Sone þey be togeder mette,
     There was strokes well isette;
     There myght men see shaftis shake,
     And many krounes all tocrake;
135 There were sheldis gylt and leyd wyth ynde,
     And baners rustland with þe wynde;
     Many nobill men vnder sheld
     Sone were slayn in þat feld.
     The kyng with Ercules mette,
140 And hard strokes on hym sette,
     And with a launce smote him þere,
     That out of his sadill he ganne hym bere.
     Sir Ercules for that dynt
     Fill downe on þe pament.
145 Thenne cam rydyng Sir Jasoun
     With a launce to Lymadown;
     Hard togeder there þey dryves,
     That ther shaftis all toreves;
     Swerdis þey drowyn in that stonde,
150 And ether gave oder grysly wonde;
     A strong batayle there beganne

Betwex Sir Jason and Lymadan.
Therewhyles þey to fyghtes,
There come of Grece to hundrid knyghtys,
155 And brought on hors Sir Ercules,
All iarmed as he was;
And whenne he was vppon his stede,
He thought he brynt as ony glede.
With a launce he com forth thenne,
160 And cometh rydant to Sir Lymadan,
And bare him thorowe þe sydes too,
And thre of his sones he slowe also;
And all here folke, owt and owte,
Sone they were to deth brought.
165 Tho the kyng was to grounde falle,
Ercules and his felous alle
Goth and robbeth that cyte;
Of no man hathe no pyte.
The kyng hath dowghters none but one,
170 That was called Dame Isyon.
Whanne her fader had loryn his lyve,
She went and hydder also blyve;
But Ercules, þat was so stought,
Anone ryght he sought her ought,
175 And lad her with him awey,
Noo wonder þow she were sory.
The gylden fell they tokyn also,
The wheche awaked all þat woo;
They token vessell, armour, and cloth,
180 Too the water forth þey gothe,
And passed ouer the salt fome,
And euery man went to his home,
And make mery, and sleu care,

And loke how þey may best fare.
185 The kyng of Troye was þus slayne.
He had a sone left in þat reaulme;
His name Sir Priamus he hitt,
He was a prince of myche myght;
The heritage him wuld befalle
190 To bene kyng of Troyens alle.
In Fygry he dwelled tho,
His wyf and his chyldryn also.
Of the discomfeture wist he nought,
How the Troyens were down brought.
195 Whan he vndirstode bothe all and summe,
His fader was slayn, Sir Lymadon,
And his thre bredryn him by,
And also his sistryn lad away, —
'Alas, who hathe my fadir slauwe,
200 And my broder brought adauwe,
And raveshed my suster, Dame Ysyon?
Alas, frendes nowe have I none;
And treuwe Troye is þus distroyed' —
He sorowed ay and was anoyed.
205 Thenne had Priamus sones þre,
Nobill men, curteys and fre:
Sir Ectour, the prynce, eldest is,
Troyell, and Alisaunder of Paryse.
That nyght that Alisaunder was begeteth,
210 A mervelous dreme his moder dremeth,
That out of her body sprong a brond
That brent Troye and all þe lond.
And whanne she waked of here dremeng,
She sent for clerkys in grete hastyng,
215 And tolde hem her dremyng eueri word,

Howe in her slepe meved was her mode;
And bad hem telle, and nought lye,
What her dreme myght synifye.
'Madame,' þey seyd, 'forsothe, iwis,
220 In thi body a chyld þere is
That shall Troy to shame bryng
Thorough his foly, withought lesyng.'
They therfore were full woo,
And thought it shuld not be soo.
225 Whanne he was born she sent him
Too an herd, to kepe swyn,
That he shuld se non armes bryght,
Ne nought lerne for to fyght.
There he was, out of knowyng,
230 Yeres fyftene, without lesyng;
But game he hadde, and grete solace,
Whoreso he sawe in ony place
Beres or bolles fyght togedere,
For soche game louid his fadere;
235 And where he sawe þoo þat were strong,
He crowned þem with a garlond.
Of all domes he was wyse,
Therefore men cleped him Parys.
The kyng of Troye herd tell of this,
240 That his sone of the lawe was so wyse;
After him he did sende,
With him to Troye for to wende;
His wiff, his chyldren, he toke with him,
And hastily into Troy they entred in.
245 And he swore and seyd in his þought
His fader deth shuld bene dere bought.
After masons he sent anone,

That were in his kyndom,
And dede hem to werke alle,
250 The town of Troye for to walle.
Veryly, withought wene,
There was no mason in þat reaume
Wold take a dragme of gold a day
But that they myght fette þere þere paye.
255 They wrought þe walles wonder hye,
Stronger neuer no man syye.
Abought the walles he did make a grete dyche,
Soo depe nowhere were hem lyche;
Too and thirty yatis he made, iwis,
260 With doubill bryg and portcolys,
And whanne the see is hye at the full,
Abought the town rynne it wull.
The dyche was soo rome and large,
Theryn myght scyle boþe bote and barge;
265 Grete sheppis þerin myght rouwe.
There was joy and myrthe inowe.
And whanne the se gothe ageyneward,
The dyches bene so ouergarde
That no man entere ne may
270 Ayen ther will, soth to say.
Strenger cyte was non vnder sone;
Soo seker it was it myght neuer be wonne
But if it be with grete tresoun.
In all this world was non sweche a town.
275 Whanne it was dyght as it shulld be,
Priamus sent for all his barons to that cite,
And dide him for to be kyng crouned tho,
And Ekeuba, his quene, alsoo;
Ector, his eldest son, takes,

280 And vnder him princes he makes;
And Alisaunder, his sone Paris,
His yonger sone that his soo wyse,
An erldom he yeveth him in honde;
And all his sones makes lordis in þat lond.
285 And thenne after al his reaulme he sent,
And maketh a ryalle parlement;
And whanne þe parlement plenor is,
Eche man seyth þanne his devis.
First speketh þenne þe kyng Priamus:
290 'Lordyngis,' he seyd, thus and thus,
'Ye wote whanne þey of Grece come,
And this lond robbed and nome,
All our elders have destroyed.
Grete cause have we to be avenged,
295 And if ye will geve þerto counsayle,
We shull hem yeve newe bataylo,
And werre on hem nyght and day.'
All the baronage tho seyd nay:
'Better is pees euer withought ende
300 Thenne eche of vs with batayle oder to shend.
Therefore, sir, do as we you desyr,
And of your barouns send thedyr
To hem that our elders sley,
And her goodis did bere awey,
305 And loke if þey wull wage
Ravnsom, or ony trevage;
And brynge ageyne þey sustir ryght,
Dame Isyon þat is so bryght;
And if þey wull, do as good is;
310 If þey ne wull, doth your avyse.'
Thenne seyd þe kyng, 'I graunt þerto;

Late be sene who may best þeder go.'
Amonge them all þey seyd anon
Sir Ectour theder most gon.
315 Sir Ectour to this greeth him,
And passeth the Grekeshe Se þat is so grym.
Nyght and day forth he ryt,
Tille he come to Greke ryght.
He cometh to Sir Ercules,
320 That mayster ouer all Aufryk was,
Sir Pollex and Sir Castor,
Sir Tallamo and Sir Nector.
'Lordyngis,' he seyde, 'I am now here,
Com from Troye as a mesenger;
325 The kyng Pryamus me hedur send,
And asketh howe ye will be demened
Of that ye comyn ayens his pees,
And slouwe his fader gyltles.
And wheche of you haue his suster hend,
330 I rede þat ye ayen her send,
For sekerly it is nought ryght
A kyngis doughter to serue a knyght;
I rede þat ye to him gone,
And in his grace put you anone.'
335 'Fye, on Develes name,' seyd Ercules,
'Soche a dispyte don to vs neuer was.
Shulld we in his grace abyde?
Nay for thing that may betyde.
Goo sey his fader did vs wrong,
340 And we him anodir also strong.
And if þou were not a mesyngere,
Too wrother hele com þou here;
And if þou þynkest hens on lyfe,

Trusse þe out of þis lond blyve.'
345 Sir Ectour sey þer was no wey,
But turned to shep and went þat day,
And told Sir Priamus eueri worde,
How he was rebuked, ende and orde.
Sir Priamus at þat time
350 He was full wrothe, it was will sene;
And sent þorought his kyndom
After his carpenters echon,
And fellith tymbir, and gene to hewe,
And fourty sheppis he ded make newe;
355 And gadered swythe be his conseyle
A nobill ost, without fayle.
Whenne þey were gedered on grete hyyng,
They com to Troye before þe kyng.
The kyng thyngketh no longer to lende,
360 But dyght him forth, redy to wende.
Ectour, the prince that was eldest,
Of all þe kyngis sones he was boldest.
'Sir,' he seyde, 'my lord the kyng,
Ye shull travayle noþyng,
365 But be at hom and meri make,
And þyn ost I wull take,
And werryn with our enmyes,
And stoughtly bryng home þe pryce.'
The kyng answerd wyth wordis still,
370 And þanked moche his sonys will,
And þenketh he wull be good werrour,
And taketh him all his power,
And bad him take his host and gone,
For to awrekyn hym of his foone.
375 Thenne comyth Alisaunder of Parys,

His yonger sone þat is so wyse.
'Sirr,' he seyd, 'my lord þe kyng,
I will you telle anoþer þyng:
If ye take yourself your ost,
380 And goth to Greke in grete bost,
Þou shalt be discomfet and ouerþrouwe,
And all þy folkys nere islawe.
Sir, I wille tellyn the anoder:
Iff ye send Ector my broder,
385 His host shall be all totore,
And þenne we be all forlore.
And if ye wull beleven here,
I wull go with your poere,
And I will batayll and werryn soo,
390 Men shall speke þerof for euermoo;
And wyn the pryce with honour,
And comon hom as conquerour.'
Thanne seyd Sir Priamus þe kyng:
'Now is þis a wondir thyng.
395 Alisaunder, son, how spekest þou?
Ector is ten so strong as þou.
Telle me now I sey the,
Wenest þou to spede better thanne he?'
'Sir,' he seyd, 'listeneth a stounde:
400 Thre goddes an apull fonde —
Juno, the lady of wysenesse,
Dame Pallas, and Dame Venesse —
That Fortune cast, withoutyn lees,
Too makyn werre þat ere was pees.
405 That appul was with gold begraue,
And seyd the fayrest it shuld have.
Thanne seyd Juno, "Myn shall it be,

For I am fayrest of vs thre."
Pallas seyd, "It shall be myn;"
410 She swore be Jubiter and Appolyn;
"For well it is knowyn and vnderstond
The fayrest I am of þat is in ony lond."
Dame Venesse seyd, "Now be stylle;
That appul is myn be ryght skylle,
415 For I am, without lees,
The fayrest that euer born was."
Dame Juno seyd, "Be Mahomid, nay.
O non wyse it may not be
That it be at our juggement,
420 For ilkone seyth his owne talent."
"Thou seyst sothe," seyde Pallas, "sekerly
Anoder man þat most jugegy,
Whyche shall have þis juell."
Thenne seyd Venus, "Þou ooyst well.
425 Paris is the trewest man
That God leyd euer lyf vppon;
Best it is our juge þat he be,
Who shall it have of vs thre."
All þey graunted þerto iwisse.
430 Juno she went onto Parysse,
And seyd, "Parys, will þou be,
For grete nede I com to the,
For an appull þat we fownde
This endir day vppon the grounde;
435 That appull Parys yef þou me,
Thou shalt be wyse, will þou ma . . ."
Parys seyd, "Soo I wille,
If þou have therto skylle."
Pallas þe wey from him has taken,

440 And Venesse to him was icomen,
    And seyd, "Parys, wele be þou ay,
    Mahomid the save þat best may.
    For þou art þe trewest knyght,
    And all þyng þou jugest ryght,
445 Therefore, Parys, I pray the
    That appull þat þou graunte me
    That we fond þis endir daye,
    As we went on our playe.
    That appull Parys graunt þou me,
450 A feyre leman I will yeve þe;
    Thou shallt haue the fayrest leman
    That euer God leyd lyf vppon."
    And thenne, sire, I beþought me so
    That Juno hadd no ryght þerto;
455 Though she were lady of wysenesse,
    She had nought so moche fayrnesse.
    Ne Pallas, sir, so mot Y the;
    Venesse was fayrer thanne þre.
    Therefore I grauntt her to have
460 That appul was with gold begraue,
    And therfore, with myn entent,
    Thus I yave þe iugegement.
    "Now, Alisaunder," seyd she,
    "Thou hast full fayre honoured mee;
465 Therefore I graunt the anone,
    Whanne thou wilt to Grece gone,
    For noþyng the ne drede,
    Without dought þou shat welle spede
    The fayrest lady þat bereth lyfe
470 Thou shat wynne to be þy wyfe."
    Therfore I have will to wend

Into Grece, all hem to shend.'
Sir Etour and his bredryn alle
Answerd Sir Priamus in his halle,
475 And seyd, 'If Alisaunder Parys
Goo too Troy to wynne the pryss,
Men of Grece will stynte no stounde
Er that Troye be brought to gronde.'
Neuerþelater, þe kyng anon
480 Graunted Alisaunder for to gon.
All his poer he him takes,
And mayster of his host makes,
And bad him bere him stowtelyche
Ouer all other, and manlyche,
485 And euermore with his myght
Meynten well his faders ryght.
Alisaunder is now in jolyte,
Seyland in þe se with ryal meyne,
With fourty shyppis good and stronge;
490 The mastes were grete and wonder long,
And hadde stremers of rede sendel,
With armes of Troye wrought full well;
The seyles were of ryche clothe.
They haddyn good wynde and forth gothe.
495 Nyght and daye forth they drives,
Comon to Grece, and there aryves.
The folke of Grece hath vndirnome
That sweche shyppis þere bene come,
And have wonder what þay wull doo,
500 Wherfore they comen, and wharrtoo.
Eueri man come hem to behold,
And curteysley asked hem what þey wold.
Sir Alisaunder seyd, and al his,

And answerd hem with wordis wyse:
505 'Marchauntis,' þey seyd, 'þat we be;
Out of the See Octaman comen wee,
And a tempest hedur vs drof;
Therfore, lordyngys, be nought wroth.
We ne dwell but a day or too,
510 Þenne we will take leue and goo;
And parauentour, so it may betyde,
We will not soo long abyde.'
Alisaunder hyeth him fast to here
Of Ercules, to wete where he were,
515 And Sir Pollex and Sir Castor,
Thalamon and Sir Nastor,
And all þe lordis euerychon
That held his ante, Dame Ysyon.
Thanne was it fallyn soo,
520 In that self tyme thoo,
The kyng of Grece, Syr Monelay,
Sooiorneyd both nyght and day
In on of þe noblest cyte
That was in all þat contre.
525 It was cleped Capharnoum;
In all þe worlde was soche a town
Saue Troye, trusty and trewe,
For that was late bygged newe.
Salamon, the conquerour,
530 Ne Dauid of more honour,
Ne þe hey kyng Alisaunder,
Of whom þer was soo grete sklaunder.
Held not soo ryal meyne
As did Sir Menaly in his cite,
535 And with him Elyn, his quene,

c

The fayre lady, bryght and shene.
Fayrer formed was neuer none
In this world, bothe blode and bone;
She was full of goodnesse,
540 Myght no man tellyn her fayrenesse, —
Virgil, þough he on lyve were,
Or Aristodill that koude more,
Or Neptanabus, that nobill clerke,
That koud most of soche werke,
545 Too diskryvyn womans fayrnes,
Here beaute, and her mekenes;
Dame Olimpias, I vnderstond,
Crowned him with a garlond,
Ouere all oder maystres to bere þe pryce
550 For that he was so good and wyse.
Dame Elyn, þe quene with myld mode,
Speketh wordes oder þanne good,
And seyd to her maydens thus:
'Moche men speke of Pryamus,
555 The kyng of Troye þat crownede is,
And of his sone, Alysaunder Paryse,
That is in our lond alyght;
Men seyen he is a nobill knyght;
And therfore, so mote I the,
560 Me longeth more him to se.
Blynne neuer I ne will
Or I have sene him my fylle.'
A spye all þis mater herd,
And told it Alisaunder, eueri word,
565 What the lady had iseyd.
Tho held Alisaunder him wel payed.
'Certis,' seyd Alisaunder also,

'Me longeth to sene here hyen too.
Glad shal I neuer be
570 Or I may her my fille se.'
On a day, Elyn the quene,
With knyghtis and ladis mo þen ten,
With her went moche grete chyualrye,
And cometh to þe temple on hye.
575 Withoutyn the temple eþer oder metis,
And gentely ether other gretis;
Ether beholdeth oder lovely
Wonder long, sekyrly.
The quene turneth and goth awey,
580 With many a knyht and many a lady.
Alisaunder seeth that she will goo,
Soore he seyeth, and his full woo;
The love of here he takys be lyve,
That his hert is poynt to ryve,
585 And swereth he will neuer ete
Or he have her with strenght gete.
Toward his ost he gynneth gone,
And cryed, 'As armes, lordyngis, echon.
Eche man make redy and arme him,
590 And take his wepyn stought and grym.'
He bad first of all þyng
Take Sir Monely the kyng,
But wheresomeuere the kyng become,
The quene algate þat she be takyn.
595 Now eueri man forthe þey shove,
For Alisaunder hir lordis love.
Alisaunder the game did begynne,
Too assayle the cite þe quene was inne.
The folke of the cite defended hem fast,

600 Begynne to shete, and stones to cast.
Alisaunder leseth many men
That lay todreve in that fenne,
But he fauht as a good baroun; -
Many grete lord he drave adown,

605 Helmes toheuwyn, sheldis torappyth,
Many hedis fro the body swappith.
He and his folke that same day
Sleeth pepill þat no man nobir may.
The kyng seeth the barouns all

610 Bene islayn and ifalle,
And doughtyth him sore of his lyf,
And fleth awey and forth he goth.
No man wote where he is becom,
And Alisaunder the quene hath takon;

615 He taketh her in her worthy wede,
And setteth here beforn him on a stede;
She wepith fast and maketh cry,
And neuerþelater he lad her awey,
And many counteys and ladies also,

620 The fayrest þat myght on erthe go.
Therewhyle his men robyn and reves,
In all the countre noþyng beleves.
Alisaunder cometh home to his faders toure;
Hys fader him welcometh with honour:

625 'How hast þou sped, sonne myn?'
'Fader,' he seyd, 'welle and fyn.
I have distroyed in all þyngis
Of Grece þe grete lordyngys;
But the kyng, Sir Monalay,

630 He is askaped so wele away.
The quene I have, whyte as flour,

With all þe maydens of her bour;
Gold and siluer, grete and small,
The tresour of þe contre all.'

635 Sir Priamus was glad tho
That Alisaunder had sped soo;
But þe quene weped sore,
And thus she seyd euermore:
'Alas, alas, þat I was bore.'

640 She wepis and wryngis euermore.
Her heer, þat shynyth as gold wyre,
She todrowe, and her nobill atyre.
'Alas, I am to long on lyfe.
Why nyll myn hert breke on fyve?'

645 But Alisaunder at the laste
Comforted here swythe faste,
And loved here as his lyve,
And wedded her to his wyfe.
First she was quene and empres,

650 And she is now but a countes.
Alisaunder hadde at his gestyng,
Of all the kyndom eueri lordyng,
And holdeth a feste, ryche and ryall,
As eueri kyngis sone shall.

655 There weryn grete yiftis, for the nons,
Of ryche gold and precious stonys.
The more myrthe þat eche man makes,
The more sorow Dame Elyn takes;
But tho that there weryn wist not all,

660 After her myrthe, whatt wuld befall.
Now reste we a litill pece,
And speke we of the kyng of Grece.
The kyng of Grece, Sir Monalay,

Syght and soroweth nyght and day;
665 He leveth in mornyng and strife,
And often he remembrith Elyn, his wyfe,
Here beaute and her fayrenesse,
Here gentil body, here lovesumnes.
'Allas,' he seyd, 'my quene is go,
670 Myne erles, barouns, slayne also,
And my lond robed and reved,
And myself in sorow leved.'
And whanne he sawe ther was non other,
He sent fast after his brodir,
675 That was cleped Agamenoun,
He was a duke, a nobil man;
And also after Euluxes,
þe best knyght in his kyndom was.
They to in all maner thyng
680 Confortedd well her lord þe kyng,
And bad him blyve þanne send
Into his kyndom, to eche ende,
Too eueri man, yong and elde,
That myght ony wepyn welde,
685 Too comyn beforne him euerichon.
The kyng graunted þerto anon.
Sir Monelay sent on hyyng
Too duke, erle, and eueri lordyng,
That eueri of hem to him bryng,
690 Too ther power in all þyng,
Of good shippis, grete and wyde,
For all be water þey must ryde;
And comyn into a certeyn stede.
And ryght soo eueri lordyng dede.
695 Sir Monaly, the kyng of Grece,

A litill man and a lene, iwis;
His hede was rede; his her also,
The queyntest man þat myght go;
IIe was egre and hardy also,
700 And loth ony wrong to ben don to.
He gadered him with his myght,
A gret ost he did him dight,
And maked him shippis an hundrid,
Sweche to sene men had wonderid.
705 His broder, Sir Agamanoun,
Þat was a duke, a nobill man,
Fayre of body, queynte, and ryche,
He was not his brodir liche;
He was duke of Messen.
710 He brought shyppis fyfty and ten,
And with him anoder oste,
Better fyghters no man neuer wost.
Sir Eluxes come wele idyght,
In armes he was a nobill knyght;
715 Noon hardier man bereth bonys,
Hende and large, for the nonys,
Glad of semlant and rody;
He was lord of Parpachy.
A fayre pepill wit him he brought,
720 Fyfty shyppis wel ywrought.
Sir Tolemew, I prey,
Four skore shyppis he brought on hye.
Sir Nectour, þe lord of Pelye,
He brought with him out of his ile
725 Full nobill folkis, I telle you before,
And good sheppis foure score.
Sir Podane of Colapy

Brought sheppis nyne and thirty.
Sir Archeley, þe lord of Boys,
730 Of all the londe he hathe þe choyse
Of good men and hardy;
He brought sheppis fyfty.
Sir Sennes of Cypres also anon
Bryngeth sheppis twenty and on.
735 And also the lorde Parpadode,
With wariours stought and goode,
Fourty sheppis he brougth on hye,
With well fayre chyualry.
Sirr Pollex and Sir Talamon,
740 That lordis were of Antaton,
Brought good sheppis of defense,
With hir vytayles and here dispense,
Foure score sheppis vppon the flode,
And whyte men in armour gode.
745 Also the lord Sirr Anys,
A lord of Grece, of mekyl pryse,
Syxty sheppis with him he brought,
With grete folke grym and stought.
Sir Askelop, þe good werere,
750 þat was lord of Orkemere,
Fourty sheppis, withoutyn fayle,
He brought with him to bataylle.
Sir Portislay of Polleke,
He goth to Troy ryght worthele;
755 Toward þat host he bryngyth more,
Fourty sheppis with seyle and ore.
Thus they gynne togeder dryve,
With twelfe hundryd sheppis, XX., aı
Thanne spake Sir Monalay þe kyng,

760 He cleped his barouns on hyynge:
    'Lordyngs,' he seyd, 'in all wyse,
    We must doone Apolyn sacrifyse.
    The better I hope we shall doo.'
    And al þe baronage graunted þertoo.
765 The kyng cheses precious stonys,
    Ryche relikis, for þe nones,
    Plente of siluer and of gold,
    And cleped Eluxes, þat was mekyl to hym hold:
    'Eluxies, take this tresour,
770 And offered to Appolyn, there sauiour,
    And herkyn at him, þat we ne fayle,
    How we shall spede at our batayle.'
    Eluxes toke þe tresour fyn,
    And goþe to þe temple of Apolyn,
775 And offered as þe maner was þo,
    And falleth adown on his knees too.
    'Lord,' he seyde, 'I þe beseche
    That þou answere with mylde speche,
    If we shull into batayle wende,
780 Whoo shall have the batayle at ende.'
    That image answered of Appolyn:
    'Gooth and werreth with leve myn,
    And loke þat ye stynt nought
    Or Troye be to erthe brought;
785 For, or this ten yere be gon,
    Ye shull ouercome hem euerichon.'
    Eluxes hereth þis tydyng,
    And cometh to Monaly þe kyng.
    He tellith him gynnyng and ende,
790 How þe ymage had iseyde.
    Sir Monaly is glad inow,

And for tho tydyns fast he low.
He cleped Agamynon his broder —
He loved hym more than ony oder —
795 And leder of his ost him makes,
And all his poer him betakes,
And comoundeth that eueri man
To be entendaunt to Agamynon;
For he shall with gret honour
800 Bene all þer gouernour.
Now is Agamynon with grete maystrie,
The kyngs broder, with his baronye.
Ouer þe see þey flyng awey,
With XII hunderd sheppis, and fyve, and twenti,
805 And be at Troye comyn to londe,
And ther they make hir sheppis stond.
Whanne they com to lond echon,
They sent to þe kyng anon,
And bad hem þat þey shuld to þem sende
810 Dame Elyn, her quene hende, —
'And if he will, soo good is,
Or we shull slene him and all his.'
The kyng of Troye, Sir Priamus,
Answerd stoughtlyche thus:
815 'Ye of Grece my fader slowe,
And my suster fro hens drewe,
And ye distroyed al my lond,
I woll you do to vndirstond;
Therfore I hold Elyne, your quene,
820 The lady that is so bryght and shene.
And moche magre com you to,
But ye loke what ye kan do;
For I have here, I vndirstond,

All þe power of my lond,
825 For to defende, vp and down,
Troye þat is my ryche town.'
The messangers sene þer is no gayn,
They have þer answer, and turne ayen.
The folke of Grece beganne to ryde,
830 To besege Troye on eueri syde,
Cryyng and blowyng and bekeryng fast;
With all maner of gonnys þey did kast.
They had an ingyn, for the nons,
That cast many full grete stonys.
835 Tho þe walles þey gonne asayle,
Almost twelve monthys, with þer bataylle.
An hundrid gynnys þey were vpset,
Of maungeneles and treybochet;
The leste of hem, the sothe to seye,
840 Myght castyn a large myle of þe way.
All abought Troye þe true,
Nyght and day þey stonys in threwe.
Att eueri tyde, the shyppis all
Yoven asaught onto þe wall,
845 Drowen vp her botis to the myd mast,
And shett men with dartis and arblast,
And sharpe quarell, and eke floon,
As þyke as ony hayle ston.
Soo strong asaught as þer beganne
850 Sawe yett neuer non erthely man
Sen Jhesu Cryst was borne,
Nether after ne beforne.
They leyden on with axis of stele,
And faught togeder hardy and wele.
855 The folke of þe cete wythynne

Defended them with many a gynne;
Eche toure is full abought þe walle
Of arblast, devise, and spryngalle,
Kenne arous, and good bouwe,
860 Slengis, stonys for to throuwe.
They without þe tourys breken,
And they þought welle to be wrekyn;
En boþe half grete folke were þrouwe down,
Of lordis that were of grete renown.
865 That first yere, with that fyght,
Many man was to deth dyght.
Of all þat yere, for no nede,
They myght neuer ayen Troye spede.
That oder yere, Sir Priamus,
870 The kyng of Troye, doth þus:
He cleped anon before him
Too of his sonys, that was so grym,
Sir Ector, that eldest is,
The toder, Alysaunder Parys:
875 'Take your host into þe feld,
The folke of Greke batayle to yelde,
And preve yourself doughti knyghtis,
And meynten well your faders ryghtis.'
And þey 'answerd him smertly,
880 'Fader,' þey seyd, 'we ar redy.'
Sir Ector and his broder stought
Brought her folke þe cete without,
And were wel armed and seker;
Thenne there beganne a newe beker.
885 Sir Ector, that bold baron,
Many a lord he dreves adown;
There was helme, shelde, ne targe

That myght stond his strokis large.
And Alisaunder beganne to hewe,
890 He fellid an hundred on a rewe;
Many a grete lord of Grece
He them heuwes al to pecie.
Grete slauter was made on eueri syde
Of hors, of men, in þe feldys wyde;
895 The valeys ron on blode,
There dyed many a frely food.
Thus they fowghtyn þen in fere
Nyne monthis of þe yere.
They of Troye rested eueri nyght,
900 And eueri morn prest to fyght;
The folke of Grece, in here syde,
Toke truce for to abyde,
Whyle they beryed the dede in ground,
And heled hem that hadde wound.
905 The kyng graunted well þertoo.
Thus the toder yere is go.
The þerde yere, Ector, þe werrour,
Brought his host wyth grete pouer,
And brought his folke into þe feld,
910 Stoughtly arayed with spere and sheld.
The folke of Grece he ascries,
And þey hem hasted and hyes.
A duke of Grece, Sir Portuflay,
As fast he preketh as he may;
915 Ayens Ector a stroke he wande,
The shafte it shevered al in his hande;
They breyd out swerdes, sharpe igrounde
Edere gave oder grymly wounde;
They streken faste hem betwene

920 With swerdes that were sharpe and kene
    That fyre out of the helmes sprong;
    Betwene them was batayll strong,
    That non man cowde þe sothe sayne
    Wheder myght þe better bene.
925 Sir Ectour thanne a stroke wonde,—
    I do you all to onderstande,
    Was neuer soche smytyng or þat day,
    Sertenlych, as I yow say;
    The fleshe quyte he paryth adown,
930 Both þorow hauberk and akton,
    And, as God gave hem grace,
    It made þe swerde somdel glace,
    Þat halvendell þe brode sheld
    Fley quytely into þe felde;
935 But Sir Ectour anon him hitte,
    That the hede fro þe body he ofsmyte.
    Thenne come a lord, Sir Padradod,
    And oder weriours, many and good,
    And all þey leyden Ectour vppon,
940 But he him defended as a leyon;
    He leyd abowt him good spede,
    Many a side he made to blede,
    Padradodes body he smote atoo,
    And many a man he slow also;
945 Thus þey faught with dolfull play
    Fourti dayes, day be day.
    Sirre Monastew of Grece þenne
    Rode to juste Ectour ageynne,
    And with a spere he yede him nyh,
950 And smote Sir Ectour þorough þe thygh.
    Ector seth his blode ryn down,

And wexith egre as ony lyon;
He gynnyth to sle with dilfull dynt
A thowsaund men or euer he stynt.
955 And Alisaunder, his broder Parys,
Fawght as manly as nede is.
The kyng of Grece him sey,
Too Alysaunder he cryed on hye:
'Tretour, sende hider my quene so bryght,
960 That thou holdest with grete onryght,
Or thou shalt sey, or þou dye,
Cursyng the tyme þat euer þou here sey.'
Alisaunder wold to him anon goo,
But for prese myght he not do soo;
965 But of a man hes bowe he toke,
And drewe an arowe vp to þe hoke,
And shet it to þe kyng anon;
It fley þorow his shulder bon;
A leche anon the arow out drow,
970 And helid the kyng wele inow.
No man myght nombryn, withoutyn les,
The folke þat on boþe sydes slayn was.
There was full of manys blode,
Thereas men rode and yode;
975 There was slayn so moche folke,
That on blod ranne eueri polke;
Men myght not fynden a bare stede
But on dede men to trede.
And whanne þe pepill beganne to fayle,
980 Thanne departed þat batayle;
They of Troye gon into þe town,
And they of Grece to pavilion;
Trews þey token in bothe the party,

Half a yere, withoutyn lye.
985 And therwhyles þe kyng full wyde
Gadered more folke, be eueri syde,
And time of trewes was come to ende,
They were redy to batayle wende.
Sir Monelay, of Grece the kyng,
990 Clepyd his barouns on hyyng:
'Lordyngis,' he seyde, 'se ye nought
How our folkys is down brought?
And but yf we fyght beter wone,
Ector will slene vs euerichone;
995 And therfor, lordyngis euerichon,
For my love, abought ye gon
To fellyn Ector, if that ye kun,
For þenne have we þe maystri wone.'
A mayster seyd, without lees —
1000 He cleped was Sir Palmydes —
He seyd onto þe kyng thoo:
'Sir, speketh ye nought soo.
In all þis world is man ifounde
That myght bryng Ector to ground
1005 But a chyld, sir, sekerly,
That was born in Parpachy;
If ye that chyld fynde mowe,
He shall him sle I will avowe;
For a man, the god of Lybye,
1010 He shewed me full vtterly
In a planete, verement,
He shall him slene with dolfull dynte.
But how Achylles was ibore,
It is nouht knowyn eueriwhere;
1015 Therfore I will a stownd dwell,

And of Achylles I will you tell.
Half hors, half man, his fader was,
And icleped Sir Pelles.
His moder was goddes of þe see,
1020 Half fishe, half women, was she;
Her name was called Dame Tytes,
On her was gotyn Achylles.
For whanne he born was, withoutyn fayle,
And that he shull be stronge in bataylle,
1025 She baþed him verament
Of water of enchauntement,
That also hard his skynne became
As ony baleyn to hewen vppon;
Save the soles of his fete,
1030 There his moders handes sett;
And sythen he was slayne þere,
As ye may sone after here.
Vppon a day, Dame Tytes
Loked vppon the furmament, withoutyn les,
1035 And sauwe þeryn, withoutyn fayle,
He xall be slayn in Troye batale.
His moder therfore was full woo,
And þought it shuld not be soo.
She sent him into Parpaty,
1040 In maydens wede, sekerly,
And seyd it was Achelles nought,
But his suster, they had brought.
Sir Likamedes hit the kyng,
And hadde a doughter, fayre and ying;
1045 Dyademades was here name,
Moche she cowd of gle and game;
She was a lovely creature,

Jentill and swete, of fayre porture;
Lovely were her eyen too,
1050 Gracious vice she had also.
Soo long was Achylles in her boure,
With the maydens of anowre,
The kyngis doughter with chylde was.'
And therafter befille a cas
1055 That knyghtis, sekerly,
Comyn to the lond Parparchi,
That comyn fro Sir Monaly;
And in that lond comyn were þey
For to sekyn Achilles,
1060 In þe contre where he was.
They aryved in þat cyte
There was þe kyng and his meyne.
The knyghtis þat day, without lesyng,
Eten with Lykamedes the kyng;
1065 They weryn servid rychely
With metis and drynkis nobeley,
With swannys and cranys and betoris,
Plover, partriche, and wyld bores,
With corlues and cormerant,
1070 With malardes wylde and fesaunt.
And whanne the clothe was idrawe,
Thanne begynnyth nowe playe;
An hundrid mynstrelles in a rewe,
Diuerse melodye for to shewe
1075 Of trumpis, tabours, and nakeres—
Pypers, sarsynners, and symbaleris;
And whanne all men etyn hadde,
The kyngis doughter þe daunce ladde—
Her name was Dyademades—

1080 And lad in her hond Achelles.
     Dyademedes was gentill and small,
     Achelles was long and grete withall,
     Brode brest and stought vysage,
     Long body and shulders large;
1085 Alle þe knyghtis þat þere was
     Behelden euermore on Achelles,
     How he was so stowght and grymme,
     And inwardly behylden him,
     And seyd it was neuer woman,
1090 So large of shappe, body, ne bone.
     The knyghtis token leve to goone,
     And tokyn her consayle euerichone:
     They wold geve maydens bothe broge and ryngɪ
     But Achilles wold þey geve noþyngs
1095 But an hawberke and a spere,
     And with hem þey wold it bere,
     And when þey comyn to þe place,
     They wold leyn it on the grasse;
     And seyden, yf he be Achilles,
1100 He wolle it have, withoutyn les;
     He wolle forsake broche and ryng,
     And taken it in al þyng.
     The toder day next suyng,
     The knyghtis etyn with the kyng,
1105 And whanne they all etyn hadde,
     The kyngis dowter the daunce ledde.
     They yaf the maydens broches and ryngs,
     But Achilles þey gave noþyngis
     But an hauberk and a spere;
1110 Vppon þe erthe þey leyd it there.
     Achilles beheld aryght

The fayre armur þat was so bryght;
Therto he lepe al in haste,
And vppon hym he hath it caste,
1115 The bryght swerd he ganne outbreyde,
And skyrmed, and abought hym leyde;
And to þe kyng he seyd thenne:
'Wenyst þow, sir, I were woman?
I am Achilles, soo mote I the,
1120 Strenger thanne ony of þy men;
And God yef me myschaunce,
Yf I go more on your daunce.
To þe batayle of Troye I will ryght,
To preve there my mayn and my myght.
1125 Yeve me hors and armis also,
And make me knyght, and late me go.'
Syr Lykamedes anon ryght
Made Achylles that day a knyght,
And yaf him armis good and sure,
1130 With a lyon of good asure,
And yave him stedes good wone,
And toke his leve to Troye to gon.
The Grekys were glad euerichon
Whanne he was to Troy come.
1135 Sir Monaly, of Grece þe kyng,
Cleped to Achilles in gret hastyng:
'Achilles,' thenne seyde he,
'Thow art hertely welcome to me.
I shall the telle, wythout lesyng,
1140 Sir Priamus, of Troy the kyng,
Thorough a sone, a nobill knyght,
A bold man he is in fyght —
There is no man in all þis londe

May stond a stroke of his hond;
1145 Therfore, Achilles, I prey þe
 With him to fyght whenne þou him se,
 For were he to grounde falle,
 We shuldyn bene maystres of hem all.'
 Achylles answer þoo:
1150 'That I may, I wul doo.
 Be the trowth þat is myn,
 The first batayle þat he cometh inne,
 Be he neuer so stout ne grym,
 He shall me slee, or I will him.'
1155 Achilles armith him anon,
 Too bataylle with his oste to gon;
 Sir Priamus the kyng, also
 Ector and Alisaunder, his sonys too;
 And comyn forth in her syde,
1160 With all that þey may go or ryde.
 Thenne com þe cowntes, Syr Ectors wyf,
 That loved her lord as her lyfe,
 Wepyng and cryng on hy:
 'Sir Priamus, merci I cry.
1165 Too-nyght, abowte mydnyght,
 In my swevyn I sey a syght:
 Sir Ectour my lord to batayle goth,
 He shall be slayne with dolfull deth;
 And therfore, sir, pur charite,
1170 Lete him dwell at home with me.'
 Thenne seyd Sir Priamus the kyng:
 'Ector, sone, on my blessyng,
 Be here with þy lady hynde;
 We be inough to batayle wende.'
1175 Ector at hom with his wyf abytt,

The kyng with his hoste to bataylle rytt.
Ether ost begynnyth oder to asayle,
There begynnyth newe batayll;
Fourty dayes þere þey fought,
1180 There togyder, strong and stought;
There myght men sene, withoutyn lesyng,
Good knyghtis be her styroppis hyng;
Many an helm þere was ofwevyd,
And many a basnett þere was cleved,
1185 Many a spere and many a sheld
Fley abowte into þe feld;
There were many wondis wyde,
And also many a blody syde,
And many on les þe hert blode,
1190 And many on þe ballis in þe hode,
Many on brayned into þe hede,
And many a good stede hys lif bereved,
Many a knyght les bothe his armes,
And many a stede trayled his tharmes,
1195 Many a doughty man in þe feld
Layne þere slayne vnder shelde;
No man myght se, for no good,
In all the feld but redde blode;
As after a flode, þe blode ganne rynne,
1200 And euer þey faught lyche yerne.
That time Achyles hath vndertakyn
That Ector is nott to batayll comyn,
He leyd abougth hym in lenght and bred‹
And cryed, 'Tretours, ye bene dede.'
1205 Achilles an erle of Troy hitt,
Bothe man and hors atoo he slette;
Anoder he clef above the shellde,

. That hors and man felle in þe felde;
The fourthe, the fyfte, þat he myght hitt,
1210 Myght no man his stroke withsitt.
The kyng of Troye saw him so ryde,
He fle awey, and myght not byde.
And certenlyche, withoutyn fayle,
Thus departed þat batayle.
1215 It was vppon þe Pentecost,
Swyche time as þe Holy Gost
Lyght adown, in forme of fyre,
Amongis his Aposteles with glad chere.
Ector stant in toure and seeth
1220 How Sir Priamus, his fader, fleeth.
'Alas,' he seyth, 'þat I was borne.
My faders honour to-day is lorn.
Shuld Y, wheder I may go or ryde,
Se my fader swyche shame betyde,
1225 And namely for a womans sweuen,
That is fals and nought to leven?'
He armith him in stelyn wede,
And leppe vppon a nobill stede;
He priketh forth with all his mayn,
1230 And al þe ost he dryveth ageyn;
He gynnyth to sle with dilfull dynt
A thousand men, or euer he stynt;
Was knyght neuer, sythyn God was born,
Neþer sythyn, ne beforn,
1235 That bettir bar him, sauncs delaye,
Thanne dede Ectour that elke day;
But sooth he was slayne with dolfull chere
As ye mown herafter here.
Sir Achilles with him is mette,

1240 Thenne were strokis well isette,
    For neuer in þis world weryn
    Too stronger kympis, as I ween ;
    First Ector Achilles smotte,
    That in his sadell onnethis he satte,
1245 And Achille, with all his mayne,
    On Ectours helme he smote agayne ;
    Soo hard he smote, I you insure,
    That al his helme scon fyre ;
    Ector seeth he is wyth his make mette,
1250 Strokes on Acheldes sore he sette,
    That his sheld to pecis fleye,
    And a side of his gambyson awey,
    Hauberke and acton alsoo,
    And his thygh well nygh in too ;
1255 In the sadell þe swerd withstode.
    Achyles is greved wel ny wode.
    He smote Ector on hellme on hye,
    That cercle and crest adown fleye,
    And a quarter of his shelde
1260 Went whytly into the feld ;
    And whanne his shelde was slowyn to nought,
    Sone him was anoder brought.
    Newe batayle, withoutyn lees,
    Beganne betwenne Ector and Achilles ;
1265 Myght no man knowe, for swerdis bryght,
    Wheder was the better knyght.
    To fyghten thus they weryn all prest
    Tille the sonne yede too reste.
    In the morn, Sir Priamus the kyng
1270 Is redy in al maner thyng.
    And all that euer doth Ector mete,

Sone þey gonne the lives lete.
That sawe sonne a champyon,
A lord of Grece, of grete renown,
1275 That was called Syr Annys,
He was a man of moche prise;
He was atyred in good armour,
That shone as gold and asure;
The helme was ryche, for the nons,
1280 Isette abowte with precious stonys,
With rubies and safers orientall,
With cassedowns, grete and small.
Fast he ganne Ector to asayle,
And he myght with strong batayle;
1285 Sir Ectour anon him hit,
Bothe helme and hede of he smette.
Sir Ectour sey þat ryche atyre,
And therto had grete desyre;
The helme to take adown he stopeth,
1290 And Achilles þenne behynd him comyth;
He smote him att the fundament —
Syr Ector dyed of that dynt.
And thenne dyed þe dowghtiest man
That euere leued seþyn þe world began.
1295 The kyng of Troye þis þenne seth,
With woo and sorow to town he fleeth;
And lyght of day beganne to fayle,
And thus departeth that batayle.
They of Troye gone town,
1300 And they of Grece to pavylion;
Treuws þey toke for that dede
Twelmonth, be botheyrs redde;
And þerwhyles þe kyng full wyde

Gadered more folke be euery syde.
1305 Sir Priamus and all his
Soroweth sore, no wonder it is,
For Ectour was so good a champyon;
Forth they gone with grete procession
Too fett him hout of the felde;
1310 They turnne vpsodown his sheld;
Syre Ectour is beryed with grete honour
Before the yate of the tour,
That all the folke of the cete
Weped and for him made grete pete.
1315 And Sir Pryamus, as I you saye,
Wepes and sorouwes, nyght and daye,
For Sir Ectour, the good weryer;
He wrong his handis and drewe his here.
'Alas,' he seyd, 'what me is woo.
1320 Why nylle myn hert broke on too?'
With þat he fille to þe grownde,
And swoned in that ilke stownde;
It was grete dole, so God me glade,
To se the weymentyng that he made.
1325 Uppon a day, Dame Pollexene,
Ectours soster, withouten wene,
Come to that ilke place
There her broder slayn was;
A lytill besyde the graue she stode,
1330 She weped and wrong hir hondis on blod.
'Alas, alas,' thenne seyd she,
'That I now this day now se.
So doughty a body in þat stownd
That soo lowe is leyd in þe ground.'
1335 Soche dolour she made for hem tho,

That ny her hert brak in too.
Here lovely fax shyned as selke,
Here lovesom face, whytte as mylke;
She all todrewe here ryche gere,
340 She rent here vice, and tare her here,
And often she cleped herself caytyf,
And seyd, 'To longe in me last lyf.'
Achilles behalt aryght
Þat may þat was soo rody and bryght;
345 Soche dole she made and pyte,
Sory in here hert was she;
The love of her he taketh be lyve,
That nygh his hert all toryve.
A knyght anon he cleped him to,
350 And bad him on his mesage to go,
To þe kyng of Troy, Sir Priamus,
And sey to him þis wordus þus:
'For a woman þis woo was waked,
And for a woman pees shall be maked;
1355 For Dame Elen, our quene of Grece,
A hundred þousand have bene hewyn to pece,
And if he will soo for his doughter,
Pes shall be euer hereafter;
If that he and his quene
1360 Woll yeue me his doughter, Pollexene,
Thenne, for that maydens sake,
Pees foreuer þenne shall I make.'
The knyght went to Kyng Priamus,
And told hem þese wordus thus;
1365 His mesage he told and seyde,
That his lord vppon him leyde.
Sir Pryamus answerd on hye,

And seyd he þat was his enymye
Shuld neuer his doughter have to wyff,
1370 For no man þat bereth lyff;
And namely that hadde sleyn his sone —
Erst he shuld be hangged and drawyn.
Troyell and Alisaunder Paryse,
The kyngis sones, bothe witti and wyse,
1375 Rebuked soo this mesanger,
That forthought þat he cam there.
Thenne answerd the gentill quene
To þat messangere, withoutyn wene:
'Goo sey thy lord Syr Achilles,
1380 If he wull make durable pees
That neuermore after shall be,
He shall have my dowter fre.'
The messanger, withoutyn lees,
Wont ayen to Achylles,
1385 And told him both ende and orde
Of his answere, eueri worde.
Achilles was bothe glad and blyþe,
And went for Sir Monaly full swythe,
And told him in all thyng
1390 How Pryamus, of Troye þe kyng,
Wull yeve him his douhter, without lees,
If þat he wull graunt pees, —
'And, sir, better is in pees and rest to wende,
Thanne leve in werre withoutyn ende.'
1395 Sir Monaly, of Grece the kyng,
Answered Achilles, without lesyng,
And seyd to him þese wordes ryght:
'Though þi love be on a lady lyght,
Amendes have I neuer þe moo

)0 Of the wrong þey have me doo,
  Of robery and ravysheng my quene,
  Elyn that is so bryght and shene,
  And yet into þis time withholdeth here there;
  But I be wrekyn it rewith me soore.'
)5 And therfore he seyd tho:
  'Consentyn shall I neuer þerto,
  Tyll I wete without fayle
  Who shall wynne the batayle.'
  Achilles turneth and goth awey,
10 And leyth in mornyng, þe soþe to sey;
  The love of Pollexene him takes,
  That grete sorow for her he makes;
  He drowpis and dares, nyght and day,
  Often he menys þat lovesum may,
15 Here fayre semblant and lovely chere,
  Here rode rede as blosom on the brere,
  Here lovely vice, here leppis swete;
  His sorow is moche and vnmete;
  And þus he syghyeth, day and nyght,
20 And often bemenyth þat swete whyte.
  Sir Monely to batayle goth,
  Achilles his left att hom for wroth.
  Sir Priamus of Troye also,
  And Alisaunder, his sone, tho
25 Comyn anon on her syde,
  With all that they may ryde;
  And his oder sone, þe yong knyght,
  Sir Troyel of moche myght,
  With erles and barons of moche pryde.
30 There beganne batayle onrydde;
  On of the gretest, I vndirstonde,

That euer befelle in ony londe;
And wosoo of the batayle here will,
Now after ye may here, if ye be stylle.

1435 All the somers day the batayll last,
Many thousaund men to deth were cast;
Alysaunder and his broder yeng
Slowyn of Grece many a grete kyng;
There men myght sone se

1440 Legges cutted be the kne,
And many a man was born þorough,
That lay welteryng meny forow;
Many an helme þere was toryven,
And many a sheld al toclovyn,

1445 Many an haweberke there was tohewyn,
And many a face with blode bewreyen,
Many was þe shert steyned with blode;
There dyed many a frely foode,
And or þe batayle were ouercome,

1450 There dyed many a moder sone.
Troyell wonded Sir Monayl þoo,
And Agamenoun, his broder, also
He wold a dryven to þe deth,
But he skaped well onneth.

1455 Monaly fley with his barouns,
And Alysaunder robbed hir pauelyons
Of grete hors and good armour,
And thre hundred shyppis he sette on fyre.
Now shull ye here of Achilles:

1460 Whenne of bed arysyn was,
Toward the batayle he came rydyng,
And mette with Monaly þe kyng;
And whanne he the kyng mette,

Full curteysly he hath him grete:
1465 'How fareth it, lord, that ye flees?'
'Houwe, merci,' he seyd, 'Sir Achilles.
A yong knyght ther is icome,
Sir Troyel, of Troye þe kyngis sone;
Sore wounded hathe he me,
1470 And my broder, as þow may se.
Also sterne he is in fyght
As a lyon outrages on heyght;
Ther is no man in all þis lond
May stond a stroke of his hond;
1475 Thorow him we have lost þis fyght,
Cowardus bene we cleped full ryght.'
Achilles answerd to þe kyng:
'Sir, I have wonder of thi talkyng
That he so strong a man is,
1480 And is not but a chyld, iwys.
Ther is no man soo strong of kynde
But he may his make fynde,
And yet to-day men shall see
Wheder of vs shall mayster be.'
1485 Achilles armeth him aryght
In armor þat shone as þe sonne bryght,
And vpon him a nobil corset,
The helme vppon þe hede is set—
Bettir wered it yet no man;
1490 It was the kyngis, Sir Limadan;
In Troye it wan Sir Ercules,
Whanne he wanne the gilden flees;
The helme was dyght rychely
With pipes of gold, and ryche pery,
1495 With charbuncles that shynes bryght,

And perytotes of moche myght,
With rubies and savers orientall,
And all was sette with ryche aumiall —
A rycher hellme was neuer onder sonne,
1500 Sethenne the world was begunne.
His sheld aboute his neke he cast,
And lepe to hors all in hast;
He smote his stede with sporis of goold,
Many a man ganne him beholde;
1505 The feyre onderneth þe stedes fete aroos.
The folke of Troye were sore agryse.
And of Troyell he hadde a syght,
And askryed him anon ryght:
'Abyde, thou yong bachelere,
1510 For þow more shall fynde here.
Or þat þou þis batayle wynne,
Anoder pley þou most begynne.
I am Acheles þat to þe speke,
Our kyng of Grece I woll awreke;
1515 Turne the heder, and fyght with me.'
'With good chere,' seyd Troyell, 'so mote Y
    thee.'
Achilles to him a stroke raught,
That his helme fley all to naught;
Sir Troyell thenne agreved was,
1520 And smotte a stroke to Acheles,
That his shelde fley to þe grounde —
Soo it is in Frenshe fownde;
Hard þey hewyn with swerdes clere,
That helme and shelde, þat strong were,
1525 They gunne to rendyn and ryve,
Soo delyd þey strokis wonder blythe.

Achelles sore beganne to smerte,
He smote Sir Troyell to þe herte,
Even ato his body he deled,
1530 Fond he no man þat him helyd.
Anoder baron he mett with,
That hors and man to þe erþe sleeth;
The þyrde, þe IIIIthe, that he may hitte,
May no man his stroke withsitte.
1535 The kyng of Troye sawe him soo ryde,
He fley awey, and durst not byde.
Achilles hunted the host alle
Too Troye, to þe cyte wall.
The quene of Troye, Sir Priamus wyfe,
1540 With grete care she ledeth her lyf;
For Troell, she weped sore,
And for Ectour moche more:
'Achilles, þat tretour, that thef,
Hath slayne my sones þat were me soo lee
1545 Myne hole herte woll tobreke
But I of him be awreke.
Alisaunder, sone, come too me.
For my love, I prey now the,
On my blessyng, doo after my rede,
1550 Awreke þy brodren þat ben dede.'
Alisaunder asked, 'Moder, how
Shulld I wrekyn my broder now?
In all þis world may man be fownde
Þat myght Achilles bryng to grownde;
1555 For as hard is his skynne and his bone
As is baleyn to hewyn vppon.
How shulld I þenne bryng him downe?'
'Oo yes, sone, with treson.

E

I tell þe, sonne, vtterly,
1560 Ther is a place of his body,
In the solis of his fete,
Thereas is modir handis sete,
Whanne she bathed him verament
With water of enchauntement;
1565 And yf þou mystest with sum wile com þerto,
Sone þou shuldest him there sloo.
He hath desyred many a day
To wede þy suster, þat fayre may;
Therfore I will to him sende,
1570 That he intoo our temple wende,
And wedde thy suster with grete honour,
Dame Pollexene, as whytte as flour.
And therfor to þe temple goo
With a hundred men or moo,
1575 And whanne Achilles is theder come,
Quyk or dede that he be nome.'
Alysaunder, vp and downne,
Men of armes of grete renown,
An hundrid men þat cowde well fyte,
1580 And did hem into þe temple be nyghte,
And helde hem þeren, close, stylle,
And þought for to have here wille.
The quene sent to Achylles þerwhyle
A mesanger that cowd of gyle;
1585 The mesanger was full of treson,
And come to Achelles in that seson,
And knelled adown, and seyd þus:
'Heder me sent Sir Priamus,
And sayde he nolde no more batayle,
1590 For his men begynneth to fayle;

But he wille acorde be þe pees,
And holy of the werre sees.
He preyeth þat ye to þe temple wende,
And wedde Dame Pollexne, þe hende,
1595 And take þe kyngdom with her.
And þerfore spede the, leve syr,
And take hem with the that þou wilt take,
And come to þe temple sekernesse to make.'
Achilles see þat he was fre,
1600 He yaf him yeftis, grete plente;
He wist noþyng of his treson,
Ne of her false conspiracoun.
Achilles dight him at wordis shorte,
For he loved þat may in herte;
1605 Too wedden her he his full prowde.
He cloþed him in ryche shrowde,
And lapped him in a ryche mantille,
And toke his swerde, and did full welle.
Of al þe oste told he none
1610 Whereabought þat he wold gone,
But a yong knyght with him he nome,
And into Troye he is come.
He cometh to the temple, and goth in;
Anone þey closed þe door with gynne.
1615 He doughteth him of no treson,
But in þe temple he knelith adown;
Therwhyle a man, wele I wote,
Smote hym in þe soles of his fete,
And yaf him a wounde onrydde;
1620 The knyghtis stert vp on euery syde,
And al þey leyden him vppon,
And cryed, 'Tretour, yeld þe anon.'

'I ne was,' he seyde, 'tretour, ne neuer I nyle.
But ye bene tretours, prove I wulle.'
1625 Abought his harme his mantill lappeth,
He drow þe swerd, and to hem swapeth;
He wondid many and did hem harmes.
His felow of his lyf was lyght,
He defended him as a nobill knyght;
1630 In sexe stedes þey yaf him a wounde,
And sixti of hem he fell to grounde;
Soo long he heuwe on helmes þoo,
That is swerde barst on too;
Thoo he was in a febell cas,—
1635 'Alas,' he seyde, 'helples, alas.'
With his fyst he leyd on fast,
That ther nekkis fast he barst.
He sterid him as nede him techith;
One, be þe shuldors, he arechith,
1640 And threwe him abought, and lete hym gon,
That he tobrake eueri bone;
Anoder, þe thirde, ayen þe walle
He dasshed him to pecis smalle;
Anodir he hent armed also stought,
1645 And at a wyndowe he cast him ought.
And as he ganne his fomen quelle,
The blode out of his body ganne swelle;
With dyntis he gann amonge hem dryve,
Of a hundrid he left but fyve;
1650 His hert blode beganne to blede,
He wax all feynt he most nede.
Alisaunder speketh him to:
'Now þou shalt þy lyf forgoo.
Þow slow Ectour, þe good werreur,

655 And Troyell, broder lefe and dere.'
    He ranne to Achilles, and him slow,
    And out of the temple he him drow,
    And comounded his men, by and by,
    That without, as hornes and with crye,
660 That men shuld bende an engynne,
    And þerevppon leyn him,
    And cast him to þe kyng of Grece,
    That houndis myght gnawyn him to pecis.
    Thus he bad fast on hyeng,
665 In dispyte of Monaly the kyng.
    And swor as deply as he myght
    He was a fend and no man in fyght.
    And þus ended Achilles þere,
    Ther was neuer in world his pere.
670 Sir Monaly, of Grece þe kyng,
    Herith telle of þis tydyng,
    How Achilles, the good baron,
    Was imordred in þe town.
    He maketh dole and his full woo,
675 And al his barons he clepeth hym to,
    And anon, 'As armes,' he cryes —
    Iche man grythet and him hyes —
    'Our good Achilles wrekyn we shall,
    Though we shull our lyves lese all.'
680 He taketh is host and forth heyes,
    And cometh to Troye, and hem ascryes.
    Sir Priamus of Troye also,
    And Alisaunder of Troye cometh forth too,
    With her meyne in her syde,
685 With all þat þey may gone or ryde.
    Euer was Alisaunder in the voward,

Ther was no lord þat he spared,
He leyd on as he ware wode;
That day was spylled so moche blode
1690 That no man myght telle
The folke þat in bothe the sydes felle;
There was many a blody syde,
And many a wounde, depe and wyde,
Many was born þorought þe long,
1695 And many thorow with sperys stong,
And many a stede was brokyn the bakke,
And many les þe hede in his iren hatte;
Soche hurtelyng was in bothe syde
That hors and man ley dede in feldis wyde;
1700 It ferd of helmes and swerdis bryght
As þough it hadde fro heven alyght.
This batayle lastid, withoutyn misse,
As bokes of gramer berith wittnesse,
Twelve dayes, day be day;
1705 Thus they faught with dollfull play.
Whanne the twelve dayes to þe ende was brought,
Thanne was þe most sorow wrought
That euer befelle in ony londe,
As that I vnderstonde,
1710 For thanne endid Sire Alisaunder.
On a time Sir Aiax, a barown,
A lorde of Grece, of grete renown,
Come dryvyng, with spere and shelde,
Too iustyn with Alisaunder in the felde.
1715 Alisaunder take a spere forth þanne,
Ayen Sir Aiax fast he ryde beganne,
And mad the spere so in him glyde
That þe hede left in his syde;

Sir Aiax is hurt full sore,
1720 And yet he þenketh to iuste more;
He come dryvyng Alisaunder ayen,
And smote a stroke þat was ongayn
Thorow the sheld, into þe hert;
Alisaunder dyed at worddis short.
1725 And þus ended that noble knyght.
Jesu, that weldeth day and nyght,
As thou dyedist for mankyn,
To washe hem out of her syn,
On her soulis have pyte,
1730 If that it þy wille be.
Knyghtis and squiers þat þer were
Toke vp Alisaunder, and home him bere,
And byried him with Ector, his broder;
His fader made grete dole, and many anoder.
1735 Sir Aiax of Grece gan home ryde,
The speris hede sat in his side;
And whyles þe hede in his side steke,
He myght bothe live and speke;
But þo it was take out, full right,
1740 Sir Aiax died as he was dight.
Thanne speketh Sir Monaly þe kyng,
To his barons on hyyng:
'Now hat Alisaunder his while
That he reste my quene with gyle,
1745 And therfore I am full siker
That none of hem will more beker.
And we bene now stiffe and stought;
Go we besege hem abowte,
And we shull slene hem at our wille,
1750 Or ells for hunger þey shull spille.'

And whanne the kyng þus sayde,
All þei dressed hem at a brayde,
Besegen Troye in ilke a side,
That no man myght out goo ne ryde
1755 Too fetche mette, ferre ne nere;
Thus is Troye beseged half a yere.
In Troye was no myrth thoo;
Sir Priamus was full of woo;
His barons he cleped before him,
1760 All þat euer was withinnen;
'Lorddyngs,' he seyde, 'were Ectour on lyve,
He wold our fomen all todryve;
Or his broder, Alisaunder Parys—
Litill durst we dowt our enmys.
1765 But I am an old man on,
I may not to batayle gone,
And ye bene bothe styff and stowght;
Take your hoste into þe feld without,
Preve þat ye bene doughty of dede;
1770 I hope ye shull ryght welle spede.'
Thenne answerd a foule faytour,
Sir Entemor, þat vile treytour:
'Lord,' he seyde, 'we woll gone
Out and sleen our foon.'
1775 Sir Entmore told þis cas
Too anoder traytour, Sir Enneas:
'Eneas,' he seyd, 'what to rede?
Wende we to batayle, we arn dede.
And if þat we defenden þis town,
1780 We shull bene slayn both al and summe.
Therfore this nyght go we out
Too the kyng of Grece that is stought,

And bidde we hem yeve vs our lyves,
Our katell, our chyldren, and our wyv<
1785 And we will him the town yelde;
Better is þanne to dyen in felde.'
Entmore and Eneas gunne hem dyght
Att a postern out be nyght,
And com to Sir Monaly þe kyng.
1790 Entmor speketh at þe begynnyng;
'Lord,' he seyde, and speketh þus:
'Ye besege Sir Priamus,
And for all þat ye mowen don euer,
Without helpe ye gete it neuer.
1795 Will ye graunt vs to our lives,
Our catell, chyldryn, and our wyfes,
Our londis fre for euermore,
And we wull late in yow and youre,
This nyght þat cometh next.
1800 And whanne ye be in, do your best.'
The kyng of Grece seyde þenne:
'Maketh me sekyr or ye goo henne.
Ether of you your trowth plyght
For to laten in vs be nyght,
1805 And as I am trewe kyng,
I will you save in all thyng,
With wyf, chyld, and with lond;
Therto I hold vp my hond.' ˙
These to traytours plyte her trouthe
1810 To trayen her lord, and that was rowt
They toke leve home to tenne;
Wist no man where þey had benne.
On morn þes tretours gon vp and dow
And comforted þe ost in the town,

1815 And bad euery man, with his myght,
Wachyn wele his ward aryght;
And bad the kyng that he not spare
To make him mery, and sle care, —
'And, sir, with your counsayle,
1820 Ye consenttyn to þis batayle.'
And þerefore þey seyde þey wold
Ayens her enmys þe town holde.
Þe kyng answerd, 'Blessed be ye,
And all my good barons fre.
1825 Welle your travayle shall ben yold,
Of reche rentis and of rede gold.'
The nyght is comyn, done is þe day,
The kyng of Grece, Sir Monaly,
Cleped before him anon ryght
1830 Achilles sone, a nobill knyght;
He was stalworth man and strong,
Prince of Macendoyne, his fader eyre;
He hit Sir Neptalamus.
The kyng to him speketh thus:
1835 'Willt þou wrekyn þy fader deth now?'
'Ye, sirre, and I wist how.'
'Take,' he seyde, 'all thin host,
And ryde still without bost;
Go even þe yate onto —
1840 The brygge is down, þe yate ondo —
Clepe Entemore and Eneas,
Save here lyves in þis cas;
Arere þi baner whanne þow art inne,
Wille þou shalt Troye wynne.
1845 Sle whytly, bothe vp and down,
All þat þow fyndest in þe town,

And we will here withoutyn be,
To kepe that non shall fle.'
Neptalamus with his host ganne dryve,
1850 And rered his baner also blyve.
These to treytours he lete oute passe,
And ells yeden to swerde, more and lesse.
Cry arosse þorough the cete;
They leyden on withought ony pyte;
1855 All the nyght full fast they sleth
All that þey fownden, with dolfull deth,
Doughter and sone, moder and fader,
And þe yong chyld in the cradell,
Olde blynde men, and all soche,
1860 And crepullis þat yeden with her croche;
Fyve dayes, þorough and þorough,
They ne dede but sle men in that borough.
In five dayes were slayn tho
On and twenti þousand and moo;
1865 There was shed soo moche blode
Þat man and hors to þe knees yode.
Thanne spekith Sir Priamus the kyng,
Stant in his towre and sethe all þyng:
'Alas,' quod he, 'treson, treson.
1870 Alas, who hath betrayed my town?
Alas,' he seyde, 'þat I was born.
Thorow treson we be all lorn.
If no treson hadde bene among vs alle,
This myschaunce had neuer befalle.
1875 Grete treson is don among vs þis day,
We may þerfore say welleawaye.
Had I hadde Ectour, or Alisaunder Parys,
It had not bene as it is.

Now have I no frend to help me blyve.
1880 Allas,' he seyde, ' to long I lyve.'
For soo grete sorow þat he saye,
He fallith adown, and þere he lay.
Knyghtis defended þe toure fast,
But Neptalamus brekith in at þe last;
1885 All that he founde there he sleth,
And sithin to þe kyng he gooth,
And heuweth atoo his lymys all,
And his body to pecis smalle.
There he taketh Dame Pollexene,
1890 Priamus doughter,. bryght and shene ;
'My fader,' he seyde, ' Sir Achilles,
For thi love slaynne he was
In the temple, with gret gyle,
And therfore shall be yolde þe þat whyle.'
1895 She cryed mercy, and is full woo,
And with his fist he smote her soo
That atoo her nekke he breke,
And all her kynnere he slowgh eke.
Erles, barons, with grete honour,
1900 Fecheth Elyn, þe quene, ought of þe toure,
And broughten her to þe kyng, þeyr lorde,
Ether kyssid oder and were acord ;
And made hem glade as þey wele cunne,
For they had þe maystry wonne.
1905 They dwelled in Troye with here hoste
A monthe, with pryde and with gret bost ;
As her owne, þatt þey foynd þey takes,
And eueri man him mery makes.
And they wold dwellyn no more,
1910 They dyght too hundred sheppis with ore,

And stoftden hem with armour and cloth,
Doth hem to water, and forth goth;
And seyled ouer þe salt fome,
And eueri man went to his home,
1915 And maketh mery, and sleth care,
And loken how þey may best fare,
And ferden well, and so don we.
God geve vs grace all well to the.
And yeve all Cristyn soulis good reste,
1920 And ours, whanne we com to that feste.
And that it may so be,
Seyth all amen, for charite.

Explicit The Seege of Troye.

CRITICAL NOTES.

The MS. is legible, except folios 2 b and 22 a, which are somewhat blurred. The few illegible words are noted among the emendations.

Every line begins with a capital letter, and twenty-four of these are illuminated in black and red. The illuminated initials occur in the following lines: 1, 21, 63, 121, 185, 239, 375, 487, 571, 661, 813, 869, 1017, 1127, 1211, 1269, 1325, 1343, 1421, 1459, 1539, 1604, 1670, 1849. The first occupies four lines; the third and fourth, three lines; the others, two lines. Initial T, 375, is evidently unfinished; and initial A, 1604, is misplaced from the preceding line. Comparison with the Analysis will show that these twenty-four initials generally indicate a new line of thought. In lines 1, 21, 1459, 1539, 1849, the illuminated initial is followed by a capital letter; and in 1670 the initial letter is repeated.

Many proper names have small initial letters (e.g., troy 6, grece 10, darras 14, grewe 18, etc.), and many common nouns begin with capitals (e.g., Clerke 20, Cosyn 26, Felle 36, etc.). The capital F resembles ff.

The spacing is as eccentric as the capitalization, distinct words being frequently written together, and syllables of the same word being separated.

There is no punctuation. An occasional flourish, resembling an elongated s (vertically after þre 205, fre 206, alsoo 278, withsitt 1210, horizontally after islawe 382), appears to be without meaning, except between the adverb and the possessive þere 254, where it may be intended to indicate that the scribe has not carelessly repeated the word. A dash follows it in 206. Apparent instances of hyphen occur in a-resond 32, a-gte 257, A-nobill 1830.

A lengthened acute accent occurs over i, I, in many instances, apparently for distinctness; in several cases a lengthened s takes the place of the acute accent.

MS. readings that I have emended are the following (Z = readings of Zietsch, Herrigs Archiv 72): vndir ston 33, a waked (written twice) 178, lesyn 230, Sctour 345, þy nost 366, sr 393, Z. ma lyve (nothing

63

legible after *ma*) 436; slkaund̃ 532, alisaunde 566, lyve 681, comy 685, qurell 847, Why 903, agryffie 1087, y 1204, Anamely 1225, I omit a badly blurred *he* after But 1237, Z. mown 1238, Z. weryn (only *we* and *y* (?) legible) 1241, Z. kympis as I (*ky.pis* legible, *as I* almost illegible) 1242, af 1286, smote (*m* imperfectly made) 1291, Anamely 1371, helme (*m* imperfectly made) 1443, IIII^the 1533, TE 1539, I omit illuminated A 1604, Alapped 1607, goo 1672, krobyn 1696, bene sege 1748, I 1878, Pollexne 1889.

The following are corrections in the MS. : *he* is written above the line, 54; before 1062 appears the following, with a line drawn through it and a series of dots below it (cf. Skeat, Twelve Old English Facsimiles, Introd. p. 10), There was þe kyng and hs myne; *he was* is repeated and a line is drawn through it, 1087; *of* inserted with caret, 1503; *o* inserted in Ander with caret, 1512; before 1737 appears the following with a line drawn through it, Ther whyles þe hede sat in his side; *wist* in left-hand margin, 1812.

Contractions. — *And* is represented by symbol, 99, 183 (2d), 348, 353 (2d), 389 (2d), 490, 510, 804 (twice), 812, 1062, 1081, 1084, 1093, 1203, 1258, 1393 (2d), 1627, 1747, 1906. þat is represented by þᵗ, 49, 284, 316, 927, 1894. *With* is represented by wᵗ, 758, 945, 1053, 1659, 1807 (2d). *Jesu*, 1726, is represented by *Ihu* with stroke through the *h* (cf. Skeat, *op. cit.*, Introd. p. 8). Final *us* is represented by a symbol resembling the figure 9, þus 185, Neptalamus 1884, and in every occurrence of *Priamus* and *Pryamus* except those in 1792, 1867. *Ar* is represented by a horizontal stroke through the tail of the *p*, Parfay 41, parauentour 511, Parparchi (1st P) 1056. Final *ur* is represented by an ill-made *u* (or *v*) written above the line, werrour 371, your 379, 819, 1803, honour 391, 1311, 1571, conquerour 392, werreur 1654. *Ra* is represented by an ill-made *a* written above the word, begraue 405, 460. *Ro* is represented by a curl at the left of the tail of the *p*, procession 1308. *Er, re, e* final after *r*, are represented by a heavy curl above the word. *Er:* neuer 8 (twice), 256, 272, 336, 479, 537, 561, 569, 618, 712, 850, 868, 927, 1089, 1153, 1233, 1241, 1369, 1381, 1399, 1406, 1499, 1623, 1669, 1794, 1874; ouercome 12, 786, 1449; eueri 16, 126, 215, 347, 501, 564, 595, 652, 654, 683, 688, 689, 694, 797, 830, 843, 893, 899, 900, 976, 986, 994, 1386, 1641, 1908, 1914; þer 21, 390, 836; ouer 24, 61, 125, 181, 268, 320, 381, 484, 1913; greter 24; euerichon 48, 72, 685, 786, 995, 1133; euerichone 1092; euery 182, 1304, 1620, 1815; oder 300; anoder 1734; Jubiter 410; euer 299, 390, 416, 426, 452, 954, 962, 1200, 1232, 1271, 1358, 1362, 1432, 1686,

1708, 1760; sklaunder 532; ouere 549; Alisaunder 564; euere 593, 1294; siluer 633, 767; euermore 485, 638, 640, 1086, 1797; maner 679, 775, 832, 1270; certeyn 693; gouernour 800; eueriwhere 1014; Diuerse 1074; merci 1164, 1466; þerto 1406, 1565; Doughter 1857. *Re:* precious 765, 1280. *E* after *r:* were 164, 176, 514, 1058; here 213, 323, 387, 962, 1045, 1338, 1340, 1403, 1510, 1582, 1905; grete 257; werre 404; where 613; there 770, 1124, 1403; Sirre 947; fayre 1044; boure 1051; chere 1218, 1237; bere 1732; toure 1900. The omission of *m, n,* and *u* is commonly indicated by a heavy curved stroke above the word, but in our MS. this is not always significant (e.g., come 59). In the name Jason 27, 31, I have therefore disregarded it. In 145 I read *Jasoun* because of the rime. L. I. MS. 25, 26, reads, Polpensoun: Jasoun. In the passages of the L. I. MS. corresponding to 885, 952, 982, 1558, 1672, where our MS. reads *-on* with the final, "unmeaning" curl, the riming word ends in *-oun.* Omission of *m:* summe 37, 195, 1780, hem 115, 1148, lovesumnes 668, hym 142, 768, 1114, 1640, him 1663, 1732, trumpis 1075, grymme 1087, sum 1565, com 1565, temple 1893. Omission of *n:* gunne 83, Troyens 117, wonne 272, queyntest 698, swannys 1067, and 1070, 1577, 1796, begynnyth 1178, gynnyth 1231, gonne 1272, gann 1648, kyng 1901, cunne 1903. Omission of *u:* Jasoun 145, tresoun 273, wounde 918. In 83, 668, 1903, there is a dot beneath the stroke. In addition to the instances mentioned above, I have disregarded the stroke in the following cases: shepp 50, shypp 51, vpp 129, Lymadan 152, myn 461, lordyngys 508, takyn 594, Apolyn 774, slene 812, fowghtyn 897, shuldyn 1148, cassedowns 1282, meny 1442, verament 1563, conspiracoun 1602, lymys 1887.

Marks in the MS. that appear to be without meaning. — Final *n, m, ng* usually, and medial *n, m, ng* occasionally, have a final upward curl (cf. Skeat, *op. cit.,* p. 9). In the combinations *gh, th, ht,* the *h* is usually crossed by a horizontal bar (cf. Skeat, *op. cit.,* p. 11); sporadically in Sertenlych 928. Final *ll, d* usually, and medial *ll, l* occasionally, are crossed by a horizontal bar, to which is sometimes appended a hook. This may signify in some cases final *e,* but in many it is certainly meaningless (e.g., rustland 136, shall 221, etc.); I have therefore disregarded it in all.

F

LITERARY NOTES.

15. *order*, perh. orde, cf. 348, 1385.

36. *weders felle*, L. I. 36, schepis skyn. The latter uniformly reads skyn for Harl. fell, felle.

48. *carpenters*, L. I. 48, wrygtes; also 352.

50. *Jaso*, L. I. 50, Jason. L. I. inserts (51–54) : —

> þe kyng dude make a sikir schip
> Aboue þeo water deop,
> And was boþe styf and god;
> þeo mast was gold þer yn stod.

Ben. 897, 898 : —

> Bele fu molt, et grant et forz,
> Et fu molt bien garniz li borz.

53. L. I. 57–60 : —

> He [Pelyas] dude hit charge wiþoute faile
> Wiþ mete and drynke and oþir vitayle,
> And also prouendre, corn and hay,
> To stedes and to palfrayes.

Ben. 951–953 : —

> Garnir la fist Peléus bien,
> Ne lor defailleit nule rien,
> De quant qu'il lor estoit mestier.

62. L. I. inserts (71, 72) : —

> þey made heore schip at hauene stand;
> Ercules and Jason wenten aland.

Ben. 969–972 : —

> El havre de Simoneta
> Sai bien que la nef arriva.
> Fors s'en issirent andui,
> Jason et Hercules o lui.

69. *swore*, L. I. 79, swar.

76. *sore*, L. I. 86, sare.

83. L. I. 93, Byfore foure barouns conne þey gon.

101. *magreth*, L. I. 111, maugre.

134. *tocrake*, L. I. 151, crakid.

172. *hydder*, L. I. 170, hudde hire.

198. *sistryn*, L. I. 218, suster. See Introd. p. xlix.

208. L. I. 226, Alisaunder Parys.

209-242. The earliest extant treatment of these events in the life of
Paris is to be found in the Alexandros fragments of Sophocles
and Euripides, of which the following are the only plain allu-
sions to the legend: "Stephanus Byzantius in Ἄστυ . . .
Σοφοκλῆς Ἀλεξάνδρῳ . . . βοτῆρα νικᾶν ἄνδρας ἀστίτας" (Dindorf's Sophocles, Vol. VIII, p. 21); Nauck (Euripides, Bib.
Teub., Vol. III, p. 14) cites the following: "Varro L. L. 7, 82 :
apud Ennium — 'quapropter Parim pastores nunc Alexan-
drum vocant.' Imitari dum voluit Euripidem et ponere ἔτυμον,
est lapsus. Nam Euripides quod Graeca posuit, ἔτυμα sunt
aperta." For the argument of the two lost tragedies, see
Hyginus, Fabulæ XCI and CCLXXIII. Cf. also Euripides,
Troades, 919-922, Andromache, 293-300 ; Apollodorus, Bibliotheca (Bib. Teub.), p. 105, ll. 3-20; Ovid, Epistulæ, XV
(Paris Helenæ), 43-52, 89-92, 357-360 ; Statius, Achilleis, I,
20-23 ; Benoît, MS. G, Malkaraume's interpolation (Joly, *op.
cit.*, Première Partie, p. 165) : —

> ains qu'anfantai
> Alixandre Paris, songeai
> Que j'anfantoie I grant brandon
> De feu ardant, qui anviron
> Ardoit de Troye la noblesse.
> Tex visions mon cuers trop blesse,
> Consilla moi à clergie ;
> Si me dirent celle maignie
> Que se Alixandres avoit fame
> De Grece, tot ardroit an flamme
> La grant cité, la noble Troye.
> Esparnier cuida cette voie ;
> Je prins Paris, et si l'anvoie
> En la forest qu'est vostre et moi,
> A la garde dou bois norrir.

For the details of L. I. MS. not found in the Harl., see Introd.
pp. xxxviii, lxix.

209. *begeteth*, L. I. 227, geten.

243. Ben. 2915, 2916 : —

> Sa femme avec lui en mena,
> Qui avoit à non Ecuba.

See Introd. p. lxxii.

259. *Too and thirty*, L. I. 293, seouen. Dares (Chap. IV) and Ben.
3129–3139, mention six.

260. L. I. 294, drawe brugge.

275. L. I. 315, When þe tour was dyȝt as hit beo schal. See Introd.
pp. xxxviii, xxxix.

293, 294. L. I. 333, 334 : —

> And al ȝoure freondis þey han distruyed ;
> Alle ȝe auȝten to beo anuyed.

316, 317. L. I. 357, 359 : —

> And tok wiþ him þat he wolde also
> *   *   *   *   *   *   *
> Nyȝt and day forþ conne þey ryden.

Ben. 3274, Et Antenor et cels qu'il meine.

338. L. I. 384, Nay þat schal ows neuer bytyde.

364. L. I. 418, Y rede ȝou trauaile to Grece no þyng.

375. L. I. 429, Alisaunder Parys. Cf. 208.

386. *be*, cf. Northern arn, L. I. 440.

396. L. I. 450, Ector is ten siþe streyngor þen þow.

400–470. The earliest extant reference to the Judgment of Paris is in
the Iliad, XXIV, 29, 30, a passage that is probably interpolated
from the Kypria, where was ' first recorded the story of the
strife for the apple and the choice of Paris as umpire ' (Lawton,
The Successors of Homer, p. 16). Cf. also Euripides, Andromache, 274–308, Iphigenia at Aulis, 1283–1309, Hecuba, 644–
656 ; Hyginus, Fabula XCII ; Ovid, Epistulæ XV (Paris
Helenæ), 53–88 ; Statius, Achilleis, II, 336–340.   For the
details of the L. I. MS. not found in the Harl., see Introd.
pp. lxxiii, lxxiv.

473-480. L. I. omits. In Ben. 3911-4150, Deyphebus and Troylus speak in favor of Paris's proposition, while Helenus speaks against it. After an army has been collected by Deyphebus and Paris in Pevoine (Pæonia), Panthus relates the warning of Euphorbus against a Greciañ wife for Paris. When the navy is prepared, Cassandra prophesies the destruction of Troy. The popular voice, however, is in favor of Paris's undertaking. Dares's narrative is similar (Chaps. VII, VIII).

473. Cf. 205, and L. I. 223, Priamus hade sones þreo. Ben. 2919 says that Priam had five sons.

489, 490. Cf. L. I. 597, 598, strange: lange.

525-550. The references to the Alexander Saga are omitted by the L. I. version.

525. Wyclif's version of St. Mark, l. 21, Cafarnaum.

543. The name Neptenabus occurs in the Trojanska Pricha, Chap. III. For an analysis of the argument of this version, see Meister's Dares, Præfatio, pp. xxxvii, xxxviii.

550. Here L. I. inserts the following (633-638) : —

> Sir Menolay of Grece kyng
> Herde telle of þat neowe tidyng
> Of Sir Alisaunder Paris,
> þeo kyngis sone of Troye ycomen is,
>
> *　*　*　*　*　*　*
> Bote he no wiste werfore no why.

See Introd. pp. lxxv-lxxvii.

560. more, L. I. 648, sore.

563. spye, L. I. 651, squyer.

568. L. I. 654, To seo hire eynen and vysage boo.

571-574. L. I. 657-662 : —

> Apon a tyme Dame Elayne þeo qwene,
> Wiþ knyȝtis and ladies þrytty and tene,
> Come to a temple wiþ mukil blys,
> And Sir Alisaunder herde telle þis,
> And greiþed him wiþ gret cheualry,
> And com to þeo temple ful hastely.

593, 594. L. I. 685, 686, bycome: ynome.

605, 606. L. I. 703, 704, offer similar syntactical difficulties :—

> Helmes ryuen and scheldis rappes,
> And mony hed fro þeo body swappes.

608. *nobir*, L. I. 710, nombre.

611, 612. L. I. 713, 714 :—

> And was adred to go to deþ,
> And fled away and forþ he geþ.

623. *toure*, cf. 275, note.

641. L. I. omits ; Ben. 5102 calls her blonde. Triggs (Lydgate's Assembly of Gods, p. 71) calls this "a favorite and tell-tale simile of Lydgate's." It occurs also in Launfal, 298, 939, and Lybeaus Disconus, 882 (Ritson, Ancient English Metrical Romances).

677. *Euluxes*, L. I. 785, Daries. See Introd. p. lxxxiv.

685. *comyn*, L. I. 793, come.

709. *Messen*, L. I. 821, Mestene.

713. *Eluxes*, L. I. 825, Daries. See 677, note.

721. L. I. 835, Sir Polipete of Empy.

723, 724. L. I. 839, 840, Pyle : yle.

733. L. I. 851, Sir Ywayn of Cipre.

770. L. I. 946, And offre hit to Appolyn oure saueour.

773. *Eluxes*, L. I. 949, Daries. See Introd. p. lxxxiv.

809. L. I. 987, And beden þat he scholde heom sende.

837–854. L. I. MS. omits ; cf. L. I. 693–696 :—

> On vche a side þeo schipes of Troye al
> ʒeuen asaute to þe wal ;
> Vche maste hade top castel,
> And asayliþ þe cite harde and wel.

861, 862. L. I. 1023, 1024 :—

> þey withoute þeo wal breken,
> And þey wiþynne heom awreken.

885, 886. L. I. 1045, 1046, baroun : adoun.

915–936. L. I. 1073, 1074 :—

> Sir Ector smytiþ him wiþ his spere
> þat out of his sadel he con him beore.

915-936. Ben. 7481-7485 : —

> Parmi la presse [Hector] broche et point,
> Protheselax trove, à lui joint,
> Tel li done parmi l'escu,
> Et par l'auberc qu'il ot vestu,
> Qu'en dous meitiez lo cuer li part.

954. *thousand.* L. I. 1090, sixty. Ben. 11537-11540 (of Hector): —

> Car bien M. chevaliers et plus
> A fet par force trere en sus :
> Ateinz en i a tex L.
> Qui tuit sont mort, veire LX.

961, 962. L. I. 1097, 1098 : —

> Or þou schalt say, er we gon,
> Ful eouel hayl þou hire won.

968. L. I. 1103, And smot þeo kyng þoruȝ þe syde. Ben. 11476, De la coisse li sans li raie.

999-1132. A reference, possibly interpolated, to a legend of Achilles' youth is to be found in the Iliad, XIX, 326. The prophecy of his early death and his choice of destinies are also alluded to (I, 352, 414-418; IX, 410-416). In the Cyclic poem called the Cypria, Achilles, landing in the isle of Scyros while on his way to Troy, "marries Deïdamia, daughter of Lycomedes, who bears him a son called Pyrrhus, afterwards surnamed Neoptolemus" (Mure, History of Grecian Literature, Chap. XVIII, sect. 9); in the Little Iliad, "Ulysses transports Neoptolemus from Scyros to Troy, and delivers over to him his father's armor" (Mure, *op. cit.*, Chap. XVIII, sect. 10). Achilles' residence in Scyros formed the subject of Sophocles' The Scyrian Women (Dindorf's Sophocles, Vol. VIII, p. 117), though none of the extant fragments throw light upon the legend. Cf. also Apollodorus, Bibliotheca (Bib. Teub.), p. 109, l. 33 to p. 110, l. 8; Hyginus, Fabula XCVI; Ovid, Ars Amatoria, I, 11-17, 681-706; Statius, Achilleis, *passim*, and especially the following : —

Harl. 1003–1012, Ach. I, 473–481
Harl. 1023–1030, Ach. I, 269, 270
Harl. 1033–1038, Ach. I, 31–38
Harl. 1041, 1042, Ach. I, 350–352
Harl. 1051–1053, Ach. I, 560–562
Harl. 1063, 1064, Ach. II, 67, 68
Harl. 1073–1080, Ach. II, 147–164
Harl. 1107–1116, Ach. II, 168–177, 200–210
Harl. 1117–1126, Ach. II, 232, 233.

For details of the L. I. MS. not found in the Harl., see Introd. p. lxxxii, and cf. Ach. II, 407–411, 429–434. The episode in our poem has the appearance of a crude interpolation; witness the abrupt close of Palmydes' narrative (1053) in both versions.

1003, 1004. L. I. 1143, 1144 : —

In þis world nys mon lyuand
þat may sle Ector wiþ dunt of sweord.

1009–1012. L. I. omits.
1026. *Of water.* L. I. 1161, In a water.
1027, 1028. L. I. 1165, 1166 : —

þat also hard bycom his skyn
As any baleyn to hewen yn.

1036. *zall.* L. I. 1186, scholde.
1055. *knyghtis:* Ulixes and Diomedes (Ach. II, 59).
1065–1076. These picturesque details omitted in L. I. MS.
1109. L. I. 1233, scheld and spere. Achilleis, II, 205, Iam clipeus breviorque manu consumitur hasta.
1115, 1116. L. I. omits.
1154. Here follow L. I. 1277–1292 : —

Achilles modir was a wiche ywis.
Heo tauȝte hire sone a fair coyntise,
How he scholde him kepe hol and sounde,
And come fro bataile wiþoute wounde.
Achilles dude þo pryuely
As his modir him tauȝte witerly.

Wiþ wiche craft and nygremancy þer til,
His modir him baþede in þe water of helle,
And was honged by þe feet and þries deopped adoun,
Body and blod, hed and croun,
Bote þeo soles of his feet,
þer his modir hondes seet.
And his hed was blak as Mahoun
Fro þeo feet to þe croun,
And al his body was hard as flynt,
þat was good agaynes dunt.

1157–1160. L. I. 1297–1300 : —

Sir Priamus of Troye kyng
Wiþ his ost was redy in al þyng,
And Ector and Alisaunder Paris,
þat weore knyȝtis of gret pris.

1160. L. I. 1124, Wiþ alle þat myȝte gon or ryde ; L. I. 1714, Wiþ al
þat myȝte gon oþir ryde ; Harl. 1685.

1167, 1168. L. I. 1307, 1308 : —

ȝef Ector my lord to bataile gos,
He wol beo slayn among his fos.

1172. L. I. 1312, Ector, for chaunse of þy wyues dremyng.   Ben.
15495–15500 : —

Bialz filz, fist il, vos remandreiz,
Sacheiz que oi là fors n'istreiz,
Sor ço qu'il a de mei à tei,
Et des Dex de la nostre lei,
Te conjur, et te faz devié
Que n'isses fors sans mon congié.

1173, 1174. L. I. 1313, 1314, hende : wende.
1175, 1176. L. I. 1315, 1316, abydes : rydes.
1181–1196. L. I. omits these details.
1199, 1200. L. I. 1326, 1327 : —

In grete ryuers þeo blod con renne
Of hors, of bodies of dede menne.

1254. L. I. 1382, þat on Achilles hed hit was sene.   Ben. 16144,
Parmi la coiffe de si près.   Cf. Introd. p. xxxi.

1269. In L. I. 1392–1427, the battle is continuous, as in Ben. 16157, 16158 : —

> Por sa plaie [Achilles] pas ne sejorne,
> En la bataille arrière torne.

1275. L. I. does not mention Sir Annys ; the helme that Hector coveted had no owner. L. I. 1426, 1427 : —

> As Ector prikede apon his way,
> He sawӡ an helm þer hit lay.

Ben. (16110–16115) says of Politenes, with whom Hector fights before meeting Achilles : —

> Et molt aveit riche conrei.
> Nus hom del sicle trespassé
> N'aveit véu si bel armé.
> D'or et de pierres precioses,
> Resplendissanz et merveilloses,
> Furent si garnement covert.

After Politenes has been overthrown, Ben. (16126–16129) says of Hector : —

> Et quant il vit les garnemenz
> Si riches, et si preciox,
> Molt fu de l'aveir coveitox,
> Oster les li voleit et traire.

During the struggle with Achilles, says Ben. (16166–16171) : —

> Hector a un rei abatu,
> Prendre le volt et retenir,
> Et as lor par force tolir :
> Par la ventaille le teneit,
> Fors de la presse le traeit,
> De son escu iert descoverz.

Hector is then slain as in Harl. 1291.

1298–1292. L. I. 1436–1440 : —

> He leonede ouer his stedis mane,
> þeo riche helm vp to tane ;
> Achilles com rydyng verrament,
> And smot him yu at þy fondement.

1330. L. I. 1468, Heo weopte and sorwede, and mony anoþir. Ben. (17481–17488) says that the anniversary of Hector's death was celebrated at his tomb by Ecuba, Polixenain, Heleine, and

> Mainte dame, mainte pucele,
> Et mainte riche dameisele.

1331–1341. L. I. omits these details.

1349–1386. L. I. version essentially the same, except that it contains no reference to Troilus and Paris. In Ben. (17724 ff.) Achilles sends his messenger to Ecuba, who wins her husband's consent.

1357. L. I. 1486, Ʒef me his douȝter ȝef he wol swa.

1388. So L. I. In Ben. (18122 ff.), Achilles makes his appeal to a "parlement."

1389–1404. L. I. makes no reference to Polyxena or Helen; Menelaus bases his refusal on his certainty of victory, now that Hector is dead.

1404. *sore.* L. I. 1518, 1519: —

> For now Ector is to deþe falle,
> Y ne ȝeue a sore for heom alle.

1411–1420. L. I. omits these details.

1420. Here follow L. I. 1522, 1523: —

> When tyme of treowenes was come to þe ende,
> Þey made heom redy to batail to wende.

Ben. 18455, La triève fu tote aconplie.

1428. *Troyel.* The literary history of Troilus from Homer to Benoît is summarized by Moland and D'Héricault, Nouvelles Françoises du XIVe Siécle, Introd. pp. xlviii–lxix, and Joly, *op. cit.*, pp. 776–778. Benoît is the ultimate extant source of the Briseïda episode, which passed from him, through Guido and Boccaccio (Il Filostrato), to Chaucer and Shakespeare.

1435. L. I. 1531, Al þat somer þeo batail con laste. Ben. 18957, Lo jor fust la guerre fenie.

1439–1450. L. I. omits these details.

1453. L. I. 1537, And wolde haue brouȝt heom til ded.

1455, 1456. L. I. 1539, 1540, barouns : pauelouns.

1462-1466. L. I. 1543-1546: —

> þe kyng of Grece com to Sir Achilles,
> And sette him doun apon his kneos,
> And saide, Sir Achilles, y crye mercy,
> þat þou ows helpe and þat in hy.

This is evidently a reminiscence of the embassy of Agamemnon and Nestor to entreat Achilles' aid, in consequence of the exploits of Troilus (Ben. 20347 ff.).

1485-1502. L. I. omits. Ben. 21060-21070: —

> Isnelement, sans demorance,
> Gete son hauberc en son dous:
> Molt a le cuer el ventre grous.
> El chief li ont son hialme assis ;
> Ne sé que plus vos en devis.
> Mès montez est el milsoldor
> Prist son escu peint de color,
> Une lance grosse poignal
> A une enseigne de cendal
> Li a baillié uns dameisials,
> Puis fait soner deus meieniax.

1521, 1522. L. I. 1559, 1560: —

> þat his scheld in peces feol to grounde,
> And Achilles smot agayn þat stounde.

Ben. 21146-21148: —

> Andui chaïrent en l'erbos ;
> Sor els verserent li cheval,
> Assez en furent par igal.

1537, 1538. L. I. 1569, 1570: —

> And Achilles folewes þeo ost al
> Ryȝt to þeo cite wal.

Cf. L. I. 1346, 1347: —

> Achilles honted þeo ost al
> Ryȝt to Troye þe castel wal.

The formula does not occur at the corresponding point of our text (1212).

1557, 1558. L. I. 1599, 1600, doun: tresoun.

1560-1566. L. I. omits. Cf. L. I. 1277-1292, quoted in note on 1154.

1591. L. I. 1621, And wol sauȝtenen al wiþ pes.

1611. *knyght*, Antilogus (Ben. 22091).

1618. L. I. omits. Cf. L. I. 1685, 1686 (at the close of this episode): —

> þey putten Achilles doun to grounde
> And vndur his feet þey ȝaf him wounde.

1625, 1626. L. I. 1647, 1648, lappes : swappes.
   harme, L. I. 1647, arm.

1627. Line omitted. L. I. 1649, 1650 : —

> And woundede heom and dude heom harm,
> And smot of hedes and eke arm.

1630. L. I. 1653-1657 : —

> þey no myȝte Achilles do no dere
> Nowþir wiþ sweord no wiþ spere ;
> He stod ful harde agayn heore dunt,
> His skyn was hard so any flynt.
> In mony steodis he ȝaf heom wounde.

   See Introd. p. **xxxi**.

1638, 1639. L. I. 1663, 1664, teches : reches.

1650. L. I. 1675, 1676 (the first admission of Achilles' vulnerability ;
   his death immediately follows) : —

> Al þe blod of that mon
> In swot out of his body hit ran.

1658-1663. L. I. 1691-1694 : —

> þe kyng of Troye comanded on hy,
> Without horn and outcry,
> Into þe feld men scholde drawe him or beore,
> þat wilde bestes myȝte him teore.

1672, 1673. L. I. 1701, 1702 : —

> How Achilles, his gode baroun,
> Was slayn wiþ foul tresoun.

1674. *his*. L. I. 1703, was.

1685. See 1160, note.

1686. *voward*. L. I. 1721, vantwarde.

1692-1710. L. I. omits these details.

734. Here follow L. I. 1745–1752 : —

> And Dame Elayne, his qwene, also
> Heo weop for him and was ful wo,
> And saide, Alisaunder, wel away,
> Why fattest þou me fro Grece away,
> Wiþ streynþe hider to beo þy wyf ?
> þerfore hastow lost þy lyf.
> Doun heo feol swowne him by,
> And knyȝtis token hire vp in hy.

Ben. (22843–22939) describes Helen's mourning, and adds (22940–22944) : —

> Altresi tost com ele i toche,
> S'espasmist si que à grant peine
> En issi puis funs ne aleine.
> Reide por morte en fu levée ;
> En un chier lit l'en ont portée.

743. *while.* L. I. 1768, mede.
756. Here follow L. I. 1779–1784 : —

> Lordyngis, saun faile,
> þus endiþ þeo tenþe bataile.
> So hit byfeol in þe bygynnyng of May,
> When foulis syngen on vche a spray,
> And blosmes breken on vche a boȝh,
> And ouer al was murþe ynowȝh.

L. I. formally registers the close of each of the ten campaigns, excepting the ninth. Such formulæ occur at the end of passages corresponding to the following divisions of the Harl. version (Analysis, Introd. pp. cxiii–cxv): I, IV, VI, VII, VIII, X (also after X, b), XII, XIV.

Similar descriptive passages are common in Ben. (e.g., 939–945, 2167–2175, 2354–2364). The occurrence of the word myrth, 1757, renders it probable that the Harl. scribe omitted such a passage here.

771–1786. L. I. similar. Ben. (24373–24648) assigns as the cause of the treason Priam's determination to kill Antenor and Æneas for proposing to restore Helen to the Greeks. Dares (Chap. XXXVIII) assigns the same cause.

1787, 1788. L. I. 1819, 1820 : —

> Antynor and Eneas anon heom dyȝt,
> And out at a postorne wente by nyȝt.

1799. *next.* L. I. 1834, nest —
1817-1822. L. I. 1853-1856 : —

> And saiden hit was by heore counsaile
> þat he bygon þat ilke bataile ;
> Forþy þey saiden þat they wolde
> Agayn his enemyes þe cite holde.

    In Ben. 24520-24561 Priam complains in council that Ante-
nor, who advocated the war, should now propose to surrender
Helen.

1831, 1832. L. I. 1867, 1868 : —

> He was a douȝty mon and feyr,
> Prynce of Murmydoun, his fadir eyr.

1839. L. I. 1875, And go to þeo cite ryȝt ful sone.
1845. *whytly.* L. I. 1881, clanly.
1855, 1856. L. I, 1895, 1896 : —

> Nyȝt and day þeo folk þey slees ;
> Al þat they founde to deþe gos.

1857, 1858. L. I. 1897, 1898, fadir : cadir.
1865, 1866. L. I. omits. See Introd. p. liii.
1872. *be.* L. I. 1910, arn. Cf. 386, note.
1885, 1886. L. I. 1935, 1936, þey conne slo : conne þey go.
1887, 1888. L. I. 1937, 1938 : —

> And heowen þe kyng on peces smal,
> And þe qwene and hire maydenes al.

    Ben. (26444-26484), following Dictys (V, 16), says that
Hecuba was stoned to death on account of her mad impreca-
tions upon the army.

1909. L. I. 1961, And when heom liked dwelle nomore.
1913. Here follow L. I. 1965-1982 : —

> þeo folk of Grece of mony a toun
> Comen wiþ caroles and wiþ processioun,
> And welcomeden hem in alle þyng,
> Sir Menolay, heore kyng,

> And Dame Elayne, his gode wyf,
> For hire was wakened mukil stryf.
> þer was ioye in vche a toun
> Of eorles and of baroun.
> Fourty dayes þeo kyng heold feste,
> þat was riche and honeste,
> Of pekoccus, feysans, and biccar;
> þer was veneson of herte and bar,
> þer was pyment of clarre.
> To riche men and heore meyne
> þer was riche seruyse,
> As riche as mon myȝte deuyse.
> And when þe feste was brouȝt to endyng,
> þey toke leue at heore kyng.

Ben. (28295–28306), describing the arrival of Menelaus in Crete, says: —

> Issi com reconte Dithis,
> Tote la gent de cel païs
> Veneient voier dame Heleine,
> Par qui li monz a trait tel peine,
> Par qui Grece est si apovrie
> De la bone chevalerie,
> Par qui li monz est en error,
> Par qui li halt et li menor
> Sont mort, vencu, et detrenchié,
> Par qui sont li renne eissillié,
> Par qui Troie est arse et fondue:
> Si fière gent ne fu véue.

1918. L. I. ends (1985–1988): —

> þus was ended þe bataile of Troye.
> God ȝeue ows alle heouene ioye.
> Such a batail as hit was oon
> Never byþ no neuer schal beo noon.

Colophon.   L. I.   þe batayle of Troye.

GLOSSARIAL INDEX.

A.

a, *indef. art.*, see **an**.

a, *v. inf., worn-down form of* **have**, 1453.

abought, *adv.*, about, 80, 103, 906, 1640; **abougth**, 1203; **abowte**, 1165, 1186, 1280, 1748.

abought, *prep.*, about, 257, 262, 841, 857, 1116, 1625; **aboute**, 1501; **abowt**, 941.

abyde, *v. inf.*, pause, remain, 337, 512, 902; 2 *s. imp.*, 1509; **abytt**, 3 *s. pr.*, 1175.

acord, *adv. or adj.*, in agreement, 1902.

acorde, *v. inf.*, come to an agreement, 1591.

acton, *s.*, a stuffed jacket worn under the mail, 1253; **akton**, 930.

adauwe, *adv.*, out of life, 200.

adown, *adv.*, down, downward, 604, 776, 886, 929, 1217, 1258, 1289, 1587, 1616, 1882.

aferd, *v. pp.*, afraid, 120.

afrayed, *v. pp.*, afraid, 118.

after, *adv.*, afterwards, later, 852, 1082, 1381, 1434.

after, *prep.*, after, according to, 241, 247, 285, 352, 677, 1199, 1549.

agayne, *adv.*, again, back, 1246; **ageyn**, 68; **ageyne**, 307; **ayen**, 82, 106, 828, 1384.

ageyn, *prep.*, against, 11, 1230; **ageynne**, 948; **ayen**, 270, 868, 1642, 1716, 1721. See **ayens**.

ageyneward, *adv.*, backward, 267.

agreved, *v. pp.*, aggrieved, vexed, 75, 1519.

agryse, *v. pp.*, terrified, 1506.

akton, see **acton**.

al, *adj., s. pl.*, all, every, 285, 503, 764, 817, 1230, 1248, 1609, 1621, 1675; **all**, *passim*; **alle**, *pl.*, 4, 166, 190, 249, 473, 1085, 1537, 1873. Phrases: **in al þyng**, at any cost, certainly (cf. N. H. G. **aller-dings**), 1102; **in al maner þyng**, in every respect, 1270; **al and summe**, one and all, 1780; **ouer all**, everywhere, 125; **all and summe**, the sum total, wholly, 195; **in all maner thyng**, 679; **in all þyng**, in every respect, 690; **in all wyse**, in every way, certainly, 761; **in all thyng**, wholly, certainly, 1389, 1806.

al, *adv.*, all, quite, 892, 916, 1113, 1444; **all**, 2, 87, 134, 148, 385, 692, 1267, 1339, 1348, 1502, 1518, 1651.

alas, *interj.*, 199, 202, 639, 643, 1221, 1319, 1331, 1635, 1869, 1870, 1871; **allas**, 669, 1880.

algate, *adv.*, in any case, 594.

almost, *adv.*, 836.

also, *adv.*, 73, 162, 177, 192, 198, 567, 619, 670, 677, 697, 699, 733, 735, 745, 944, 1050, 1125, 1157, 1188, 1423, 1452, 1682; **alsoo**, 278, 1253; **also**, *equivalent to* **as**, 340, 1644; *used correlatively with* **as**, 1027, 1471. Phrase: **also blyve**, as soon as possible, 172, 1850.

alyght (O. E. **ālihtan**), *v. pp.*, arrived, 557.

alyght (O. E. **onlīhtan**), *v. pp.*, lightened (?), 1701.

alyve, *adj.*, alive, 70.

am, see **be**, *v.*

amen, *s.*, 1922.

amendes, *s. pl.*, compensation, 1399.
among, *prep.*, 43, 99, 1873, 1875;
amonge, 313, 1648. See **amongis**.
amongis, *prep.*, amongst, 1218;
amongs, 4.
an, *indef. art.*, 226, 283, 400, 433, 703,
837, 890, 966, 1073, 1095, 1109, 1183,
1205, 1443, 1445, 1579, 1660; **a**,
passim.
and, *conj.*, *passim*; *conditional*,
1284 (?), 1836.
anoder, *adj.*, another, 422, 711, 1512,
1531, 1776; **anoþer**, 378.
anoder, *pron.*, another, 24, 57, 383,
1207, 1262, 1642; **anodir**, 340, 1644.
anon, *adv.*, 32, 313, 479, 686, 733, 808,
871, 935, 963, 967, 969, 1155, 1285,
1349, 1425, 1622, 1676; **anone**, 59,
247, 334, 465, 1614; **anoonne**, 44;
anon ryght, immediately, 1127,
1508, 1829; **anone ryght**, 174.
anour, *s.*, honor, 92; **anowre**, 1052.
See **honour**.
anoyed, *v. pp.*, annoyed, troubled,
204.
Answer, *s.*, 828; **answere**, 1386.
answer, *v.*, 3 *s. pr.* (?), answers, 1149;
answere, 2 *s. pr. subj.*, 778; **answerd**, 3 *s. pt.*, 369, 814, 1367, 1377,
1477, 1771, 1823; **answered**, 781,
1396; **answerd**, 3 *pl. pt.*, 474, 504;
answerdyn, 3 *pl. pt.*, 97.
ante, *s.*, aunt, 518.
Aposteles, *s. pl.*, Apostles, 1218.
appul, *s.*, apple, 405, 414, 460; **appull**, 433, 435, 446, 449; **apull**, 400.
ar, see **be**, *v.*
arayed, *v. pp.*, arrayed, 910.
arblast, *s.*, "a cross-bow, consisting
of a steel bow fitted to a wooden
shaft, furnished with special mech-
anism for drawing and letting slip
the bowstring, and used for the
discharge of arrows, bolts, stones,
etc."—Oxf. Dic., 846, 858.
arechith, *v.*, 3 *s. pr.*, lays hold of,
1639.
arere, *v.*, 2 *s. imp.*, raise, 1843;
arerith, 3 *pl. pr.*, 60.

aresond, *v.*, 3 *s. pt.*, addressed words
to, 32.
ariues, *v.*, 3 *pl. pr.*, arrive at, reach
(*trans., by omission of prep.*), 114;
aryves, arrive (*intrans.*), 496;
3 *s. pr.*, causes to arrive, brings to
port (*trans.*), 62; **aryved**, 3 *pl. pt.*,
arrived (*intrans.*), 1061.
arme, *v.*, 3 *s. pr. subj.*, put on armor,
589; **armeth**, 3 *s. pr. ind.*, 1485;
armith, 127, 1155, 1227; **armed**,
3 *pl. pt.*, 115; *pp.*, 883, 1644; **iarmed**,
156.
armes (*a*), *s. pl.*, the upper limbs,
1193.
armes (*b*), *s. pl.*, weapons, armor,
126, 227, 714, 1578; **armis**, 1125,
1129; **armes**, armorial bearings,
492; **as armes**, to arms, 588,
1676.
armor, *s.*, 1486; **armore**, 110; **armour**, 179, 744, 1277, 1457, 1911;
armur, 1112.
arn, see **be**, *v.*
aroos, *v.*, 3 *s. pt.*, arose, 1505; **arose**,
119; **arosse**, 1853; **arysyn**, *pp.*,
1460.
arow, *s.*, arrow, 969; **arowe**, 966;
arous, *pl.*, 859.
art, see **be**, *v.*
aryght, *adv.*, rightly, 127, 1111, 1343,
1485, 1816.
as, *rel. adv.*, *passim*. Phrase: **so**
. . . **as**, whereas, 78.
asaught, *s.*, assault, attack, 844, 849.
asayle, *v. inf.*, assail, 835, 1177, 1283;
assayle, 598.
ascries, *v.*, 3 *s. pr.*, challenges, 911;
ascryes, 1681; **askryed**, 3 *s. pt.*,
1508.
ashamed, *v. pp.*, 76.
as hornes (O. Fr.), with horns, 1659.
askaped, *v. pp.*, escaped, 630.
asketh, *v.*, 3 *s. pr.*, 326; **asked**, 3 *s.
pt.*, 502, 1551.
asure, *s.*, azure, 1130, 1278.
at, *prep.*, *passim*; to, *after* **herkyn**,
771; **att**, 62, 843, 1291, 1422, 1788;
atte, at the, 87.

to, *adv.,* in two, 1529; **atoo,** 943, 1206, 1887, 1897.

atyre, *s.,* attire, 642, 1287.

atyred, *v. pp.,* attired, 1277.

aumiall, *s.,* enamel, 1498.

auntres, *s. pl.,* adventures, 116.

avenged, *v. pp.,* 294.

avyse, *s.,* opinion, plan, 310.

awaked, *v.,* 3 *s. pt.,* caused, 178.

away, *adv.,* 198, 630; **awey,** 175, 304, 579, 612, 618, 803, 1212, 1252, 1409, 1536.

awreke, *v. inf.,* avenge, 1514; 2 *s. imp.,* 1550; *pp.,* revenged, 1546; **awrekyn,** *inf.,* 374.

axis, *s. pl.,* battle-axes, 853.

ay, *adv.,* ever, 204, 441.

ayen, *adv.,* see **agayne.**

ayen, *prep.,* see **ageyn.**

ayens, *prep.,* against, 327, 915, 1822. See **ageyn,** *prep.*

B.

bachelere, *s.,* bachelor, "a young knight, not old enough, or having too few vassals, to display his own banner, and who therefore followed the banner of another; a novice in arms."—Oxf. Dic., 1509.

bad, *v.,* 3 *s. pt.,* bade, 49, 71, 217, 373, 483, 591, 1350, 1664; 3 *pl. pt.,* 681, 809, 1815, 1817.

bakke, *s.,* back, 1696.

baleyn, *s.,* whalebone, 1028, 1556.

ballis, *s. pl.,* **ballis in þe hode,** *humorous expression for* 'heads,' 1190.

baner, *s.,* banner, 1843, 1850; **baners,** *pl.,* 136.

bare, *v.,* see **bere.**

bare, *adj.,* 977.

barge, *s.,* "a small seagoing vessel with sails," 264.

baron, *s.,* 885, 1531, 1672; **baroun,** 603; **barown,** 1711; **barons,** *pl.,* 83, 276, 1429, 1675, 1742, 1759, 1824, 1899; **barouns,** 302, 609, 670, 760, 990, 1455.

baronage, *s.,* body of barons, 298, 764.

baronye, *s.,* body of barons, 802.

barst, *v.,* 3 *s. pt.,* burst, broke, 1633 (*intrans.*), 1637 (*trans.*).

basnett, *s.,* "a small, light, steel headpiece, in shape somewhat globular, terminating in a point raised slightly above the head, and closed in front with a ventail or visor."—Oxf. Dic., 1184.

batale, *s.,* battle, war, 1036; **batayle,** 6, 10, 15, 151, 296, 300, 772, 779, 780, 876, 980, 988, 1123, 1152, 1167, 1174, 1214, 1263, 1284, 1298, 1408, 1421, 1430, 1433, 1449, 1461, 1511, 1589, 1702, 1766, 1778, 1820; **batayll,** 922, 1178, 1202, 1435; **bataylle,** 752, 836, 1024, 1156, 1176.

batayll, *v. inf.,* fight, 389.

bathed, *v.,* 3 *s. pt.,* 1563; **baþed,** 1025.

be, *prep.,* by, at, 355, 410, 414, 417, 583, 692, 946, 986, 1151, 1182, 1302, 1304, 1347, 1440, 1580, 1591, 1639, 1704, 1788, 1804; **by,** 107.

be, *v. inf.,* 77, 90, 224, 275, 277, 294, 312, 326, 365, 371, 381, 385, 407, 409, 418, 470, 569, 798, 862, 1024, 1036, 1038, 1168, 1358, 1381, 1484, 1553, 1847, 1894, 1921; 2 *s. pr.,* 1800; 1 *pl. pr.,* 386, 505, 1174, 1872; 2 *pl. pr.,* 1434; 3 *pl. pr.,* 131, 805; 2 *s. pr. subj.,* 431, 441; 3 *s. pr. subj.,* 273, 419, 427, 594, 784, 785, 1099, 1153, 1404, 1546, 1576, 1730; 2 *pl. pr. subj.,* 1823; 2 *s. imp.,* 413, 1173; 2 *pl. imp.,* 508; **ben,** *inf.,* 700, 1825; 3 *pl. pr.,* are, 82, 1550; **bene,** *inf.,* 5, 40, 190, 246, 800, 924, 1148, 1780; 1 *pl. pr.,* 1476, 1747; 2 *pl. pr.,* 1204, 1624, 1767, 1769; 3 *pl. pr.,* 89, 93, 122, 129, 268, 498, 610; *pp.,* 1356, 1873, 1878; **benne,** *pp.,* 1812; **beth,** 3 *pl. pr.,* 65; **am,** 1 *s. pr.,* 323, 408, 412, 415, 1119, 1513, 1745, 1765, 1805; **art,** 2 *s. pr.,* 443, 1138, 1843; **is,** 3 *s. pr., passim;* **his,** 282, 582, 1422, 1605, 1674, **ar,** 1 *pl. pr.,* 880; **arn,**

blede, *v. inf.*, bleed, 942, 1650.
blessed, *adj.*, 1823.
blessyng, *s.*, 1172, 1549.
blod, *s.*, blood, 976, 1330; blode, 538, 895, 951, 973, 1189, 1198, 1199, 1446, 1447, 1647, 1650, 1689, 1865.
blody, *adj.*, bloody, 1188, 1692.
blosom, *s.*, blossom, 1416.
blowyng, *v. pr. part.*, blowing (horns?), 831.
blynde, *adj.*, blind, 1859.
blynne, *v. inf.*, cease trying or wishing, 561.
blythe, *adv.*, gladly, 1526.
blyþe, *adj.*, glad, 1387.
blyve, *adv.*, quickly, 172, 344, 681, 1850, 1879. See lyve, *s.*
body, *s.*, 28, 211, 220, 606, 668, 707, 936, 943, 1084, 1090, 1333, 1529, 1560, 1647, 1888.
bokes, *s. pl.*, books, 1703.
bold, *adj.*, 29, 885, 1142.
boldest, *adj.*, 362.
bolles, *s. pl.*, bulls, 233.
bon, *s.*, bone, 968; bone, 538, 1090, 1555, 1641; bones, *pl.*, 28; bonys, 715.
bores, *s. pl.*, boars, 1068.
born, see bere.
borne, see bere.
borough, *s.*, fortified town, 1862.
bost, *s.*, outcry, clamor, 380, 1838, 1906.
bote, *s.*, boat, 264; botis, *pl.*, 845.
both, *adv.*, 522; bothe, 1374, 1387, 1738, 1767, 1845; boþe, 30, 264.
both, *adj.*, 930, 1385, 1780; bothe, 195, 538, 983, 1093, 1193, 1206, 1286, 1691, 1698; boþe, 863, 972.
botheyrs, *adj. gen.*, of both, 1302.
bought, *v. pp.*, atoned for, 246; ibought, 89.
bour, *s.*, bower, 632; boure, 1051.
bowe, *s.*, bow, 965; bouwe, *pl.*, 859.
brayde, *s.*, moment, short space of time, 1752.
brayned, *v. pp. (aux. om.)*, brained, 1191.
brede, *s.*, breadth, 1203.

bredryn, see broder.
breke, *v. inf.*, break, 644, 1320; 3 *s. pt.*, 1897; brekith, 3 *s. pr.*, 1884; brak, 3 *s. pt.*, 1336; breken, 3 *pl. pt.*, 861; brokyn, *pp.*, 1696.
brent, *v.*, 3 *s. pt.*, burnt, 212; brynt, 158.
brest, *s.*, breast, 1083.
brere, *s.*, briar, 1416.
breyd, *v.*, 3 *pl. pt.*, drew quickly, 917.
broche, *s.*, brooch, 1101; broches, *pl.*, 1107; broge, *pl.* (?), 1093.
brode, *adj.*, broad, 933, 1083.
broder, *s.*, brother, 384, 703, 793, 802, 881, 955, 1328, 1437, 1452, 1470, 1655, 1733, 1763; brodir, 674, 708; broder, *pl.*, 200, 1552; brodren, 1550; bredryn, 197, 473.
brokyn, see breke.
brond, *s.*, brand, 211.
bryg, *s.*, bridge, 260; brygge, 1840.
bryght, *adj.*, 227, 308, 536, 820, 959, 1112, 1115, 1265, 1344, 1402, 1486, 1700, 1890.
bryght, *adv.*, brightly, 1495.
bryng, *v. inf.*, 39, 46, 221, 368, 1004, 1554, 1557; 3 *s. pr. subj.*, 689; brynge, *inf.*, 307; bryngeth, 3 *s. pr.*, 734; bryngyth, 755; brought, 3 *s. pt.*, 710, 719, 724, 728, 732, 747, 752, 908, 909; 3 *pl. pt.*, 155, 741, 882; *pp.*, 164, 194, 200, 478, 784, 902, 1042, 1262, 1706; broughten, 3 *pl. pt.*, 1901; brougth, 3 *s. pt.*, 722, 737.
brynt, see brent.
but, *prep.*, except, 169, 1005, 1095, 1109, 1198.
but, *conj. advers.*, *passim;* conj., unless, 89, 273, 993, 1404, 1546; that not, 254, 978, 1482; *adv. conj.*, *with* ne *or* not, 509, 650 (*neg. omitted*), 1480, 1862.
by, see be, *prep.*
by and by, *adv. phrase*, straightway, 1658.
byde, *v. inf.*, wait, remain, 1212, 1536.

bygged, *v. pp.*, built, 528.
byried, see **beryed**.

C.

called, *v. pp.*, named, 22, 170, 1275.
cam, see **com**.
care, *s.*, 183, 1540, 1818, 1915.
carpenters, *s.pl.*, carpenters, 48, 352.
cas, *s.*, chance, condition, 1054, 1634, 1775, 1842.
cassedowns, *s. pl.*, chalcedony, 1282.
cast, *v. inf.*, throw, 600, 1662; 3 *s. pt.*, 403, 834, 1501, 1645; 3 *pl. pt.* (with about), turned their ship's course, 80; *pp.*, 1436; **caste**, 1114; **castyn**, *inf.*, 840; **kast**, 832.
catell, *s.*, property, 1796; **katell**, 1784.
cause, *s.*, reason, 294.
caytyf, *s.* or *adj.*, wretch *or* wretched, 1341.
cercle, *s.*, "a band or wreath surmounting or encircling a knight's helmet."—Oxf. Dic., 1258.
certis, *adv.*, certainly, 567.
certeyn, *adj.*, determined, 693.
certenlyche, *adv.*, certainly, 1213.
cete, see **cite**.
champyon, *s.*, 1273, 1307.
charbuncles, *s.pl.*, carbuncles, 1495.
charite, *s.* In phrases: **pur charite**, 1169; **for charite**, 1922.
chere, *s.*, expression of the face, frame of mind, 1218, 1237, 1415, 1516.
cheses, *v.*, 3 *s. pr.*, chooses, 765.
choyse, *s.*, choice, 730.
chyld, *s.*, 220, 1005, 1007, 1480, 1807, 1858; **chylde**, 1053; **chyldren**, *pl.*, 243, 1784; **chyldryn**, 192, 1796.
chyualry, *s.*, a body of knights or horsemen equipped for battle, 738; **chyualrye**, 573.
cite, *s.*, city, 119, 276, 534, 598, 599; **cete**, 855, 882, 1313, 1853; **cyte**, 167, 271, 1061, 1538; *pl.*, 523.
clef, *v.*, 3 *s. pt.*, cleft, hewed asunder, 1207; **cleved**, *pp.*, 1184.
clepe, *v.*, 2 *s. imp.*, call, 1841; **clepeth**, 3 *s. pr.*, 48, 1675; **cleped**, 3 *s.*

pt., 31, 760, 768, 793, 871, 1136, 1341, 1349, 1759, 1829; 3 *pl. pt.*, 238; *pp.*, 14, 525, 675, 1000, 1476; **clepyd**, 3 *s. pt.*, 990; **icleped**, *pp.*, 1018.
clere, *adj.*, bright, 1523.
clerke, *s.*, scholar, 20, 543; **clerkys**, *pl.*, 214.
close, *adj.*, concealed, 1581.
closed, *v.*, 3 *pl. pt.*, 1614.
cloth, *s.*, 179, 1911; **clothe**, 493, 1071.
cloþed, *v.*, 3 *s. pt.*, 1606.
com, *v. inf.*, come, 1565; 1 *s. pr.*, 432; 1 *pl. pr.*, 1920; 2 *pl. pr.*, 821; 3 *s. pt.*, 159, 1161; 3 *pl. pt.*, 358, 807, 1789; 2 *s. pt. subj.*, 342; *pp.*, 66, 324; **come**, 3 *pl. pr.*, 59; 3 *s. pt.*, 318, 501, 713, 937, 1327, 1586, 1713, 1721; 3 *pl. pt.*, 154, 291; 2 *s. imp.*, 1547, 1598; *pp.*, 82, 498, 987, 1134, 1575, 1612; **comen**, *inf.*, 99; 1 *pl. pr.*, 506; 3 *pl. pr.*, 500; **comon**, *inf.*, 392; 3 *pl. pr.*, 496; **comyn**, 3 *pl. pr.*, 1159, 1425; 2 *pl. pt.*, 327; 3 *pl. pt.*, 1056, 1057, 1097; 3 *pl. pt. subj.*, 693; *inf.*, 685; *pp.*, 74, 805, 1058, 1909, 1897; **cometh**, 3 *s. pr.*, 100, 310, 574, 623, 788, 1152, 1613, 1681, 1799; 3 *pl. pr.*, 1683; **comyth**, 3 *s. pr.*, 375, 1290; **cam**, 3 *s. pt.*, 145, 1376; **came**, 1461; **icome**, *pp.*, 1467; **icomen**, 440; **icomyn**, 122.
comforted, *v.*, 3 *s. pt.*, 646; 3 *pl. pt.*, 1814; **confortedd**, 680.
comondeth, *v.* 3 *s. pr.*, commandeth, 67; **comoundeth**, 797; **comounded**, 3 *s. pt.*, 1658.
conquerour, *s.*, 392, 529.
consayle, *s.*, plan, opinion, advice, 1092; **conseyle**, 355; **counsayle**, 295, 1819.
consentyn, *v. inf.*, consent, 1406; **consenttyn**, 2 *pl. imp.* (with *sing.* meaning), 1820.
conspiracoun, *s.*, conspiracy, 1602.
contre, *s.*, country, 524, 634, 1060; **countre**, 622.
corlues, *s. pl.*, curlews, 1069.
cormerant, *s. pl.*, cormorants, 1069.
corset, *s.*, corslet, 1487.

cosyn, *s.*, kinsman, nephew, 26.

countes, *s.*, countess, 650; **cowntes**, 1161; **counteys**, *pl.*, 619.

cowardus, *s. pl.*, cowards, 1476.

cowd, see **kanne**.

cradell, *s.*, cradle, 1858.

cranys, *s. pl.*, cranes, 1067.

creature, *s.*, 1047.

crepullis, *s. pl.*, cripples, 1860.

crest, *s.*, ornament worn on a knight's helmet, 1258.

croche, *s.*, crutch, 1860.

crowned, *v.*, 3 *s. pt.*, 236, 548; **crownede**, *pp.*, 555; **crouned**, 277.

cry, *s.*, 617, 1853; **crye**, 119, 125, 1659.

cry, *v.*, 1 *s. pr.*, cry, beg, 1164; **cryes**, 3 *s. pr.*, 1676; **cryng**, *pr. part.*, 1163; **cryyng**, 831; **cryed**, 3 *s. pt.*, 588, 958, 1204, 1895; 3 *pl. pt.*, 1622.

cunne, see **kanne**.

cursyng, *v. pr. part.*, 962.

curteys, *adj.*, courtly, gracious, 29, 206.

curteysley, *adv.*, politely, 502; **curteysly**, 1464.

cutted, *v. pp.*, cut, 1440.

D.

dame, *s.*, lady, mistress, 170, 201, 308, 402, 413, 417, 518, 547, 551, 658, 810, 1021, 1033, 1325, 1355, 1572, 1594, 1889.

dares, *v.*, 3 *s. pr.*, lies motionless from grief, 1413.

dartis, *s. pl.*, pointed missiles, as arrows and spears, 846.

dasshed, *v.*, 3 *s. pt.*, dashed, 1643.

daunce, *s.*, dance, game, 1078, 1106, 1122.

day, *s.*, 253, 297, 317, 346, 434, 509, 522, 571, 607, 664, 842, 927, 946, 1033, 1063, 1103, 1128, 1236, 1297, 1325, 1332, 1413, 1419, 1435, 1567, 1689, 1704, 1726, 1827, 1875; **daye**, 447, 495, 1316; **dayes**, *pl.*, 946, 1179, 1704, 1706, 1861, 1863.

ded, see **do**.

dede, *s.*, deed, 1769.

dede, *adj.*, dead, 903, 978, 1204, 1550, 1576, 1699, 1778. *The phrase,* **for that dede**, 1301, *though its syntax is uncertain, refers to the burial of the dead.*

defende, *v. inf.*, 825; **defenden**, 1 *pl. pr.*, 1779; **defended**, 3 *s. pt.*, 940, 1629; 3 *pl. pt.*, 599, 856, 1883.

defense, *s.*, 741.

degre, *s.*, rank, 23.

delaye, *s.*, 1235.

dele, *s.*, part, 16.

deled, *v.*, 3 *s. pt.*, separated, 1529; **delyd**, 3 *pl. pt.*, delivered, 1526.

demened, *v. pp.*, behaved, *i.e.*, how you will conduct yourself, 326.

departeth, *v.*, 3 *s. pr.*, endeth, 1298; **departed**, 3 *s. pt.*, 980, 1214.

depe, *adj.*, deep, 258, 1693.

deply, *adv.*, with strong feeling, 1666.

dere, *adj.*, dear, 1655.

dere, *adv.*, dearly, 246.

destroyed, *v. pp.*, 293; **distroyed**, 203, 627; 2 *pl. pt.*, 817.

desyr, *v.*, 1 *pl. pr.*, desire, 301; **desyred**, *pp.*, 1567.

desyre, *s.*, 1288.

deth, *s.*, death, 164, 246, 866, 1168, 1436, 1453, 1835, 1856.

Develes, *s. gen.*, the Devil's, 335.

devis, *s.*, opinion, mechanical contrivance, 288; **devise**, 858.

dide, see **do**.

died, see **dye**.

dight, *v. inf.*, prepare, 702; 3 *s. pt.*, prepared, clothed, 1603, 1740; **dyght**, *inf.*, make themselves ready to go, 1787; 3 *s. pt.*, 360; 3 *pl. pt.*, 1910; *pp.*, adorned, 275, 1493 (**to deth dyght**, killed), 866; **idyght**, 128, 713.

dignite, *s.*, dignity, 24.

dilfull, see **dolfull**.

discomfet, *v. pp.*, defeated, 381.

discomfeture, *s.*, defeat, 193.

diskryvyn, *v. inf.*, describe, 545.

dispense, *s.*, supplies, 742.
dispyte, *s.*, scorn, outrage, 336, 1665.
diuerse, *adj.*, 1074.
do, *v.* *Five uses of the verb occur:*
   transitive, intransitive, causal,
   periphrastic, substitutional. Trans.
   inf., effect, 42, 822; *2 s. imp.*, 1800;
   subst. inf., 964; *intrans.*, *2 s. imp.*,
   301, 309; *caus. inf.*, cause, 107, 818,
   926; doo, *trans. inf.*, 499, 1150;
   pp., done, 1400; *intrans. inf.*, 763;
   2 s. imp., 1549; don, *trans. inf.*,
   1793; *pp.*, 336, 700, 1875; *subst.*,
   1 pl. pr. subj., 1917; done, *trans.*
   inf., 102; *special use of the pp.*,
   finished, 1827; doone, *trans. inf.*,
   762; doth, *trans.*, *3 pl. pr.*, put,
   1912; *2 s. imp.*, 310; *intrans.*, *3 s.*
   pr., 870; *periph.*, *3 pl. pr.*, 1271;
   did, *trans.*, *3 s. pt.*, 339, 1627; put,
   1580; *intrans.*, 1608; *periph.*, 241,
   257, 597, 702; *3 pl.*, 107, 304, 832;
   subst., *3 s.*, 534; dide, *caus.*, *3 s.*,
   caused, 277; ded, *periph.*, 354;
   dede, *caus.*, 249; *subst.*, 694,
   1990.
dole, *s.*, sorrow, lamentation, 1323,
   1345, 1674, 1734.
dolfull, *adj.*, dismal, 945, 1012, 1168,
   1257, 1856; dollfull, 1705; dilfull,
   963, 1231.
dolour, *s.*, grief, lamentation, 1335.
domes, *s. pl.*, acts of judging, 237.
don, see do.
doo, see do.
doone, see do.
door, *s.*, 1614.
doubill, *adj.*, double, 260 (*prob.*
   drawbridge).
dought, *s.*, doubt, 468.
doughter, *s.*, daughter, 332, 1044,
   1063, 1078, 1357, 1360, 1369, 1857,
   1860; douhter, 1391; dowter, 1106,
   1382; dowghters, *pl.*, 169.
doughteth, see dowt.
doughty, *adj.*, valiant, stout, 1195,
   1333, 1769; doughti, 877.
douhter, see doughter.
dowghters, see doughter.

dowghtiest, *adj.*, most valiant, 1293.
down, *adv.*, 129, 194, 825, 863, 951,
   992, 1813, 1840, 1845; downe, 144,
   1557; downne, 1577.
dowt, *v. inf.*, fear, 1764; doughteth,
   3 s. pr. reflex., 1615; doughtyth,
   611.
dowter, see doughter.
dragme, *s.*, drachm, 253
drede, *v. reflex.*, *2 s. imp.*, fear, 467.
dreme, *s.*, dream, 210, 218.
dremeng, *s.*, dreaming, 213; dremyng, 215.
dremeth, *v.*, *3 s. pr.*, dreameth, 210.
dressed, *v. reflex.*, *3 pl. pt.*, prepared,
   1752.
dreves, see dryve.
drewe, *v.*, *3 s. pt.*, drew, 966, 1318;
   2 pl. pt., 816; drow, *3 s. pt.*, 969,
   1626, 1657; drowen, *3 pl. pt.*, 845;
   drowyn, 149; drawyn, *pp.*, 1372;
   idrawe, 1071.
drof, see dryve.
drow, see drewe.
drowpis, *v.*, *3 s. pr.*, becomes dis-
   pirited, 1413.
drynkis, *s. pl.*, drinks, 1066.
dryve, *v. inf.*, 106, 757, 1648, 1849;
   dryveth, *3 s. pr.*, 1230; drives,
   113; *3 pl. pr.*, 495; dreves, *3 s. pr.*,
   886; dryves, 61; *3 pl. pr.*, 147;
   drave, *3 s. pt.*, 604; drof, 507;
   dryvyng, *pr. part.*, 1713, 1721.
duke, *s.*, 676, 688, 706, 709, 913.
durable, *adj.*, permanent, 1380.
durst, *v.*, *3 s. pt.*, 1536; *1 pl. pr. subj.*,
   1764.
dwell, *v. inf.*, remain, delay, 79,
   1015, 1170; *1 pl. pr.*, 509; dwellyn,
   inf., 1909; dwelled, *3 s. pt.*, 191;
   3 pl. pt., 1905.
dyche, *s.*, ditch, 257, 263; dyches,
   pl., 268.
dye, *v. inf.*, die, 72; *2 s. pr. subj.*,
   951; dyen, *inf.*, 1786; dyedist, *2 s.*
   pt., 1727; died, *3 s. pt.*, 1740; dyed,
   896, 1292, 1293, 1448, 1450, 1724.
dynt, *s.*, stroke, 143, 953, 1231, 1292;
   dynte, 1012; dyntis, *pl.*, 1648.

E.

eche, *adj.*, each, 120, 288, 589, 657, 682, 857; iche, 1677; eche, *as pron.*, 90, 300. See ilke (*b*).

echon, *indef. pron.*, each one, 352, 588, 807.

edere, see ether.

egre, *adj.*, fierce, 699, 952.

eke, *adv.*, also, 847, 1898.

elde, *adj.*, old, 683. See old.

elders, *s. pl.*, parents, 293, 303.

eldest, *adj.*, 207, 279, 361, 873.

elke, see ilke (*a*).

ells, *adv.*, otherwise, besides, 1750, 1852; els, 93.

empres, *s.*, empress, 649.

en, *prep.* in, 863. See in, *prep.*

enchauntement, *s.*, enchantment, 1026, 1564.

ende, *s.*, 15, 87, 299, 348, 682, 780, 789, 987, 1385, 1394, 1706.

ended, *v.*, 3 *s. pt.*, ended (life), 1668, 1725; endid, 1710.

endir, *adj.* In the phrase: endir day, day recently past, 434, 447.

Englyshe, *s.*, English language, 20.

engynne, *s.*, bier (?), 1660; ingyn, machine, 833.

enmyes, see enymye.

entendaunt, *adj.*, attentive, 798.

entent, *s.*, deliberate intention, 461.

entere, *v. inf.*, enter, 269; entred, 3 *pl. pt.*, 244; entreth, *pp.*, 66.

enymye, *s.*, enemy, 1368; enmyes, *pl.*, 367; enmys, 1764, 1822.

er, *conj.*, before, 478.

ere, *adv.*, formerly, 404.

erldom, *s.*, earldom, 283.

erle, *s.*, earl, 688, 1205; erles, *pl.*, 670, 1429, 1899.

erst, *adv.*, first, 1372.

erthe, *s.*, earth, 2, 620, 784, 1110; erþe, 1532.

erthely, *adj.*, earthly, 850.

ete, *v. inf.*, eat, 585; eten, 3 *pl. pt.*, 1064; etyn, 1104; *pp.*, 1077, 1105.

ether, *adj. and adj. pron.*, either, 150, 576, 577, 1177, 1803, 1902; eþer, 575; edere, 918.

euer, *adv.*, 299, 416, 426, 452, 954, 962, 1200, 1232, 1271, 1358, 1432, 1686, 1708, 1760, 1793; euere, 1294.

eueri, *adj.*, every, 16, 126, 215, 347, 501, 564, 595, 652, 654, 683, 688, 694, 797, 830, 843, 893, 899, 900, 976, 986, 1386, 1641, 1908, 1914; euery, 182, 1304, 1620, 1815; eueri, *as pron.*, each one, 689.

euerichon, *indef. pron.*, every one, 48, 72, 685, 786, 995, 1133; euerichone, 994, 1092; euerychon, 517.

eueriwhere, *adv.*, everywhere, 1014.

euermore, *adv.*, 485, 638, 640, 1086, 1797; euermoo, 390.

euery, see eueri.

evel, *adv.*, distressfully, exceedingly (?), 118.

even, *adv.*, quite, directly, 1529, 1839.

explicit, *v.*, 3 *s. pr.*, here ends, Colophon.

eyen, *s. pl.*, eyes, 1049; hyen, 568.

eyre, *s.*, heir, 1832.

F.

face, *s.*, 1338, 1446.

fader, *s.*, father, 171, 196, 328, 339, 624, 626, 815, 880, 1017, 1220, 1224, 1734, 1835, 1857, 1891; fadere, 234; fadir, 199; fader, *gen.*, 246, 1832; faders, 486, 623, 878, 1222.

falleth, *v.*, 3 *s. pr.*, 776; fallith, 1882; fill, 3 *s. pt.*, 144; fille, 1321; felle, 3 *pl. pt.*, 1208, 1691; falle, *pp.*, 165, 1147; fallyn, 519; ifalle, 610.

fals, *adj.*, false, 1226; false, 1602.

fare, *v. inf.*, prosper, 184, 1916; fareth, 3 *s. pr. impers.*, happeneth, 1465; ferd, 3 *s. pt.*, acted, appeared, 1700; ferden, 3 *pl. pt.*, prospered, 1917.

fast, *adv.*, quickly, intently, 513, 599, 617, 674, 831, 914, 1283, 1636, 1637, 1664, 1716, 1855, 1883; faste, 646, 919.

1107, 1630; **yave**, 1 *s. pt.*, 462; 3 *s.
pt.*, 1131; **yoven**, 3 *pl. pt.*, 844.

glace, *v. inf.*, glance aside, 932.

glad, *adj.*, happy, 569, 635, 791, 1133, 1387; **glade**, 1903; brilliant, 717, 1218.

glade, *v.*, 3 *s. pr. subj.*, make glad, 1323.

gle, *s.*, music, 1046.

glede, *s.*, burning coal, 158.

glyde, *v. inf.*, 1717.

gnawyn, *v. inf.*, gnaw, 1663.

go, *v. inf.*, 312, 388, 620, 698, 1126, 1160, 1223, 1350; 1 *s. pr.*, 1122; 1 *pl. pr. subj.*, 103, 1748, 1781; 2 *s. imp.*, 1839; *pp.*, 669, 906; **goo**, *inf.*, 83, 510, 581, 963, 1754; 2 *pl. pr.*, 1802; 3 *s. pr. subj.*, 476; 2 *s. imp.*, 339, 1379, 1573; **gon**, *inf.*, 314, 480, 1132, 1156, 1640; 3 *pl. pt.*, 981, 1813; 2 *pl. imp.*, 996; *pp.*, 785; **gone**, *inf.*, 47, 71, 99, 333, 373, 466, 587, 1610, 1685, 1706, 1773; 3 *pl. pt.*, 1299, 1308; **gonne**, *inf.*, 43, 60; **goone**, *inf.*, 1091; **goth**, 3 *s. pr.*, 579, 612, 754, 1167, 1409, 1491, 1610, 2 *pl. pr.* (*with sing. reference*), 380; 3 *pl. pr.*, 167, 1912; **gothe**, 3 *s. pr.*, 267; 3 *pl. pr.*, 180, 494; **goþe**, 3 *s. pr.*, 774; **gooth**, 1886; 2 *pl. imp.*, 782.

god, *s.*, 1009.

goddes, *s.*, goddess, 1019; *pl.*, 400.

gode, see **good**.

gold, *s.*, 39, 253, 405, 460, 633, 656, 767, 1278, 1494, 1826; **goold**, 1503.

gold, *adj.*, 641.

gon, see **go**.

gonne, see **go**; **gynneth**.

gonnys, *s. pl.*, guns, machines for casting stones (*maungeneles*), 832.

good, *s.*, good thing. In the phrase: for no good, on no account, 1197.

good, *adj.*, 108, 110, 309, 371, 489, 494, 550, 552, 603, 691, 726, 731, 741, 749, 811, 859, 938, 941, 1129, 1130, 1131, 1182, 1192, 1277, 1307, 1317, 1457, 1516, 1672, 1678, 1824, 1919; **goode**, 736; **gode**, 744.

goodis, *s. pl.*, possessions, 304.

goodnesse, *s.*, 539.

goold, see **gold**, *s.*

goone, see **go**.

Gost, *s.*, Ghost, 1216.

gotyn, see **gete**.

gouernour, *s.*, governor, 800.

grace, *s.*, favor, 334, 337, 931, 1918.

gracious, *adj.*, beautiful, 1050.

gramer, *s.*, grammar, 1703.

grasse, *s.*, 1098.

graue, *s.*, 1329.

graunt, *v. inf.*, grant, consent, 1392, 1795; 1 *s. pr.*, 311, 465; 2 *s. imp.*, 449; **graunte**, 2 *s. pr. subj.*, 446; **grauntt**, 1 *s. pt.*, 459; **graunted**, 3 *s. pt.*, 480, 686, 764, 905; 3 *pl. pt.*, 429.

greeth, *v.*, 3 *s. pr.*, is pleased, agreeth, 315.

grete, *adj.*, great, 123, 214, 231, 257, 265, 273, 294, 357, 380, 432, 490, 532, 573, 604, 628, 633, 655, 691, 748, 801, 834, 863, 864, 891, 893, 908, 960, 1082, 1274, 1282, 1288, 1308, 1311, 1314, 1323, 1412, 1438, 1457, 1540, 1571, 1578, 1600, 1712, 1734, 1875, 1881, 1899; **gret**, 84, 702, 799, 1136, 1893, 1906.

greter, *compar. adj.*, greater, 24.

gretest, *superl. adj.*, greatest, 1431.

gretis, *v.*, 3 *s. pr.*, greets, 576; **grete**, *pp.*, 1464.

greved, *v. pp.*, vexed, 1256.

ground, *s.*, 903, 1004, 1334; **gronde**, 478; **grounde**, 165, 434, 1147, 1521, 1631; **grownde**, 1321, 1554.

grym, *adj.*, fierce, cruel, 11, 123, 316, 590, 748, 872, 1153; **grymme**, 1087.

grymly, *adj.*, cruel, 918.

grysly, *adj.*, horrible, 150.

grythet, *v.*, 3 *s. pr.*, gets ready, prepares himself, 1677.

gunne, see **gynneth**.

gyle, *s.*, guile, 1584, 1744, 1893.

gylt, *v. pp.*, gilded, 135.

gyltles, *adj.*, guiltless, 328.

gynne, *s.*, contrivance, snare, 37, 856, 1614; **gynnys**, *pl.*, 837.

gynneth, *v.*, 3 *s. pr.*, beginneth, 587; gynnyth, 953, 1231; gyneth, 3 *pl. pr.*, 60; gynne, 757; gan, 3 *s. pt.*, 88, 1735; gann, 1648; ganne, 142, 1115, 1199, 1283, 1504, 1646, 1647, 1849; gene, 353; gunne, 3 *pl. pt.*, 83, 1525, 1787; gonne, 835, 1272.

gynnyng, *s.*, beginning, 789.

H.

half, *s.*, 984, 1017, 1020, 1756; *pl.*, sides, 863.

halle, *s.*, 474.

halvendell, *s.*, the half part, 933.

hande, *s.*, 916; hond, 1080, 1144, 1474, 1808; honde, 283; handes, *pl.*, 1030; handis, 1318, 1562; hondis, 1330.

hangged, *v. pp.*, 1372.

hard, *adj.*, cruel, hard, 140, 1027, 1555.

hard, *adv.*, violently, 147, 1247, 1523.

hardier, *compar. adj.*, bolder, 715.

hardy, *adj.*, brave, 29, 56, 57, 699, 731.

hardy, *adv.*, bravely, 854.

harme, *s.*, arm, 1625.

harmes, *s. pl.*, injuries, 1627.

haste, *s.*, 1113.

hasted, *v.*, 3 *pl. pt.*, hastened, 912.

hastily, *adv.*, 244.

hastyng, *s.*, haste, 214, 1136.

hat, see have.

hatte, *s.*, hat, 1697.

hauberk, *s.*, coat of mail, 930, 1109; hauberke, 1253; hawberke, 1095; haweberke, 1445.

have, *v. inf.*, 406, 423, 428, 459, 780, 1100, 1369, 1382, 1582; 1 *s. pr.*, 202, 471, 562, 627, 631, 823, 1399, 1478, 1879; 2 *s. pr.*, 438; 3 *s. pr.*, 586; 1 *pl. pr.*, 294, 998, 1475; 3 *pl. pr.*, 3, 293, 499, 828, 1356, 1400; 2 *s. imp.*, 1729; haue, *inf.*, 451; 3 *s. pr.*, 329; hast, 2 *s. pr.*, 464, 625; has, 3 *s. pr.*, 439; hath, 169, 614, 1114, 1201, 1464, 1544, 1567, 1870; hathe, 34, 121, 199, 730, 1469; hat, 1743; hath, 3 *pl. pr.*, 497; hathe, 168; had, 3 *s. pt.*, 26, 171, 186, 205, 456, 565, 636, 790, 1050, 1288; 3 *pl. pt.*, 833, 1042, 1812, 1904; 1 *s. pt. subj.*, 1877; 3 *s. pt. subj.*, 1874, 1878; 3 *pl. pt. subj.*, 704; hadd, 3 *s. pt.*, 454; hadde, 231, 651, 1044, 1371, 1507; 3 *pl. pt.*, 491, 904, 1077, 1105; 3 *s. pt. subj.*, 1701, 1873; *pp.*, 1877; haddyn, 3 *pl. pt.*, 494.

havon, *s.*, haven, 62, 114.

hawberke, see hauberk.

hayle, *s.*, hail, 848.

he, *pers. pron.*, *passim;* him, *passim;* hem, 258, 931, 1335, 1364, 1783; hym, 140, 142, 374, 794, 1114, 1116, 1203, 1618, 1640, 1675.

hede, *s.*, head, point, 697, 936, 1191, 1286, 1488, 1697, 1718, 1736, 1737; hedis, *pl.*, 606.

heder, *adv.*, hither, 1515, 1588; hedur, 325, 507; hider, 959.

heer, *s.*, hair, 641; her, 697; here, 1318, 1340.

hele, *s.*, health, prosperity, 342.

heled, *v.*, 3 *pl. pt.*, healed, 904; helid, 3 *s. pt.*, 970; helyd, 1530.

hellme, *s.*, helmet, 1257, 1409; helm, 1183; helme, 887, 1246, 1248, 1279, 1286, 1289, 1443, 1488, 1493, 1518, 1524; helmes, *pl.*, 605, 921, 1632, 1700.

help, *v. inf.*, 1879; helpith, 2 *pl. imp.*, 91.

helpe, *s.*, 1794.

helples, *adj.*, helpless, 1635.

hem, *pers. pron. s. and pl.*, see he, they.

hemself, *reflex. pron. pl.*, themselves, 107.

hend, *adj.*, courteous, prompt, gentle, 329; hende, 29, 57, 716, 810, 1594; hynde, 1173.

henne, *adv.*, hence, 1802.

hens, *adv.*, hence, 343, 816.

hent, *v.*, 3 *s. pt.*, seized, 1644.

her, *s.*, see heer.

her, *poss. pron. fem.*, *passim;* hir, 1330; here, 213, 546, 568, 667, 668, 1337, 1338, 1339, 1340, 1346, 1415, 1416, 1417.

her, *poss. pron., pl.* their, *passim :*
hir, 596, 742, 806, 1456; here, 163,
742, 901, 1582, 1842, 1905. See ther,
poss. pron.

herd, *s.*, swineherd, 226.

here, *s.*, see heer.

here, *v. inf.*, hear, 44, 513, 1032,
1238, 1433, 1434, 1459; hereth, 3 *s.*
pr., 47, 787; herith, 1671; herd, 3
s. pt., 65, 239, 563.

here, *poss. pron. fem. s. and poss.*
pron. pl., see her.

here, *pers. pron.*, see she.

here, *adv.*, 323, 342, 387, 823, 1173,
1510, 1847.

hereafter, *adv.*, 1358; herafter,
1238.

heritage, *s.*, inheritance, 189.

herkyn, *v. inf.*, hearken, listen for,
116; 2 *s. imp.*, 771.

herself, *reflex. pron.*, 1341.

hert, *s.*, heart, 584, 644, 1320, 1336,
1346, 1348, 1723; herte, 1528, 1545,
1604; hert, *gen.*, 1189, 1650.

hertely, *adv.*, heartily, 1138.

hes, see his.

heven, *s.*, heaven, 2, 1701.

hewe, *v. inf.*, hew, 353, 889; heuwe,
3 *s. pt.*, 1632; hewen, *inf.*, 1028;
hewyn, 1556; 3 *pl. pt.*, 1523; *pp.*,
1356; heuweth, 3 *s. pr.*, 1887;
heuwes, 892.

hey, see hy.

heyes, see hyes.

heyght, *s.*, height. *In the phrase on*
heyght, aloft, on high, 1472.

hider, see heder.

himsilf, *pers. pron.* (*emphatic*), 127.

hir, *poss. pron. fem. s., and poss.*
pron. pl., see her.

his, *poss. pron., passim;* is, 1562,
1633, 1680; hys, 66, 624, 1192; hes,
965.

his, *v.*, see be, *v.*

hit, *v.*, 3 *s. pt.*, was called, 26, 85,
1043, 1833; hitt, 187.

hitt, *v. inf.*, hit, strike, 1209; hitte,
1533; hit, 3 *s. pt.*, 1285; hitt,
1205; hitte, 935.

hode, *s.*, head, 1190.

hoke, *s.*, barb of an arrow, 966.

hold, *adj.*, faithful, 768.

holde, *v. inf.*, estimate, 94, 1822;
hold, 1 *s. pr.*, 819, 1808; holdest,
2 *s. pr.*, 960; holdeth, 3 *s. pr.*, 653;
held, 3 *s. pt.*, 533, 566; 3 *pl. pt.*,
518; helde, 3 *s. pt.*, 1581; 3 *pl. pt.*,
10.

hole, *adj.*, whole, 1545.

Holy, *adj.*, 1216.

holy, *adv.*, wholly, 1592.

home, *s.*, 182, 368, 623, 1170, 1732,
1735, 1811, 1914; hom, 365, 392,
1175, 1422.

hond, see hande.

honour, *s.*, 391, 530, 624, 799, 1222,
1311, 1571, 1899. See anour.

honoured, *v. pp.*, 464.

hope, *v.*, 1 *s. pr.*, expect, 763, 1770.

hornes, *s. pl.*, 1659.

hors, *s.*, horse, 126, 155, 1017, 1125,
1206, 1208, 1502, 1532, 1699, 1866;
pl., 894, 1457.

host, *s.*, army, 373, 385, 482, 755, 875,
908, 1537, 1680, 1837, 1849; hoste,
1176, 1768, 1905; ost, 123, 356, 366,
379, 587, 702, 795, 1177, 1230, 1814;
oste, 711, 1156, 1609.

houndis, *s. pl.*, 1663.

hout, see out.

houwe, *interj.*, ho, 1466.

how, *inter. adv.*, 395, 625, 1465, 1551,
1557.

how, *rel. adv.*, 184, 194, 348, 772, 790,
992, 1013, 1087, 1220, 1390, 1672,
1836, 1916; howe, 216, 326.

hundred, *card. num.*, 890, 1356, 1458,
1574, 1910; hunderd, 804; hundrid,
154, 703, 837, 1073, 1579, 1649; hundryd, 758.

hunger, *s.*, 1750.

hunted, *v.*, 3 *s. pt.*, 1537.

hurt, *v. pp.*, 1719.

hurtelyng, *s.*, clashing together,
1698.

hy, *adj.*, high, 23; hey, 531; hye,
255, 261. In the phrase: on hy,
aloud, 1163; on hye, 958, 1367.

hydder, v., 3 s. pt., contraction of hid herself, 172.

hye, s., haste, 112, 574, 722, 737, 1257.

hyen, see eyen.

hyeng, s., haste, 1664; hyyng, 357, 687, 990, 1742; hyynge, 760.

hyes, v., 3 s. pr., hastens, 1677; heyes, 1680; hyes, 3 pl. pr., 912; hyeth, 3 s. pr., 513.

hynde, see hend.

hyng, v. inf., hang, 1182.

hyyng, see hyeng.

I.

I, pers. pron., passim; Y, 457, 1223, 1516; me, passim; mee, 464; we, passim; wee, 506; vs, passim.

i-, prefix, see simple verbs.

iche, see eche.

if, conj., passim; iff, 384; yf, 993, 1099, 1122, 1565.

igrounde, v. pp., ground, 917.

ile, s., isle, 724.

ilke (a), adj., same, very, 1322, 1327; elke, 1236.

ilke (b), adj., each, every, 1753. See eche.

ilkone, pron., each one, 420.

image, s., 781; ymage, 790.

imordred, v. pp., murdered, 1673.

ingyn, see engynne.

in, prep., passim; inne, 598, 1152. See en.

in, adv., within, 244, 1613, 1798, 1800, 1804; inne, 1843.

inough, adj., enough, 1174; inowe, 266.

inow, adv., enough, 791, 970.

insure, v., 1 s. pr., assure, 1247.

into, prep., passim; unto, 1403; intoo, 1570.

inwardly, adv., earnestly, 1088.

iren, adj., iron, 1697.

is, v., see be, v.

is, poss. pron., see his.

it, pers. pron., passim.

iugegement, see juggement.

iuste, see juste.

iwis, adv., certainly, 219, 259, 696; iwisse, 429; iwys, 1480.

J.

jentill, see gentil.

jolyte, s., jollity, 487.

joy, s., 266.

juell, s., jewel, 423.

jugegy, v. inf., judge, 422; jugest, 2 s. pr., 444.

juge, s., judge, 427.

juggement, s., judgment, 419; iugegement, 462.

juste, v. inf., joust, 948; justyn, 1714; iuste, 1720.

K.

kanne, v., 1 s. pr., can, 42; kan, 2 pl. pr., 822; kun, 997; cunne, 3 pl. pr., 1903; koud, 3 s. pt., knew, 514; koude, 542; cowd, knew, was able, 1046, 1584; cowde, 923; 3 pl. pt., 1579.

kast, see cast.

katell, see catell.

kene, adj., sharp, 920; kenne, 859.

kepe, v. inf., watch, 226, 1848.

kne, s., knee, 1440; knees, pl., 776, 1866.

knelith, v., 3 s. pr., kneeleth, 1616; knelled, 3 s. pt., 1587.

knowe, v. inf., 1265; knowyn, pp., 411, 1014.

knowyng, s., knowledge, 229.

knyght, s., 13, 56, 332, 443, 558, 678, 714, 1126, 1128, 1141, 1193, 1233, 1266, 1349, 1363, 1427, 1467, 1611, 1629, 1725, 1830; knyht, 580; knyghtis, pl., 572, 877, 1055, 1063, 1085, 1091, 1104, 1182, 1620, 1731, 1883; knyghtys, 154.

konyng, adj., skilful, 17.

koud, see kanne.

krounes, s. pl., heads, 134.

kun, see kanne.

kympis, s. pl., champions, warriors, 1242.

kynde, s., nature, 1481.

730, 805, 1143, 1432, 1708; **londis**, *pl.*, 1797.

long, *s.*, lung, 1694.

long, *adj.*, 490, 1082.

long, *adv.*, 81, 512, 578, 643, 1051, 1632, 1880; **longe**, 1342.

longer, *compar. adv.*, 359; **lenger**, 79.

longeth, *v.*, 3 *s. pr. impers.*, desireth, 560, 568.

lord, *s.*, 363, 377, 604, 680, 718, 723, 729, 745, 746, 750, 777, 886, 891, 937, 1162, 1167, 1274, 1366, 1379, 1465, 1687, 1773, 1791, 1810; **lorde**, 735, 1712, 1901; **lordis**, *gen.*, 596; *pl.*, 84, 284, 517, 740, 864.

lordyng, *s.*, lord, sir, 652, 688, 694; **lorddyngs**, *pl.*, 1761; **lordyngis**, 21, 290, 323, 588, 991, 995; **lordyngs**, 761; **lordyngys**, 508, 628; **lordyns**, 87. *Usually vocative in the plural.*

lorn, see **lese**.

losengers, *s. pl.*, flatterers, cowards (?), 94.

lost, see **lese**.

loth, *adj.*, loath, 700.

louid, see **loveth**.

love, *s.*, 583, 596, 996, 1347, 1398, 1411, 1548, 1892.

lovely, *adj.*, 1047, 1337, 1415, 1417.

lovely, *adv.*, with love, 577.

lovesom, *adj.*, lovable, 1338; **lovesum**, 1414.

lovesumnes, *s.*, lovableness, 668.

loveth, *v.*, 3 *s. pr.*, 35; **louid**, 3 *s. pt.*, 234; **loved**, 647, 794, 1162, 1604; 3 *pl. pt.*, 30.

low, *v.*, 3 *s. pt.* (O. E. **hlôh**, *pt. of* **hliehhan**), laughed, 792.

lowe, *adv.*, 1334.

lyche, *adv.* In the phrase: **lyche yerne**, eagerly, 1200.

lye, *s.*, 984.

lye, *v. inf.*, 217.

lyf, *s.*, life, 426, 452, 611, 1342, 1540, 1628, 1653; **lyfe**, 343, 469, 643, 1162; **lyff**, 1370; **lif**, 1192; **lyve**, 171, 541, 647, 1761. In the phrase: **be lyve**, quickly, 583, 1347; **lyves**, *pl.*, 1679, 1783, 1842; **lives**, 1272, 1795.

lyght, *s.*, 1297.

lyght, *adj.*, lightminded, 1398.

lyght, *v.*, 3 *s. pt.* (O. E. **lihtan**), alighted, descended, 1217; *pp.*, made light, relieved, 1628.

lymys, *s. pl.*, members, 1887.

lyon, *s.*, 952, 1130, 1472; **leyon**, 940.

lytill, *s.*, little time, 1329.

lyve, *s.*, see **lyf**.

lyve, see **leve**, *v.*

M.

mad, see **make**.

Madame, *s.*, 219.

magre, *s.*, ill-will, displeasure, 821.

magre, *prep.*, in spite of, 100.

magreth, *prep.*, in spite of, 101.

make, *s.*, mate, equal, 1249, 1482.

make, *v. inf.*, 50, 125, 257, 354, 365, 1362, 1380, 1598, 1818; 2 *s. imp.*, 1126; 3 *s. pr. subj.*, 589; 3 *pl. pr.*, 183, 806; **makyn**, *inf.*, 404; **maketh**, 3 *s. pr.*, 286, 617, 1674, 1915; 2 *pl. imp.*, 1802; **makes**, 3 *s. pr.*, 280, 284, 482, 657, 795, 1412, 1908; **maked**, 3 *s. pt.*, 703; *pp.*, 1354; **made**, 3 *s. pt.*, 259, 932, 942, 1128, 1324, 1345, 1734; 3 *pl. pt.*, 1314, 1903; *pp.*, 893; **mad**, 3 *s. pt.*, 1717.

malardes, *s. pl.*, mallards, 1070.

man, *s.*, 28, 64, 120, 126, 182, 256, 288, 422, 425, 501, 540, 589, 595, 608, 613, 657, 676, 683, 696, 698, 706, 712, 715, 797, 850, 923, 944, 965, 971, 1003, 1009, 1017, 1142, 1143, 1195, 1197, 1206, 1208, 1210, 1265, 1276, 1293, 1370, 1441, 1473, 1479, 1481, 1489, 1504, 1530, 1532, 1534, 1553, 1617, 1667, 1677, 1690, 1699, 1754, 1765, 1812, 1815, 1831, 1866, 1908, 1914; **manys**, *gen.*, 973; **men**, *pl.*, 10, 65, 133, 137, 206, 238, 390, 554, 558, 601, 704, 731, 744, 846, 894, 954, 974, 977, 978, 1077, 1120, 1181, 1232, 1436, 1439, 1483, 1574, 1578, 1579, 1590, 1658, 1660, 1859, 1862.

maner, *s.*, kind, way, 679, 775, 832, 1270.

H

mankyn, *s.*, mankind, 1727.

manly, *adv.*, 45, 92, 97, 103, 956; manlyche, 484.

mantill, *s.*, mantle, 1625; mantille, 1607.

many, *adj.*, 57, 580, 604, 606, 619, 834, 856, 866, 886, 891, 896, 938, 942, 944, 1183, 1184, 1185, 1187, 1188, 1189, 1190, 1191, 1192, 1193, 1194, 1195, 1436, 1438, 1441, 1443, 1444, 1445, 1446, 1447, 1448, 1450, 1504, 1567, 1627, 1692, 1693, 1694, 1695, 1696, 1697, 1734; manye, 3; meny, 1442.

manys, see man.

marchauntis, *s. pl.*, merchants, 505.

mason, *s.*, 252; masons, *pl.*, 247.

mast, *s.*, 845; mastes, *pl.*, 490.

mater, *s.*, matter, 563.

maungeneles, *s. pl.* (O. Fr. mangonel), machine for throwing stones, 838.

may, *v.*, 1 *s. pr.*, can, 45, 570, 1150, 1223, 1766; 2 *s. pr.*, 1470; 3 *s. pr.*, 269, 312, 338, 418, 442, 608, 914, 1474, 1482, 1533, 1534, 1553, 1001; 1 *pl. pr.*, 1070, 2 *pl. pr.*, 1032, 1434; 3 *pl. pr.*, 184, 1160, 1426, 1685, 1916; 3 *s. pr.*, may, 511; maye, 3 *s. pr.*, 5; mowe, 2 *pl. pr.*, 1007; mowen, 1793; mown, 1238; myght, 3 *s. pt.*, 218, 272, 540, 620, 684, 698, 840, 888, 924, 964, 971, 1004, 1197, 1209, 1210, 1212, 1265, 1284, 1554, 1666, 1690, 1738, 1754; 3 *pl. pt.*, 133, 254, 265, 868, 977, 1181, 1439, 1663; mystest, 2 *s. pt.* (*error for* my5test), 1565.

may, *s.*, maid, 1344, 1414, 1568, 1604.

maydens, *s. gen.*, 1040, 1361; *pl.*, 553, 632, 1052, 1093, 1107.

mayn, *s.*, strength, 67, 1124, 1229; mayne, 1245.

mayster, *s.*, master, ruler, 17, 320, 482, 999, 1484; maystres, *pl.*, 549, 1148.

maystry, *s.*, mastery, 1904; maystrie, 801; maystri, 998.

mekenes, *s.*, meekness, 546.

mekyl, *adj.*, great, 746; moche, 456, 573, 821, 975, 1046, 1276, 1418, 1428, 1429, 1496, 1689, 1865; myche, 188.

mekyl, *adv.*, greatly, very, 768; moche, 370, 554, 1542.

melodye, *s.*, melody, 1074.

menys, *v.*, 3 *s. pr.*, bemoans, 1414.

mercy, *s.*, 1895; merci, 1164, 1466.

mervayles, *s. pl.*, marvels, 44.

mervelous, *adj.*, marvellous, 210.

mery, *adj.*, 183, 1818, 1908, 1915; meri, 365.

mesage, *s.*, 1350, 1365.

mesenger, *s.*, 324; mesanger, 1375, 1584, 1585; messanger, 1383; messangere, 1378; mesyngere, 341; messangers, *pl.*, 827.

mete, *v. inf.*, meet, 1271; metis, 3 *s. pr.*, 575; mett, 3 *s. pt.*, 1531; mette, 130, 1462, 1463; *pp.*, 131, 1239, 1249.

mette, *s.*, meat, food, 1755; metis, *pl.*, 1066.

meved, *v. pp.*, moved, 216.

meyne, *s.* (O. Fr. maisnée), household, followers, army, 128, 488, 533, 1062, 1684.

meynten, *v. inf.*, maintain, 486; 2 *pl. imp.*, 92, 878.

misse, *s.*, fail, 1702.

mo, see more.

moche, see mekyl.

mode, *s.*, mind, 216, 551.

moder, *s.*, mother, 210, 1019, 1037, 1551, 1857; moder, *gen.*, 1450; moders, 1030; modir, 1562.

monthe, *s.*, 1906; monthis, *pl.*, 898; monthys, 836.

more, *adj.*, 530, 542, 657, 658, 755, 966, 1304, 1510, 1589, 1952; mo, 572; moo, 1399, 1574, 1864.

more, *adv.*, 560, 794, 1122, 1542, 1720, 1746, 1909.

morn, *s.*, 900, 1269, 1813.

mornyng, *s.*, mourning, 665, 1410.

most, *superl. adj.*, 544, 1707.

mot, *v.*, 1 *s. pr. subj.*, may, shall, 457; mote, 559, 1119, 1516; 3 *s. pr. subj.*, 69; most, 2 *s. pt.*, must,

1512; 3 *s. pt.*, 314, 422, 1651; **must**, 1 *pl. pt.*, 762; 3 *pl. pt.*, 692.

mote, see **mot**.

mowe, see **may**.

must, see **mot**.

my, *poss. pron.*, 199, 200, 201, 363, 377, 384, 562, 570, 669, 671, 815, 816, 817, 824, 826, 959, 996, 1124, 1166, 1167, 1172, 1222, 1224, 1382, 1401, 1470, 1544, 1548, 1549, 1552, 1744, 1808, 1824, 1870, 1891; **myn**, 407, 409, 414, 461, 625, 644, 782, 1151, 1320; **myne**, 670, 1545.

myche, see **moche**.

myd, *adj.*, middle, 845.

mydnyght, *s.*, 1165.

myght, *s.*, 67, 188, 485, 701, 1124, 1428, 1496, 1815.

myld, *adj.*, 551; **mylde**, 778.

myle, *s.*, 840.

mylke, *s.*, 1338.

mynstrelles, *s. pl.*, 1073.

myrth, *s.*, 1757; **myrthe**, 266, 657, 660.

myschaunce, *s.*, ill luck, 1121, 1874.

mysdedon, *v.*, 3 *pl. pt.*, acted amiss, 78.

myself, *reflex. pron.*, 672.

myspayed, *v. pp.*, displeased, 117.

mystest, see **may**, *v.*

N.

nakeres, *s. pl.*, kettledrums, 1075.

name, *s.*, 187, 335, 1021, 1045, 1079.

namely, *adv.*, especially, 1225, 1371.

naught, *s.*, 1518; **nought**, 2, 52, 90, 1261.

nay, *adv.*, 298, 338, 417.

ne, *adv.*, not, 269, 310, 467, 509, 561, 771, 1862.

ne, *conj.*, neither, nor, 228, 457, 530, 531, 852, 887, 1090, 1153, 1234, 1602, 1623, 1754, 1755.

nede, *adv.*, necessarily, 1651.

nede, *s.*, need, 432, 867, 956, 1638.

nekke, *s.*, neck, 1897; **neke**, 1501; **nekkis**, *pl.*, 1637.

nere, *adv.*, near, 382, 1755.

nether, *conj.*, neither, 852; **neþer**, 1234.

neuer, *adv.*, 8, 256, 272, 336, 537, 561, 569, 712, 868, 927, 1089, 1153.

neuermore, *adv.*, 1381.

neuerþelater, *adv.*, nevertheless, 479, 618.

new, *adj.*, 108; **newe**, 296, 884, 1178, 1263; **nowe**, 1072.

newe, *adv.*, newly, 354, 528.

next, *adv.*, 1103, 1799.

no, *adj.*, *passim*; **noo**, 176; **non**, 227, 271, 274, 418, 673, 850, 923; **none**, 169, 202; **noon**, 715.

nobeley, *adv.*, nobly, 1066.

nobir, see **nombryn**.

noble, *adj.*, 104, 1725; **nobil**, 111, 676, 1487; **nobill**, 50, 137, 206, 356, 543, 558, 642, 706, 714, 725, 1141, 1228, 1629, 1830.

noblest, *superl. adj.*, 523.

nolde, *v.*, 3 *s. pt.*, would not, 1589.

nombryn, *v. inf.*, number, 971; **nobir**, 608.

nome, *v.*, 3 *s. pt.*, took, seized, 1611; 3 *pl. pt.*, 292; *pp.*, 81, 1576.

non, *adj.*, see **no**.

non, *indef. pron.*, no one, 1848; **none**, 70, 537, 1609, 1746.

none, *adj.*, see **no**, **non**.

nons, *adv.*, used only in the phrase: **for the nons**, for the occasion, 27, 655, 833, 1279; **nones**, 766; **nonys**, 716.

noon, see **no**.

nor, *conj.*, 8.

not, see **nought**, *adv.*

noþyng, *s.*, 622; **noþyngs**, *pl.*, 1094; **noþyngis**, 1108.

nothyng, *adv.*, in no wise, 78; **noþyng**, 364, 467, 1601.

nought, *adv.*, not, 5, 79, 193, 217, 228, 331, 456, 508, 783, 991, 1002, 1041, 1226; **nouht**, 1014; **not**, *passim*; **nott**, 1202.

now, *adv.*, 19, 323, 394, 397, 413, 650, 661, 801, 1332; **nowe**, 103, 202.

nowe, *adj.*, see **new**, **now**.

nowhere, *adv.*, 258.

nygh, *adv.*, 1254, 1348; **ny**, 1256, 1336.
nyght, *s.*, 209, 297, 317, 495, 522, 664, 842, 899, 1316, 1413, 1419; **nyghte**, 1580.
nyh, *prep.*, 949.
nyle, *v.*, 1 *s. pr.*, will not, 1623; **nyll**, 3 *s. pr.*, 644; **nylle**, 1320.
nyne, *card. num.*, 728, 898.

O.

o, see **of**, **on**, *prep.*
oder, *adj.*, second, other, 549, 552, 869, 938, 1427.
oder, *indef. pron.*, see **other**.
of, *prep.*, *passim*; with that, because, 327; during, 867; in, 1026; for, 1400, 1401; on, 1546; with, 1700; by means of, 1826; from, 1460; **o**, 122.
of, *adv.*, off, 1286.
offered, *v.*, 3 *s. pt.*, 770, 775.
ofsmyte, *v.*, 3 *s. pt.*, smote off, 936.
often, *adv.*, 666, 1341, 1414, 1420.
ofwevyd, *v. pp.*, shaken off, 1183.
old, *adj.*, 30, 1765, **olde**, 1659. See **elde**.
on, *prep.*, *passim*; in, into, 335, 343, 357, 541, 643, 644, 687, 1122, 1320, 1633, 1761, 1813; with, 895, 976; **on blod**, so that blood came, 1330; **o**, 418.
on, *adv.*, 853, 1765, 1854.
on, *card. num.*, one, 734, 1864; **one**, 169.
on, *indef. pron.*, one, 523, 1189, 1190, 1191, 1431; **one**, 1639.
onder, see **vnder**.
onderneath, *prep.*, underneath, 1505.
onderstande, see **vnderstond**.
ondo, *v. pp.*, unfastened, 1840.
one, see **on**.
ongayn, *adj.*, perilous, dreadful, 1722.
onneth, *adv.*, with difficulty, 1454; **onnethis**, 1244.
onrydde, *adj.*, enormous, cruel, 1430, 1619.
onryght, *s.*, wrong, 960.

onto, *prep.*, unto, 430, 844, 1001, 1839.
ony, *adj.*, any, 158, 232, 306, 412, 684, 700, 794, 848, 952, 1028, 1432, 1708, 1854.
ony, *indef. pron.*, any one, 1120.
oo, *interj.*, oh, 1558.
or, *conj.*, *passim*; until, before, 562, 570, 586, 784, 785, 954, 961, 1232, 1449, 1511, 1802.
or, *prep.*, before, 927.
orde, *s.*, beginning, 348, 1385.
order, *s.*, 15.
ordeyn, *v. inf.*, prepare, 107.
ore, *s. pl.*, oars, 756, 1910.
orientall, *adj.*, 1281, 1497.
ost, see **host**.
other, *indef. pron.*, 576, 673; *pl.*, 484; **oder**, 150, 300, 575, 577, 794, 918, 1177, 1902.
ouer, *prep.*, *passim*; **ouere**, 549; **ouer all**, everywhere, 125.
ouercome, *v. inf.*, 786; 3 *pl. pt.*, 12; *pp.*, 1449.
ouergarde, *adv.*, crosswise, 268.
ouerþrouwe, *v. pp.*, overthrown, 381.
ought, see **out**.
our, *poss. pron.*, 92, 293, 303, 367, 419, 772, 992, 1355, 1514, 1570, 1678.
ours, *poss. pron.*, 1920.
out, *adv.*, 5, 130, 142, 344, 506, 724, 969, 1647, 1657, 1728, 1739, 1754; **oute**, 1851; **ought**, 174, 1645, 1900; **owt**, 163; **owte**, 163; **hout**, 1309.
outbreyde, *v. inf.*, draw out, 1115.
outrages, *v.*, 3 *s. pr.*, runs riot, 1472.
owne, *adj.*, 420, 1907.

P.

pament, *s.*, pavement, 144.
parauentour, *adv.*, perchance, 511.
parfay, *adv.*, by my faith, 41.
parlement, *s.*, parliament, 286, 287.
partriche, *s. pl.*, partridges, 1068.
party, *s. pl.*, sides, 983.
paryth, *v.*, 3 *s. pr.*, cutteth, 929.
passe, *v. inf.*, pass, 1851; **passed**, 3 *pl. pt.*, 181; **passeth**, 3 *s. pr.*, 316.
pavilion, *s.*, 982; **pavylion**, 1300; **pauelyons**, *pl.*, 1456.

paye, *s.*, 254.

payed, *v. pp:*, satisfied, 566.

pece, *s.*, piece, time, 661; *pl.*, 1356; pecie, 892; pecis, 1251, 1643, 1663, 1888.

pees, *s.*, peace, 299, 327, 404, 1354, 1362, 1380, 1392, 1393, 1591; pes, 1358.

pepill, *s.*, people, 608, 719, 979.

pere, *s.*, equal, 1669.

pery, *s.*, precious stones, 1494 (O. F. perrée).

perytotes, *s. pl.*, peridot, chrysolite, 1496.

pete, see pyte.

pipes, *s. pl.*, rolls or quills on which gold thread was wound for embroidery, or (*as here*) for ornament, 1494.

place, *s.*, 232, 1097, 1327, 1560.

planete, *s.*, planet, 1011.

play, *s.*, battle, sword-play, 945, 1705; playe, sport, 448, 1072; pley, 1512.

plenor, *adj.*, full, 287.

plente, *s.*, plenty, 767, 1600.

plover, *s. pl.*, 1068.

plyght, *v.*, 2 *s. imp.*, pledge, 1803; plyte, 3 *pl. pt.*, 1809.

poer, see power.

polke, *s.*, small pool, 976.

portcolys, *s.*, portcullis, 260.

porture, *s.*, bearing, 1048.

postern, *s.*, 1788.

power, *s.*, ability, 690; military forces, 372, 824; pouer, might, 908; poer, military forces, 481, 796; poere, 388.

poynt, *s.*, 584 (*here used adverbially*), on the point of.

pray, *v.*, 1 *s. pr.*, 445; prey, 1 *s. pr.*, 1145, 1548; preyeth, 3 *s. pr.*, 1593.

precious, *adj.*, 656, 765, 1280.

preketh, see priketh.

prese, *s.*, throng, 964.

prest, *v.*, 3 *pl. pt.*, pressed forward, 900.

prest, *adj.*, ready, 1267.

preve, *v. inf.*, prove, 1124; 2 *pl. imp.*, 877, 1769; prove, *inf.*, 1624.

prey (?), 721, see Literary Notes.

priketh, *v.*, 3 *s. pr.*, rideth, 1229; preketh, 914.

prince, *s.*, 188, 361, 1832; prynce, 207; princes, *pl.*, 280.

prise, *s.*, price, value, 1276; pryse, 746; pryce, prize, 368, 391, 549; pryss, 476.

procession, *s.*, 1308.

prove, see preve.

prowde, *adj.*, proud, 1605.

pryde, *s.*, 1429, 1906.

pur, *prep.* (Fr. pour), for the sake of, 1169.

put, *v.*, 2 *pl. pr. subj.*, place, 334.

pypers, *s. pl.*, 1076.

pyte, *s.*, 168, 1729, 1854; lamentation, 1345; pete, 1314.

Q.

quarell, *s. pl.*, square bolts, 847.

quarter, *s.*, 1259.

quelle, *v. inf.*, kill, 1646.

quene, *s.*, 278, 535, 551, 571, 579, 594, 598, 614, 631, 637, 649, 669, 810, 819, 959, 1355, 1359, 1377, 1401, 1539, 1583, 1744, 1900.

queynte, *adj.*, famous, 707.

queyntest, *superl. adj.*, most elegant, 698.

quod, *v.*, 3 *s. pt.*, said, 1869.

quyk, *adj.*, alive, 1576.

quyte, *adv.*, wholly, 929.

quytely, *adv.*, wholly, 934.

R.

ranne, see ryn.

raught, *v.*, 3 *s. pt.*, reached, 1517.

raveshed, *v. pp.*, ravished, 201; ravysheng, *pr. part.*, 1401.

ravnson, *s.*, ransom, 306.

reaulme, *s.*, realm, 186, 285; reaume, 252.

rebuked, *v.*, 3 *pl. pt.*, 1375; *pp.*, 77, 348.

reche, see ryche.

rede, *s.*, advice, counsel, 1549; redde, 1302.

rede, *adj.*, red, 491, 697, 1416, 1826; redde, 1198.

rede, *v. inf.*, advise, 1777; 1 *s. pr.*, 330, 333.

redy, *adj.*, ready, 51, 360, 589, 880, 988, 1270.

relikis, *s. pl.*, relics, 766.

remembrith, *v.*, 3 *s. pr.*, remembereth, 666.

rendyn, *v. inf.*, rend, tear, 1525; rent, 3 *s. pt.*, 1340.

renown, *s.*, 864, 1274, 1578, 1712.

rentis, *s. pl.*, revenues, 1826.

rered, *v.*, 3 *s. pt.*, raised, 1850.

rest, *s.*, 1393; reste, 1268, 1919.

reste (*a*), *v.*, 1 *pl. pr. subj.*, 661; rested, 3 *pl. pt.*, 899.

reste (*b*), *v.*, 3 *s. pt.*, wrested, 1744.

reves, *v.*, 3 *pl. pr.*, rob, plunder, 621; reved, *pp.*, 671.

rewe, *s.*, row, line, 890, 1073.

rewith, *impers. v. pr.*, grieveth, 1404.

robbeth, 3 *pl. pr.*, rob, 167; robyn, 621; robbed, 3 *s. pt.*, 1456; 3 *pl. pt.*, 292; robed, *pp.*, 671.

robery, *s.*, robbery, 1401.

rode, *s.*, complexion, 1416.

rody, *adj.*, ruddy, 717, 1344.

rome, *adj.*, spacious, 263.

ron, see ryn.

rought, *s.*, company, 104.

rouwe, *v. inf.*, sail, 265.

rowth, *s.*, pity, 1810.

rubies, *s. pl.*, 1281, 1497.

rustland, *v. pr. part.*, rustling, 136.

ryal, *adj.*, royal, 488, 533; ryall, 653; ryalle, 286.

ryche, *adj.*, 493, 653, 656, 707, 766, 826, 1279, 1287, 1339, 1494, 1498, 1606, 1607; reche, 1826.

rychely, *adv.*, 1005, 1490.

rycher, *compar. adj.*, 1499.

ryde, *v. inf.*, 692, 829, 1160, 1211, 1223, 1426, 1535, 1685, 1716, 1735, 1754; 2 *s. imp.*, 1838; ryt, 3 *s. pr.*, 317; rytt, 1176; rode, 3 *s. pt.*, 948; 3 *pl. pt.*, 974; rydant, *pr. part.*, 160; rydyng, 145, 1461.

ryght, *s.*, 454, 486; ryghtis, *pl.*, 878.

ryght, *adj.*, 331, 414.

ryght, *adv.*, 97, 754, 1770; straightway, 174, 307, 1123, 1127, 1508, 1739, 1829; precisely, 318, 694, 1397; justly, 444, 1476.

ryn, *v. inf.*, run, 951; rynne, 262, 1199; ranne, 3 *s. pt.*, 976, 1656; ron, 3 *pl. pt.*, 895.

ryng, *s.*, 1101; ryngs, *pl.*, 1093, 1107.

ryt, see ryde.

ryve, *v. inf.* (*aphetic form of* arrive), arrive, go, 70, 105.

ryve, *v. inf.*, pierce, tear, 1525; *intrans.*, break, fall asunder, 584.

S.

sacrifyse, *s.*, 762.

sadell, *s.*, saddle, 1244, 1255; sadill, 142.

safers, *s. pl.*, sapphires, 1281; savers, 1497.

sake, *s.*, 1361.

salt, *adj.*, 181, 1913.

same, *adj.*, 607.

sarsynners, *s. pl.*, players upon the psaltery (M. E. sautrie) or the dulcimer (?), 1076.

sat, *v.*, 3 *s. pt.*, 1736; satte, 1244; sete, 1562; sett, 3 *pl. pt.*, 1030.

saunce, *prep.*, without, 1235.

sauiour, *s.*, 770.

sauwe, see se, *v.*

save, *v. inf.*, 1806; 3 *s. pr. subj.*, 442; 2 *s. imp.*, 1842.

save, *prep.*, except, 1029; saue, 527.

savers, see safers.

say, *v. inf.*, say, speak, 270, 1876: 1 *s. pr.*, 928; saye, 1315; sey, *inf.*, 961, 1352, 1410; 1 *s. pr.*, 397; 2 *s. imp.*, 309, 1379; seye, *inf.*, 839; sayne, *inf.*, 923; seyst, 2 *s. pr.*, 421, 424; seyth, 3 *s. pr.*, 288, 420, 1221; 2 *pl. imp.*, 1922; seyen, 3 *pl. pr.*, 558; sayde, 3 *s. pt.*, 1589, 1751; seyd, 33, 41, 245, 290, 298, 311, 335, 406, 407, 409, 626, 638, 669, 761, 999, 1001, 1041, 1117, 1171, 1319, 1331, 1342, 1368, 1397, 1405,

1466, 1516, 1587 ; 3 *pl. pt.*, 87, 98,
219, 313, 475, 880, 1089 ; **seyde**, 3
s. pt., 13, 323, 363, 421, 777, 991,
1137, 1365, 1623, 1635, 1761, 1773,
1791, 1801, 1837, 1871, 1880, 1891 ;
3 *pl. pt.*, 1821 ; **seyden**, 1099 ; **iseyd**,
pp., 565 : **iseyde**, 790.
scon, see **shynyth**.
score, *s.*, 726, 743 ; **skore**, 722.
se, *s.*, sea, 61, 267, 316, 488 ; **see**, 59,
113, 261, 506, 803, 1019.
se, *v. inf.*, see, 227, 560, 570, 1197,
1224, 1324, 1439, 1470 ; 1 *s. pr.*, 1332 ;
2 *pl. pr.*, 991 ; 2 *s. pr. subj.*, 1146 ;
see, *inf.*, 133, 1483 ; 3 *s. pt.*, 1599 ;
sene, *inf.*, 568, 704, 1181 ; 3 *pl. pr.*,
827 ; *pp.*, 312, 350, 562 ; **seeth**, 3 *s.
pr.*, 581, 609, 1219, 1249 ; **seth**, 951,
1295 ; **sethe**, 1868 ; **saw**, 3 *s. pt.*,
1211 ; **sawe**, 15, 232, 235, 673, 850,
1273, 1535 ; **sauwe**, 1035 ; **saye**,
1881 ; **sey**, 1 *s. pt.*, 1166 ; 3 *s. pt.*,
345, 957, 962, 1287 ; **syye**, 256.
sees, *v. inf.*, cease, 1592.
seker, *adj.*, strong, sure, 272, 883 ;
sekyr, 1802 ; **siker**, 1745.
sekerly, *adv.*, surely, 331, 421, 1005,
1040, 1055 ; **sekyrly**, 578.
sekernesse, *s.*, assurance, 1598.
sekyn, *v. inf.*, seek, 1059 ; **sought**,
3 *s. pt.*, 174.
self, *adj.*, same, 520.
selke, *s.*, silk, 1337.
semblant, *s.*, aspect, 1415 ; **semlant**,
717.
sen, *conj.*, since, 851.
send, *v. inf.*, 681 ; 3 *s. pr.*, 325 ; 2 *pl.
pr.* (*with sing. reference*), 384 ;
2 *s. imp.*, 302 ; 2 *pl. pr. subj.* (*with
sing. reference*), 330 ; **sende**, *inf.*,
241, 809, 1569 ; 2 *s. imp.*, 959 ; **sent**,
3 *s. pt.*, 214, 225, 247, 276, 285, 351,
674, 687, 1039, 1583, 1588 ; 3 *pl. pt.*,
808.
sendel, *s.*, a thin silk, 491.
sertenlych, *adv.*, certainly, 928.
serue, *v. inf.*, 332 ; **servid**, *pp.*, 1065.
seson, *s.*, time, 1586.
sete, see **sat**.

seth, see **se**, *v.*
sethenne, *conj.*, since, 1500 ; **seþyn**,
1294 ; **sithyn**, 1 ; **sythyn**, 1233, 1234.
sett, see **sat**.
setteth, *v.*, 3 *s. pr.*, 616 ; **sette**, 3 *s.
pt.*, 140, 1250, 1458 ; *pp.*, 1498 ; **set**,
pp., 1488 ; **isette**, 132, 1240, 1280.
sexe, *card. num.*, six, 1630.
sey, see **say** ; **se**, *v.*
seyeth, see **syghyeth**.
seyle, *s.*, sail, 60, 756 ; **seyles**, *pl.*, 493.
seyle, *v. inf.*, sail, 68, 264 ; **seyled**, 3
pl. pt., 1913 ; **seyland**, *pr. part.*, 488.
shafte, *s.*, spear-haudle, 916 ; **shaftis**,
pl., 133, 148.
shake, *v. pp.*, shaken, 133.
shall, *v.*, 1 *s. pr.*, 1362, 1406 ; 2 *s. pr.*,
1510 ; 3 *s. pr.*, 70, 221, 385, 407, 409,
423, 428, 654 ; 1 *pl. pr.*, 763, 1678 ;
3 *pl. pr.*, 390, 1483 ; **shal**, 1 *s. pr.*,
569 ; **shalt**, 2 *s. pr.*, 381, 436, 961,
1653 ; **shallt**, 451 ; **shat**, 468, 470 ;
xall, 3 *s. pr.*, 1036 ; **shull**, 90, 1024 ;
1 *pl. pr.*, 296, 779, 812, 1679, 1749 ;
2 *pl. pr.*, 304, 786, 1459, 1770 ; 3 *pl.
pr.*, 1750 ; **shuld**, 1 *s. pt.*, 1223 ; 3 *s.
pt.*, 40, 224, 227, 246, 406, 1038, 1369,
1372 ; 3 *pl. pt.*, 49, 68, 72, 809, 1660 ;
shulld, 1 *s. pt.*, 1552, 1557 ; 3 *s. pt.*,
275 ; 1 *pl. pt.*, 337 ; **shuldest**, 2 *s.
pt.*, 1566 ; **shuldyn**, 1 *pl. pt.*, 1148.
shame, *s.*, 221, 1224.
shappe, *s.*, form, 1090.
sharpe, *adj.*, 847, 920.
sharpe, *adv.*, 917.
shat, see **shall**.
she, *pers. pron.*, *passim* ; her, *passim* ; **here**, 583, 616, 646, 647, 962,
1403.
shed, *v. pp.*, 1865.
sheld, *s.*, shield, 137, 910, 933, 1185,
1251, 1310, 1444, 1501, 1723 ; **shelde**,
887, 1196, 1259, 1261, 1521, 1524,
1713 ; **shellde**, 1207 ; **sheldis**, *pl.*,
135, 605.
shend, *v. inf.*, revile, destroy, 88,
300, 472.
shene, *adj.*, beautiful, splendid, 536,
820, 1402, 1890.

shep, s., ship, 80, 112, 346; shepp,
50; shypp, 51; sheppis, pl., 108,
265, 354, 726, 728, 732, 734, 737, 741,
743, 747, 751, 756, 758, 804, 806,
1910; shippis, 691, 703; shyppis,
489, 498, 710, 720, 722, 843, 1458.

shert, s., shirt, 1447.

shete, v. inf., shoot, 600; shet, 3 s.
pt., 967; shett, 3 pl. pt., 846.

shevered, v., 3 s. pt., splintered,
916.

shewe, v. inf., show, 1074; shewed,
3 s. pt., 1010.

shippis, see shep.

short, adj., 1724; shorte, 1603.

shove, v., 3 pl. pr., pushed, 595.

shrowde, s., garment, 1606.

shuld, see shall.

shulder, s., shoulder, 968; shulders,
pl., 1084, 1639.

shynyth, v., 3 s. pr., shineth, 641;
shynes, 3 pl. pr., 1495; shone, 3
s. pt., 1486; soon, 1248; shyned,
1337.

shypp, see shep.

side, s., 942, 1252, 1736, 1707, 1753;
syde, 830, 893, 901, 986, 1159, 1188,
1304, 1425, 1620, 1684, 1718; sydes,
pl., 161, 972, 1691.

siker, see seker.

siluer, s., 633, 767.

sir, s., passim; sire, 453, 1710; sirr,
377, 739, 745; sirre, 947, 1836; syr,
521, 1127, 1161, 1275, 1292, 1379,
1596; syre, 1311.

sistryn, see suster.

sithin, adv., afterwards, 1886; syþyn,
17; sythen, 1031.

sithyn, conj., see sethenne.

sixti, card. num., 1631; syxty, 747.

skaped, v., 3 s. pt., escaped, 1454.

sklaunder, s., scandal, 532.

skylle, s., reason, reasonable claim,
414, 438.

skynne, s., skin, 1027, 1555.

skyrmed, v., 3 s. pt., fenced, 1116.

slauter, s., slaughter, 893.

sle, v. inf., slay, 953, 1008, 1231, 1818,
1862; 2 s. imp., 1845; slee, inf.,

1154; slene, 812, 994, 1012, 1749;
sleen, 1774; sloo, 1566; sleeth, 3
s. pr., 1532; 3 pl. pr., 608; sleth,
3 s. pr., 1885, 1915; 3 pl. pr., 1855;
slow, 2 s. pt., 1654; 3 s. pt., 944,
1656; slowe, 162; 2 pl. pt., 815;
slouwe, 328; sleu, 3 s. pt., 183;
slowgh, 1898; sley, 3 pl. pt., 303;
slowyn, 1438; pp., beaten, 1261;
slauwe, 199; slayn, 138, 196, 972,
975, 1036, 1328, 1780, 1863; slayne,
185, 670, 1031, 1168, 1196, 1237,
1544; slaynne, 1892; sleyn, 1371;
islayn, 610; islawe, 382.

slengis, s. pl., slings, 860.

slepe, s., 216.

slette, v., 3 s. pt., split, 1206.

small, adj., 633, 1081, 1282; smalle,
1643, 1888.

smerte, v. inf., smart, 1527.

smertly, adv., quickly, 879.

smote, v., 3 s. pt., 141, 943, 950, 1246,
1247, 1257, 1291, 1503, 1528, 1618,
1722, 1896; smotte, 1243, 1520;
smette, 1286.

smytyng, s., 927.

so, soo, adv., passim.

soche, adj., such, 7, 234, 336, 526,
544, 927, 1335, 1345, 1698, 1859;
sweche, 274, 498, 704; swyche,
1216, 1224.

socour, s., help, 91.

solace, s., amusement, 231.

soles, s. pl., 1029, 1618; solis, 1561.

somdel, adv., somewhat, 932.

somers, s. gen., summer's, 1435.

somtime, adv., once, 21.

son, s., 279, 395; sone, 186, 240, 281,
282, 376, 556, 654, 1141, 1172, 1371,
1424, 1427, 1450, 1468, 1547, 1556,
1830, 1857; sonne, 625; sones, pl.,
162, 205, 284, 362, 1374, 1544; sonys,
872, 1158; gen. sing., 370.

sone, s., sun, 271; sonne, 1268, 1486,
1499.

sone, adv., soon, 131, 138, 164, 1032,
1262, 1272, 1439, 1566; sonne, 1273.

sooiorneyd, v., 3 s. pt., dwelt,
522.

soore, *adv.*, sorely, 582, 1404; **sore**, 75, 76, 611, 637, 1250, 1306, 1469, 1506, 1527, 1541, 1719.

sooth, *adv.*, truly, 1237.

sorouwes, *n.*, 3 *s. pr.*, sorrows, 1316; **soroweth**, 3 *s. pr.*, 664; 3 *pl. pr.*, 1306; **sorowed**, 3 *s. pt.*, 204.

sorow, *s.*, 658, 672, 1296, 1412, 1418, 1707, 1881.

sory, *adj.*, 176, 1346.

soster, see **suster**.

soth, *s.*, truth, 270; **sothe**, 421, 839, 923; **soþe**, 1410.

sought, see **sekyn**.

soulis, *s. pl.*, souls, 1729, 1919.

spare, *v.*, 3 *s. pr. subj.*, 1817; **spared**, 3 *s. pt.*, 1687.

speche, *s.*, 778.

spede, *v. inf.*, prosper, hasten, 398, 468, 772, 868, 1770; 2 *s. imp.*, 1596; **sped**, *pp.* 625, 636.

spede, *s.* In the adverbial phrase: good **spede**, with rapidity, 941.

speke, *v. inf.*, 390, 1738; 1 *s. pr.*, 1513; 3 *pl. pr.*, 554; 1 *pl. pr. subj.*, 662; **spekest**, 2 *s. pr.*, 395; **speketh**, 3 *s. pr.*, 289, 552, 1652, 1741, 1790, 1791, 1834; 2 *pl. imp.* (*with sing. reference*), 1002; **spekith**, 3 *s. pr.*, 1867; **spake**, 3 *s. pt.*, 759.

spere, *s.*, spear, 910, 949, 1095, 1109, 1185, 1713, 1715, 1717; **speris**, *gen.*, 1736; **sperys**, *pl.*, 1695.

spille, *v. inf.*, perish, 1750; **spylled**, *pp.*, lost, 1689.

sporis, *s. pl.*, spurs, 1503.

sprong, *v.*, 3 *s. pt.*, sprung, 211, 921.

spryngalle, *s.*, an engine for casting stones, 858.

spye, *s.*, 563.

squiers, *s. pl.*, esquires, 1731.

squyery, *s.*, company of esquires, 111.

stalworth, *adj.*, stalwart, 56, 1831.

stant, see **stond**.

stede (*a*), *s.*, steed, 157, 616, 1192, 1194, 1228, 1503, 1696; **stedes**, *gen.*, 1505; *pl.*, 1131.

stede (*b*), *s.*, stead, place, 693, 977; **stedes**, *pl.*, 1630.

steke, *v.*, 3 *s. pt.*, stuck, 1737.

stele, *s.*, steel, 853.

stelyn, *adj.*, steel, 1227.

sterid, *v.*, 3 *s. pt.*, guided, 1638.

sterne, *adj.*, severe, 1471.

stert, *v.*, 3 *pl. pt.*, started, 1620.

steyned, *v. pp.*, stained, 1447.

stiffe, *adj.*, strong, 1747; **styff**, 1767.

still, *adj.*, 369; **stylle**, 413, 1434, 1581.

still, *adv.*, 1838.

stode, see **stond**.

stoffed, *v.*, 3 *pl. pt.*, stuffed, 109; **stoftden**, 1911.

ston, *s.*, stone, 848; **stones**, *pl.*, 600; **stonys**, 656, 765, 834, 842, 860, 1280.

stond, *v. inf.*, stand, remain, endure, 806, 888, 1144, 1474; **stant**, 3 *s. pr.*, 1219, 1868; **stode**, 3 *s. pt.*, 1329.

stonde, see **stounde**.

stong, *v. pp.*, punctured, 1695.

stopeth, *v.*, 3 *s. pr.*, stoopeth, 1289.

stought, *adj.*, strong, violent, 6, 123, 173, 590, 736, 748, 881, 1083, 1747, 1782; **stout**, 1153; **stowght**, 1087, 1767.

stought, *adv.*, violently, 1180, 1644.

stoughtly, *adv.*, strongly, 98, 368, 910; **stoughtlyche**, 814; **stowtelyche**, 483.

stounde, *s.*, time, hour, 399, 477; **stonde**, 149; **stownd**, 1015, 1333; **stownde**, 1322.

streken, *v.*, 3 *pl. pt.*, struck, 919.

stremers, *s. pl.*, streamers, 491.

strenger, see **stronger**.

strenght, *s.*, strength, 586.

strife, *s.* (O. N. strīth), grief, 665.

stroke, *s.*, 915, 925, 1144, 1210, 1474, 1517, 1520, 1534, 1722; **strokes**, *pl.*, 132, 140, 1250; **strokis**, 888, 1240, 1526.

strong, *adj.*, strong, violent, 151, 235, 340, 396, 849, 922, 1284, 1479, 1481, 1524, 1831; **stronge**, 489, 1024.

strong, *adv.*, violently, 1180.

stronger, *compar. adj.*, 256, 1242; **strenger**, 271, 1120.

stynte, *v. inf.*, pause, 477; **stynt**, 3 *s. pr.*, 954, 1232; 2 *pl. pr. subj.*, 783.

styroppis, *s. pl.*, stirrups, 1182.

sued, *v.*, 3 *pl. pt.*, pursued, 130; **suyng**, *pr. part.*, following, 1103.

sum, *adj.*, some, any, 1565; **summe**, 37.

summe, *indef. pron.* In the phrase: **all and summe**, all and sundry, one and all, entirely, 195, 1780.

sure, *adj.*, secure, 1129.

sure, *adv.*, securely, 109.

suster, *s.*, sister, 201, 329, 816, 1042, 1568, 1571; **sustir**, 307; **soster**, 1326; **sistryn**, *pl.*, 198.

swannys, *s. pl.*, swans, 1067.

swapeth, *v.*, 3 *s. pr.*, swoopeth, sweepeth, 1626; **swappith**, 606.

sweche, see **soche**.

swelle, *v. inf.*, flow, 1647.

swerd, *s.*, sword, 1115, 1255, 1626; **swerde**, 932, 1608, 1633, 1852; **swerdes**, *pl.*, 917, 920, 1523; **swerdis**, 149, 1265, 1700.

swereth, *v.*, 3 *s. pr.*, sweareth, 585; **swor**, 3 *s. pt.*, 1666; **swore**, 69, 245, 410.

swete, *adj.*, 1048, 1417, 1420.

sweuen, *s.*, dream, 1225; **swevyn**, 1106.

swoned, *v.*, 3 *s. pt.*, swooned, 1322.

swyche, see **soche**.

swyn, *s. pl.*, swine, 226.

swythe, *adv.*, quickly, 68, 71, 355, 1388; very, 646.

syght, *v.*, see **syghyeth**.

syght, *s.*, 1166, 1507.

syghyeth, *v.*, 3 *s. pr.*, sigheth, 1419; **syght**, 664; **seyeth**, 582.

symbaleris, *s. pl.*, players upon cymbals, 1076.

syn, *s.*, 1728.

synifye, *v. inf.*, signify, 218.

sythen, **syþyn**, see **sithin**.

sythyn, *conj.*, see **sethenne**.

syye, see **se**, *v.*

T.

taboura, *s. pl.*, small drums, 1075.

take, *v. inf.*, take, seize, 49, 253, 366, 373, 510, 592, 1289, 1597; 3 *pl. pr.* (*with sing. reference*), 379; 3 *s. pt.*, 1715; 2 *s. imp.*, 769, 1597, 1837; 2 *pl. imp.*, 875, 1768; 3 *s. pr. subj.*, 590; 2 *pl. pr. subj.* (*with sing. reference*), 1595; *pp.*, 1739; **taken**, *inf.*, 1102; *pp.*, 439; **takon**, 614; **takyn**, 594; **takes**, 3 *s. pr.*, 279, 658, 1411; offers, gives, 481; **takys**, 583; 3 *pl. pr.*, 1907; **taketh**, 3 *s. pr.*, 54, 55, 615, 1347, 1680, 1889; offereth, giveth, 372; **toke**, 3 *s. pt.*, 243, 773, 965, 1608; gave, 1132; 3 *pl. pt.*, 902, 1301, 1732, 1811; **token**, 179, 983, 1091; **tokyn**, 177, 1092.

talent, *s.*, desire, 420.

talkyng, *s.*, saying, 1478.

tare, *v.*, 3 *s. pt.*, tore, 1340.

targe, *s.*, small shield, 887.

techith, *v.*, 3 *s. pr.*, teacheth, 1638.

tell, *v. inf.*, 239, 1016; 1 *s. pr.*, 1559; **telle**, *inf.*, 65, 217, 378, 1139, 1671, 1690; 1 *s. pr.*, 725; 2 *s. imp.*, 397; **tellyn**, *inf.*, 383, 540; **tellith**, 3 *s. pr.*, 789; **told**, 3 *s. pt.*, 347, 564, 1364, 1365, 1385, 1389, 1609, 1775; *pp.*, estimated, 90; **tolde**, 3 *s. pt.*, 215.

tempest, *s.*, 507.

temple, *s.*, 574, 575, 774, 1570, 1573, 1580, 1593, 1598, 1613, 1616, 1657, 1893.

ten, *card. num.*, 396, 572, 710, 785.

tenne, *v. inf.*, go, 1811.

þ = th.

than, *conj.*, 794; **thanne**, **þanne**, 398, 458, 552, 1120, 1236, 1394, 1786; **þen**, 572; **thenne**, 300.

þanked, *v.*, 3 *s. pt.*, 370.

thanne, *adv.*, then, 393, 407, 519, 759, 925, 980, 1072, 1707, 1710, 1741, 1867; **þanne**, 125, 288, 681, 1715; **þen**, 897; **thenne**, 145, 159, 205, 285, 311, 375, 424, 453, 884, 937,

1117, 1137, 1161, 1171, 1240, 1293, 1331, 1361, 1377, 1519, 1771; **þenne,** 41, 289, 386, 510, 947, 998, 1290, 1295, 1362, 1557, 1801.

thanne, þanne, *conj.,* see **than.**

tharmes, *s. pl.,* bowels, 1194.

that, þat, *conj., passim.*

that, þat, *dem. pron., passim.*

that, þat, *rel. pron.,* that, what, *passim;* **þatt,** 1907.

þatt, see **that,** *rel. pron.*

þay, see **þey.**

the, *pers. pron.,* see **thou.**

the, þe, *def. art., passim.*

the, *dem. pron. instr.,* 657, 658, 763; **þe,** 1399.

the, *v. inf.,* prosper, 457, 559, 1119, 1918; **thee,** *inf.,* 1516.

theder, *adv.,* thither, 314, 1575; **þeder,** 312; **thedyr,** 302.

thef, *s.,* thief, 1543.

þei, see **they.**

þen, see **than, thanne.**

thenke, see **þynkest.**

þenketh, see **þynkest.**

thenne, see **than, thanne.**

thens, *adv.,* thence, 70, 71.

ther, *adv.,* there, 83, 673, 806, 1467, 1560; **þer,** 13, 21, 24, 345, 532, 827, 849; **there,** 70, 132, 496, 655, 659, 884, 887, 1110; **þere,** 141, 220, 254, 498, 1031.

ther, *poss. pron.,* their, 148, 270, 690, 1637; **þer,** 800, 828, 836; **there,** 770; **þere,** 254; **þeyr,** 1901. See **her.**

therafter, *adv.,* thereafter, 1054.

therde, *adj.,* third, 86; **þerde,** 907; **thirde,** 1642; **þyrde,** 1533.

there, þere, *adv.,* see **ther.**

there, *rel. adv.,* where, 1030, 1062, 1328.

there, þere, *poss. pron.,* see **ther.**

thereas, *rel. adv.,* there where, 974, 1562.

therefore, *adv.,* 238, 301, 445, 459, 465; **þerefore,** 1821; **therefor,** 91; **therfor,** 995, 1573; **therfore,** 223, 461, 471, 508, 559, 819, 1015, 1037,

1145, 1169, 1405, 1569, 1745, 1781, 1894; **þerfore,** 1596, 1876.

þeren, see **þerin.**

þerevppon, *adv.,* thereupon, 1661.

therewhyle, *adv.,* meanwhile, 621; **þerwhyle,** 1583; **therwhyle,** 1617; **therwhyles,** 985; **þerwhyles,** 1303.

therewhyles, *conj.,* whilst, 153.

þerin, *adv.,* 66, 265; **þeren,** 1581; **theryn,** 264; **þeryn,** 1035.

þerof, *adv.,* 390.

therto, *adv.,* 438, 1113, 1288, 1808; **þerto,** 295, 311, 429, 454, 686, 1406, 1565; **þertoo,** 764, 905.

these, þese, *dem. pron. pl.,* 89, 1364, 1397, 1809, 1851; **þes** 1813; **þis,** 1352.

they, þey, *pers. pron., passim;* **þei, thei,** 68, 81; **þay,** 499; **them, þem,** 4, 236, 313, 809, 856, 892; **hem,** *passim.*

þey, *poss. pron.,* see **thi.**

þeyr, see **ther.**

thi, *poss. pron.,* 220, 1478, 1892; **thy,** 40, 1379, 1571; **þy,** 382, 470, 1120, 1173, 1550, 1568, 1653, 1730, 1835; **þey,** 307; **thin,** 1837; **þyn,** 366.

thing, *s.,* 338; **thyng,** 394, 679, 1270, 1389, 1806; **þyng,** 35, 378, 444, 591, 690, 1102, 1868; **þyngis,** *pl.,* 627.

thirde, see **therde.**

thirty, *adj.,* 209, 728; **thurtty,** 9.

this, þis, *dem. pron., passim.*

þis, *dem. pron. pl.,* see **these.**

tho, *dem. pron. pl.,* those, 659, 792; **þoo,** 235.

tho, *adv.,* then, 191, 277, 298, 566, 635, 835, 1335, 1405, 1424, 1863; **þo,** 775; **thoo,** 84, 520, 1001, 1634, 1757; **þoo,** 74, 1149, 1451, 1632.

tho, *conj.,* when, 165; **þo,** 1739.

thorough, *prep.,* through, 222, 1141; **þorough,** 950, 1853; **thorow,** 1475, 1723, 1872; **þorow,** 930, 968; **thorowe,** 161.

þorough, *adv.,* through, 1441, 1861; **thorow,** 1695.

þorought, *prep.,* throughout, 351, 1694; **thorowout,** 119.

thou, þou, *pers. pron.*, *passim*;
thow, 1138; þow, 1118, 1470, 1510,
1654, 1843, 1846; the, þe, 344, 383,
387, 432, 442, 445, 450, 465, 467,
777, 1139, 1145, 1513, 1515, 1548,
1559, 1596, 1622, 1894; you, *passim*;
yow, 928, 1798; ye, *passim*.

though, *conj.*, 455, 1398, 1679;
þough, 541, 1701; þow, 176.

þought, *s.*, mind, 245.

thought, see þynkest.

þousand, *s.*, 1356, 1864.

thousand, *adj.*, 1232, 1436; thowsaund, 954.

thow, þow, see thou, though.

thre, *s.*, 162, 408, 428; þre, 458.

thre, *adj.*, 197, 400, 1458; þre, 205.

throuwe, *v. inf.*, throw, 860; þrouwe,
pp., 853; threwe, 3 *s. pt.*, 1640; 3
pl. pt., 842.

thryve, *v. inf.*, 69.

thurtty, see thirty.

thus, þus, *adv.*, *passim*.

thygh, *s.*, 950, 1254.

þyke, *adj.*, thick, 848.

þynkest, *v.*, 2 *s. pr.*, thinkest to
go, 343; þenketh, 3 *s. pr.*, 371,
1720; thyngketh, purposeth, 359;
thenke, 3 *pl. pr.*, 124; thought, 3
s. pt., 158; þought, 1038; thought,
3 *pl. pt.*, 224; þought, 862, 1582.

þyrde, see therde.

tille, *conj.*, 318, 1268; tyll, 1407.

timber, *s.*, 49; tymbir, 353.

time, *s.*, 349, 987, 1216, 1403, 1711;
tyme, 520, 962.

to, *prep.*, *passim*; too, 180, 226, 342,
404, 476, 545, 598, 683, 685, 688,
690, 958, 1156, 1268, 1309, 1538,
1547, 1605, 1714, 1755, 1776, 1792.

to, *card. num.*, two, 153, 154, 679,
1795, 1809, 1851; too, 9, 161, 259,
509, 568, 776, 872, 1049, 1158, 1242,
1254, 1320, 1336, 1633, 1910.

to, *adv.*, too, 643, 1342, 1880; too,
1683.

tobreke, *v. inf.*, break in pieces,
1545; tobrake, 3 *s. pt.*, 1641.

toclovyn, *v. pp.*, cleft asunder, 1444.

tocrake, *v. pp.*, cracked, 134.

to-day, *adv.*, 1222, 1483.

toder, *indef. pron.*, other, second,
85, 874, 906, 1103.

todrewe, *v.*, 3 *s. pt.*, drew asunder,
tore in pieces, 1339; todrowe, 642.

todryve, *v. inf.*, drive asunder, 1762;
todreve, *pp.*, 602.

togeder, *adv.*, together, 131, 147, 757,
854; togedere, 233; togyder, 1180.

toheuwyn, *v. pp.*, hewn in pieces,
605; tohewyn, 1445.

toke, see take.

ton, *indef. pron.*, one, 85.

too, *prep.*, *card. num.*, *adv.*, see to.

too-nyght, *adv.*, 1165.

torappyth, *v.*, 3 *s. pr.*, seizeth violently, 605.

toryve, *v. intrans.*, 3 *s. pr.*, breaks
in pieces, 1348; toreves, 3 *pl. pr.*,
148; toryven, *pp.*, 1443.

totore, *v. pp.*, torn in pieces, 385.

tour, *s.*, tower, 1312; toure, 623, 857,
1219, 1883, 1900; towre, 1868;
tourys, *pl.*, 861.

toward, *prep.*, 587, 755, 1461.

town, *s.*, 130, 250, 262, 274, 826, 981,
1296, 1673, 1779, 1785, 1814, 1822,
1846, 1870; *used adverbially*, 1299.

travayle, *s.*, toil, 1825.

travayle, *v. inf.*, toil, *perh.* travel,
364.

trayen, *v. inf.*, betray, 1810.

trayled, *v.*, 3 *s. pt.*, trailed, 1194.

traytour, *s.*, traitor, 1776; tretour,
959, 1543, 1622, 1623; treytour,
1772; traytours, *pl.*, 1809; tretours, 1204, 1624, 1813; treytours,
1851.

trede, *v. inf.*, tread, 978.

treson, *s.*, treason, 1558, 1585, 1601,
1615, 1869, 1872, 1873, 1875; tresoun, 273.

tresour, *s.*, treasure, 53, 634, 769,
773.

tretour, see traytour.

treuwe, see true.

treuws, see truce.

trevage, *s.*, tribute, 306.

trewe, see true.

trewes, see truce.

trewest, *superl. adj.*, truest, 425, 443.

trews, see truce.

treybochet, *s.* (O. Fr. trebuchet), engine for casting stones, 838.

treytour, see traytour.

trouthe, *s.*, troth, faith, 1809; trowth, 1151, 1803.

truce, *s.*, 902; treuws, 1301; trewes, 987; trews, 983.

true, *adj.*, 841; treuwe, 203; trewe, 527, 1805.

trumpis, *s. pl.*, trumpets, 1075.

trusse, *v.*, 2 *s. imp.*, pack up, begone, 344.

trusty, *adj.*, 527.

turne, *v.*, 3 *pl. pr.*, 828; 2 *s. imp.*, 1515; turnne, 3 *pl. pr.*, 1310; turneth, 3 *s. pr.*, 579, 1409; turned, 3 *s. pt.*, 18, 346; 3 *pl. pt.*, 80.

twelmonth, *s.*, twelvemonth, 1302.

twelve, *card. num.*, 836, 1704, 1706; twelfe, 108, 758.

twenti, *card. num.*, 804, 1864; twenty, 734.

tyde, *s.*, 843.

tydyng, *s.*, 787, 1671; tydyns, *pl.*, 792.

U (V, vowel).

vnder, *prep.*, 137, 271, 280, 1196; onder, 1499.

vnderstond, *v.*, 1 *s. pr.*, understand, 547; vnderstonde, 1709; vndirstond, 33, 823; vndirstonde, 1431; vnderstond, *pp.*, 411; vndirstond, *inf.*, 818; onderstande, *inf.*, 926; vndirstode, 3 *s. pt.*, 195.

vndertakyn, *v. pp.*, taken in, heard, understood, 121, 1201.

vndernome, *v. pp.*, perceived, 497.

vnmete, *adj.*, immoderate, 1418.

vp, *adv.*, 105, 825, 845, 1620; vpp, 129.

vpon, *prep.*, 1487; vppon, 105, 157, 426, 743, 1215, 1488; uppon, 1325.

vppon, *adv.*, upon, 939, 1028, 1556.

vpset, *v. pp.*, set or placed up, 837.

vpsodown, *adv.*, upside down, 1310.

vtterly, *adv.*, fully, 1010, 1559.

V (consonant).

vaileth, *v.*, 3 *s. pr. (aphetic form of availeth)*, availeth, 79.

valeys, *s. pl.*, 895.

verament, *adv.*, verily, 1025, 1563; verement, 1011.

veryly, *adv.*, 251.

vessell, *s.*, 179.

vice, *s.* (O. Fr. vis), look, face, 1050, 1340, 1417.

vile, *adj.*, 1772.

vitayl, *s.*, victual, 110; vytayles, *pl.*, 742.

voward, *s.*, vanward, advance guard, 1686.

vysage, *s.*, 1083.

W.

wachyn, *v. inf.*, watch, 1816.

wage, *v. inf.*, pledge, 305.

waked, *v.*, 3 *s. pt.*, awoke, 213; *pp.*, aroused, 1353.

wall, *s.*, 844, 1538; walle, 857, 1642; walles, *pl.*, 255, 257, 835.

walle, *v. inf.*, surround with a wall, 250.

wan, see wyn.

wande, *v.*, 3 *s. pt.*, turned, twisted, 915; wonde, 925.

ward, *s.*, charge, 1816.

ware, see be, *v.*

wariours, see werere.

was, see be, *v.*

washe, *v. inf.*, 1728.

water, *s.*, 180, 692, 1026, 1564, 1912.

wax, see wexith.

way, *s.*, means, journey, 840; wey, 81, 345, 439.

wedden, *v. inf.*, wed, 1605; wede, 1568; wedde, 3 *s. pr. subj.*, 1571; 2 *pl. pr. subj. (with sing. reference)*, 1594; wedded, 3 *s. pt.*, 648.

wede, *s.*, clothing, 615, 1040, 1227.

wede, *v.*, see **wedden**.

weders, *s. gen.*, wether's, 36.

ween, *v.*, 1 *s. pr.*, think, 1242; **wenest**, 2 *s. pr.*, 398; **wenyst**, 1118.

wel, *adv.*, **well**, very, 566, 720, 883, 1256; **wele**, 35, 630, 713, 854, 970, 1617, 1816, 1903; **well**, 40, 45, 109, 115, 128, 132, 411, 424, 680, 738, 878, 905, 1240, 1254, 1454, 1579, 1917, 1918; **welle**, 468, 626, 862, 1608, 1770, 1825; **will**, 350; **wille**, 1844.

welcome, *adj.*, 1138.

welcometh, *v.*, 3 *s. pr.*, 624.

welde, *v. inf.*, wield, handle, 684; **weldeth**, 2 *s. pr.*, rulest (ruleth), 1726.

wele, *adj.*, fortunate, 441; **will**, 431.

wele, *adv.*, see **wel**.

well, *v.*, see **will**.

welleawaye, *interj.*, alas, 1876.

welteryng, *pr. part.*, rolling about, 1442.

wend, *v. inf.*, go, 471; **wende**, 58, 242, 360, 779, 968, 1174, 1393; 1 *pl. pr.*, 1778; 3 *s. pr. subj.*, 1570; 2 *pl. pr. subj.* (*with sing. reference*), 1593; **went**, 3 *s. pt.*, 172, 182, 346, 430, 573, 1260, 1363, 1384, 1388, 1914; 1 *pl. pt.*, 448; 3 *pl. pt.*, 112, 115.

wene, *s.*, doubt, 251, 1326, 1378.

wenest, see **ween**.

went, see **wend**.

wepes, *v.*, 3 *s. pr.*, weeps, 1316; **wepis**, 640; **wepith**, 617; **weped**, 3 *s. pt.*, 637, 1330, 1541; 3 *pl. pt.*, 1314; **wepyng**, *pr. part.*, 1163.

wepyn, *s.*, weapon, 590, 684.

were, see **be**, *v.*

wered, *v.*, 3 *s. pt.*, wore, 1489.

werere, *s.*, warrior, 749; **werreur**, 1654; **werrour**, 371, 907; **weryer**, 1317; **wariours**, *pl.*, 736; **weriours**, 938.

werke, *s.*, matters, 544.

werke, *v. inf.*, make, 249; **wrought**, 3 *s. pt.*, 1; 3 *pl. pt.*, 255; *pp.*, 51, 492, 1707; **ywrought**, 720.

werre, *s.*, war, 7, 404, 1394, 1592.

werre, *v. inf.*, war, fight, 297; **werryn**, 367, 389; **werreth**, 2 *pl. imp.*, 782.

weryn, see **be**, *v.*

wete, *v. inf.*, know, 514; 1 *s. pr.*, 1407; **wote**, 1617; 3 *s. pr.*, 19, 613; 2 *pl. pr.*, 291; **wist**, 1 *s. pt.*, 1836; 3 *s. pt.*, 193, 1601, 1812; 3 *pl. pt.*, 659; **wost**, 3 *s. pt.*, 712.

wexith, *v.*, 3 *s. pr.*, groweth, becometh, 952; **wax**, 3 *s. pt.*, 1651.

wey, see **way**.

weymentyng, *s.*, lamentation, 1324.

whan, *conj.*, when, 195; **whanne**, 51, 171, 213, 225, 261, 267, 275, 287, 291, 466, 673, 807, 979, 1023, 1071, 1077, 1105, 1134, 1261, 1463, 1492, 1563, 1575, 1706, 1751, 1800, 1843, 1920; **when**, 1097; **whenne**, 157, 357, 1146, 1460.

wharrtoo, *inter. pron.*, to what end, 500.

what, *rel. pron.*, 218, 565, 822; **whatt**, 660.

what, *inter. pron.*, 499, 502, 1777; *in exclamation*, 1319.

wheche, *rel. pron.*, which, 84, 178; **whyche**, 423.

wheche, *indef. rel. pron.*, whichever, 329.

wheder, *rel. pron.*, which of two, 924, 1266, 1484.

wheder, *conj.*, if, 1223.

when, see **whan**.

whenne, see **whan**.

where, *conj.*, 235, 514, 613, 1060, 1812.

whereabought, *rel. adv.*, to what place, 1610.

whereso, *rel. adv.*, wheresoever, 232.

wheresomeuere, *rel. adv.*, wheresoever, 593.

wherfore, *inter. adv.*, why, 500.

while, *s.*, reward, 1743; **whyle**, 1894; labor, trouble, 40.

who, *rel. pron.*, 106, 312, 428, 1408; **whoo**, 780; **whom**, 532.

who, *inter. pron.*, 199, 1870.

whom, *indef. rel. pron.*, whomever, 54.

why, *inter. adv.*, 644, 1320.

whyche, see wheche, *rel. pron.*

whyle, *conj.*, while, 903; whyles, 1737.

whyte, *s.*, creature, 1420.

whyte, *adj.*, 631; brave, 744; whytte, white, 1338, 1572.

whytly, *adv.*, nimbly, 1260; vigorously, 1845.

wiff, see wyf.

wile, *s.*, trick, 1565.

will, *v.*, *passim*; wille, 1 *s. pr.*, 383, 437; 3 *s. pr.*, 1591; well, 1 *pl. pr.*, 102; woll, 1 *s. pr.*, 43, 818, 1514; 3 *s. pr.*, 1545; 1 *pl. pr.*, 1773; 3 *pl. pr.*, 94, 1360; wolle, 3 *s. pr.*, 1100, 1101; wull, 1 *s. pr.*, 46, 366, 388; 3 *s. pr.*, 47, 262, 371, 1380, 1391, 1392; 1 *pl. pr.*, 1798; 2 *pl. pr.* (*with sing. reference*), 387; 3 *pl. pr.*, 124, 305, 309, 310, 499; wul, 1 *s. pr.*, 1150; wulle, 42, 1624; wilt, 2 *s. pr.*, 466, 1597; willt, 1835; wuldest, 2 *s. pt.*, 37; wold, 3 *s. pt.*, 253, 963, 1453, 1610; 3 *pl. pt.*, 98, 502, 1093, 1094, 1096, 1098, 1821, 1909; wuld, 3 *s. pt.*, 189, 660.

will, *adj.*, see wele, *adj.*

will, *adv.*, see wel.

wille, *v.*, *s.*, *adv.*, see will.

wist, see wete.

with, *prep.*, *passim*; wit, 719; wyth, 135, 369, 908, 1249.

withall, *adv.*, besides, 1082.

withholdeth, *v.*, 3 *pl. pr.*, withhold, 1403.

withinnen, *adv.*, within, 1760; wythynne, 855.

without, *prep.*, 9, 356, 415, 468, 882, 999, 1063, 1391, 1396, 1407, 1838; withought, 222, 251, 299, 1854; wythout, 1139.

without, *adv.*, outside, 861, 1659, 1768.

withouten, *prep.*, without, 1326; withoutyn, 403, 575, 751, 971, 984, 1023, 1034, 1035, 1100, 1181, 1213, 1263, 1378, 1383, 1394, 1702

withoutyn, *adv.*, without, 1847.

withsitt, *v. inf.*, resist, 1210; withsitte, 1534.

withstode, *v.*, 3 *s. pt.*, stood still, 1255.

witti, *adj.*, 1374.

wittnesse, *s.*, 1703.

wode, *adj.*, mad, furious, 1256, 1688.

wold, see will, *v.*

woman, *s.*, 1089, 1118, 1353, 1354; women, 1020; womans, *gen.*, 545, 1225.

wonde, *s.*, see wound.

wonde, *v.*, see wande.

wonded, see wounded.

wonder, *s.*, 176, 499, 1306, 1478; wondris, *pl.*, 3.

wonder, *adj.*, wonderful, 35, 38; wondir, 394.

wonder, *adv.*, wonderfully, 64, 255, 490, 578, 1526.

wonderid, *v. pp.*, wondered, 704.

wone, *s.*, hope, plenty; beter wone, with better hope or energy, 993; good wone, great plenty, 1131.

wone, *v.*, see wyn.

woo, *s.*, 178, 1296, 1319, 1353, 1758.

woo, *adj.*, sorrowful, 223, 582, 1037, 1674, 1895.

word, *s.*, 215, 564; worde, 347, 1386; worddis, *pl.*, 1724; wordes, 552, 1397; wordis, 76, 89, 369, 504, 1603; wordus, 1352, 1364.

world, *s.*, 274, 538, 1003, 1241, 1294, 1500, 1553, 1669; worlde, 1, 526.

worthele, *adv.*, worthily, 754.

worthy, *adj.*, rich, 615.

wosoo, *indef. rel. pron.*, whosoever, 1433.

wost, see wete.

wote, see wete.

wound, *s.*, 904; wonde, 150; wounde, 918, 1619, 1630, 1693; wondis, *pl.*, 1187.

wounded, *v. pp.*, 1469; wonded, 3 *s. pt.*, 1451; wondid, 1627.

wrekyn, *v. inf.*, avenge, 1552, 1678, 1835; *pp.*, 862, 1404.

wrong, *s.*, 339, 700, 1400.

wrong, see wryngis.

wrot, v., 3 s. pt., wrote, 16; wrote, 20.

wroth, s., wrath, 1422.

wroth, adj., 508; wrothe, 350; wrother (O. E. dat., wràþere), bad, 342.

wrought, see werke, v.

wryngis, v., 3 s. pr., wrings the hands, 640; wrong, 3 s. pt., 1318, 1330.

wul, see will, v.

wyde, adj., 691, 894, 1187, 1693.

wyde, adv., 985, 1303.

wyf, s., wife, 192, 1161, 1175, 1807; wiff, 243; wyfe, 470, 648, 666, 1539; wyff, 1369; wyfes, pl., 1796; wyves, 1784.

wyld, adj., 1068; wylde, 1070.

wyn, v. inf., 391; wynne, 38, 470, 476, 1406, 1844; 2 s. pr., 1511; wan, 3 s. pt., 1491; wanne, 1492; wonne, pp., 272, 1904; wone, 998.

wyndowe, s., 1645.

wynde, s., 61, 113, 136, 494.

wyntyr, s. pl., winters, 9.

wyre, s., 641.

wyse, s., 418, 761.

wyse, adj., 64, 237, 240, 282, 376, 436, 504, 550, 1374.

wysenesse, s., wisdom, 401, 455.

X

xall, see shall

Y (vow. and cons.).

Y, see I.

yaf, see geve.

yate, s., gate, 1312, 1839, 1840; yatis, pl., 259.

yave, see geve.

ye, adv., yea, verily, 1836. See yes.

yede, v., 3 s. pt., went, 949, 1268; yeden, 3 pl. pt., 1852, 1860; yode, 974, 1866.

yef, see geve.

yeftis, s. pl., gifts, 1600; yiftis, 655.

yelde, v. inf., yield, 876, 1785; yeld, 2 s. imp., 1622; yold, pp., recompensed, 1825; yolde, 1894; iyold, 40.

yeng, see yong.

yere, s., year, 865, 867, 869, 898, 906, 907, 984, 1756; pl., 785; yeres, 230.

yerne, adv., eagerly, 1200.

yes, adv., 1558.

yet, adv., still, notwithstanding, 1403, 1483, 1489, 1720; yett, 850; yit, 25.

yeve, see geve.

yf, see if.

yiftis, see yeftis.

ying, see yong.

yit, see yet.

ymage, see image.

ynde, s., indigo, 135.

yode, see yede.

yold, see yelde.

yong, adj., young, 30, 683, 1427, 1467, 1509, 1611, 1858; yeng, 1437; ying, 1044.

yonger, compar. adj., younger, 282, 376.

your, poss. pron., 302, 310, 379, 388, 819, 875, 878, 1122, 1768, 1800; youre, 1798.

yourself, reflex. pron., 379; pl., yourself, 877.

yoven, see geve.

yow, see thou.

ywrought, see werke, v.

INDEX OF PROPER NAMES.

I.

Troell, Troilus, 1541; Troyel, 1428, 1468; Troyell, 208, 1373, 1451, 1507, 1516, 1519, 1528, 1655.

Troy, 6, 221, 244, 476, 754, 1134, 1140, 1205, 1351; Troye, 11, 34, 58, 62, 63, 88, 114, 121, 185, 203, 212, 239, 242, 250, 324, 358, 478, 492, 527, 555, 784, 805, 813, 826, 830, 841, 868, 870, 899, 981, 1036, 1123, 1132, 1211, 1295, 1299, 1390, 1423, 1468, 1491, 1506, 1538, 1539, 1612, 1681, 1682, 1683, 1753, 1756, 1757, 1844, 1905, Colophon.

Troyens, Trojans, 93, 99, 117, 190, 194; Troyeaunce, 43.

Tytes, Thetis, 1021, 1033.

Venus, 424; Venesse, 402, 413, 440, 458.

Virgil, 541.

Ysyon, Hesione, 201, 518. See Isyon.

II.

Æneas, see Eneas.
Africa, see Aufryk.
Agamemnon, see Agamanoun.
Ajax Telamonius, see Aiax; Talamon (b).
Alexander the Great, see Alisaunder (a).
Alexander Paris, see Alisaunder (b); Paris.
Anectanabus, see Neptanabus.
Antenor, see Entemore.
Anthedon, see Antaton.
Apollo, see Apolyn.
Arcesilaus, see Archeley.
Aristotle, see Aristodill.
Ascalaphus, see Askelop.

Bœotia, see Boys.

Cyphus, see Cypres.
Cythera, see Capharnoum.

Dares Phrygius, see Darras.
Deidamia, see Dyademades.

Greece, see Grece.
Greek language, see Greu.
Greek, adj., see Crekkyshe, Grekeshe.
Greeks, see Grekys.
Guneus, see Sennes.

Hector, see Ector.
Hecuba, see Ekeuba.
Helen, see Elen.

Hercules, see Ercules.
Hesione, see Isyon, Ysyon.

Jason, see Jaso.
Jesus, see Jesu.
Jesus Christ, see Jhesu Cryst.
Jupiter, see Jubiter.

Laomedon, see Lamatan.
Latin, see Latyn.
Libya, see Lybye.
Lycomedes, see Likamedes.

Macedonia, see Macendoyne.
Mahomet, see Mahomid.
Menelaus, see Menaly.
Menestheus, see Monastew.
Mycene, see Messen.

Neoptolemus, see Neptalamus.

Olympias, see Olimpias.
Orchomenus, see Orkemere.

Palamedes, see Palmydes.
Patroclus, see Padradod.
Peleus, see Pelles (b).
Pelias, see Pelles (a).
Peloponnesus, see Pelpeson.
Phrygia, see Fygry.
Phylace, see Colapy, Polleke.
Podarces, see Podane.
Pollux, see Pollex (a).
Polypoetes, see Annys.

BIBLIOGRAPHY.

[A selected list of printed books and articles relating to the mediæval Troy Cycle.]

Albertus Stadensis, Troilus, ed. Merzdorf, Leipzig, 1875.

Amador de los Rios, Historia Critica de la Literatura Española, Madrid, 1863.

D' Ancona, Due Farse del Secolo XVI, Scelta di Curiosità Lett., Disp. 187 ; Studi di Critica Storia e di Letteraria, Bologna, 1880.

Audigier, L'Origine des François et de leur Empire, Paris, 1676.

Barbour's des Schottischen Nationaldichters Legendensammlung, nebst den Fragmenten seines Trojaner Krieges, ed. Horstmann, Heilbronn, 1881–82.

Bartoli, I Codici Francesi della Biblioteca Marciana di Venezia, Venice, 1872 ; I Poemi del Ciclo Trojano, Archivio Veneto, III, Venice, 1872 ; Storia della Letteratura Italiana, Florence, 1878.

Bartsch, Albrecht von Halberstadt und Ovid im Mittelalter, Quedlinburg, 1861.

Beauvois, Histoire Légendaire des Francs et des Burgondes aux III et IV Siècles, Paris, 1867.

Benoît de Sainte-More et le Roman de Troie, ed. Joly, Paris, 1870–71.

    Fischer, Der Altfranzösische Roman de Troie des Benoît de Sainte-More als Vorbild für die Mittelhochdeutschen Troja-Dichtungen des Herbort von Fritzlâr und des Konrad von Würzburg, Neuphilologische Studien, Heft 2, Paderborn, 1883.

    Jäckel, Dares Phrygius und Benoît de Sainte-More, Breslau, 1875.

    Joseph, Dares Phrygius als Quelle für die Briseida-Episode im Roman de Troie des Benoît de Sainte-More, Gröbers Zeit. für Rom. Philol., VIII, 177.

    Fromman, Herbort von Fritzlâr und Benoît de Sainte-More, Germania, II, 39.

    Constans, La Langue du Roman de Troie, Revue des Universités du Midi, Tome I, No. 16.

Papa, Giornale Storico della Lett. Ital., II, 192 (Ital. prose version of Benoît).

Settegast, Benoît de Sainte-More, die Chronique des Ducs de Normandie und der Roman de Troie, Breslau, 1876.

Bernhardus Floriacensis, De Excidio Troiæ, ed. Du Méril, Poésies Populaires Latines Antérieures au Douzième Siècle, Paris, 1843.

Dunger, Phil. Anz., V.

Ovidii Erotica, ed. Goldast, 193.

Bernhardy, Grundriss der Griech. Lit., Halle, 1852–59 ; Grundriss der Röm. Lit., Halle, 1830.

Birch-Hirschfeld, Über die den Provenzalischen Troubadours des 12. und 13. Jahrhunderts Bekannten Epischen Stoffe, Halle, 1878.

Boccaccio, Filostrato, Opere Volgari, Florence, 1831.

Bartoli, I Precursori del Boccaccio, Florence, 1876.

Crescini, Contributo agli Studi sul Boccaccio, Turin, 1887.

Hortis, Studi sulle Opere Latine del Boccaccio, Triest, 1879.

Körting, Boccaccios Leben und Werke, Leipzig, 1880.

Novati, Istoria di Patroclo e d' Insidoria, Turin, 1888. (Imitation of Boccaccio.)

De la Borderie, L' Historia Britonum Attribué à Nennius et l' Historia Britannica avant Geoffroi de Monmouth, Paris, 1883.

Braun, Die Trojaner am Rhein, Bonn, 1856.

Ten Brink, History of English Literature, Eng. Trans., New York, 1889–96.

Brunet, Manuel du Libraire et de l'Amateur de Livres, Paris, 1860–65, 1878–80.

Carmina Burana, Bibl. Soc. Lit. Stutgardiensis, 1847.

Caxton, The Recuyell of the Historyes of Troye, translated from Raoul Lefèvre, ed. Sommer, London, 1894.

Chassang, Histoire du Roman dans l'Antiquité Grecque et Latine, Paris, 1862.

Chaucer, Troilus and Criseyde, ed. Skeat, Complete Works of Geoffrey Chaucer, Oxford, 1894.

Lounsbury, Studies in Chaucer, New York, 1892.

Ten Brink, Chaucer, Studien zur Geschichte seiner Entwickelung, Münster, 1870.

Kissner, Chaucer in seinen Beziehungen zur Italienischen Literatur, Bonn, 1867.

Eitner, Die Troilusfabel in ihrer Literaturgeschichtlichen Entwickelung, Shakesp.-Jahrb., III, 252.

Belleza, Introduzione allo Studio dei Fonti Italiani di G. Chaucer.
Hertzberg, Shakesp.-Jahrb., III, 252; VI, 169.
Delius, Dryden und Shakespeare, Shakes.-Jahrb., IV, 23.
Mamroth, Geoffrey Chaucer, seine Zeit und seine Abhängigkeit von Boccaccio, Berlin, 1872.
Sandras, Étude sur Chaucer Consideré comme Imitateur des Trouvères, Paris, 1859.
Koch, Chaucer im Verhältnis zu seinen Quellen, Sitz. der Berl. Gesellsch. für das Stud. der Neueren Sprachen, 1887–88.
Schipper, Chaucer's Troilus und Criseyde, Oesterreich. Rundschau, Heft 1.
Furnivall, Trial Forewords, Chauc. Soc. Pub., Series II, No. 6.
Rossetti, Chauc. Soc. Pub., Series I, Nos. 44 and 65 (comparison of Troilus and Criseyde with the Filostrato).
Broatch, Indebtedness of Chaucer's Troilus to Benoît's Roman, Journ. Germ. Philol., II.
Cholevius, Geschichte der Deutschen Poesie nach ihren Antiken Elementen, Leipzig, 1854–56.
Chronicon Altinate, ex Ms. Codice Regiæ Bibliothecæ Dresdensis, Archivio Storico Italiano, Appendice, V, 37.
Comparetti, Vergilio nel Medio Evo, Livorno, 1872.
Dütschke, Vergil im Mittelalter (trans. of Comparetti), Leipzig, 1875.
Constans, La Légende d'Oedipe, Étudiée dans l'Antiquité, au Moyen Âge, et dans les Temps Modernes, Paris, 1881.
Dares Phrygius, De Excidio Troiæ Historia, ed. Smids, Amsterdam, 1702; Dederich, Bonn, 1835; Meister, Leipzig, 1873.
Collilieux, Étude sur Dictys de Crète et Darès de Phrygie, Grenoble, 1836; Deux Éditeurs de Virgile, Grenoble, 1887.
Dunger, Anzeige von Meisters Dares-Ausgabe, Fleckeisen's Jahrb., 1873, Heft 7.
Haupt, Dares, Malalas, und Sisyphos, Philologus, XL, 107.
Meister, Dares Phrygius, Breslau, 1871.
Paris, Historia Daretis de Origine Francorum, Romania, III, 129; Revue Critique, 1874, No. 19.
Wagener, Beitrag zur Dares Phrygius, Philologus, XXXVIII.
See Dictys.
Dederich, Der Franckenbund, Hannover, 1873.
Dernedde, Ueber die den Altfranzoesischen Dichtern Bekannten Epischen Stoffe aus dem Alterthum, Erlangen, 1887.

Dictys Cretensis, Ephemeridos Belli Trojani Libri Sex, ed. Mercerus, Paris, 1618; Dederich, Bonn, 1833; Meister, Leipzig, 1872.

Dunger, Dictys-Septimius, Ueber die Ursprüngliche Abfassung und die Quellen der Ephemeris Belli Trojani, Dresden, 1878.

Körting, Dictys und Dares, ein Beitrag zur Geschichte der Troja-Sage in ihren Uebergange aus der Antiken in die Romantische Form, Halle, 1874.

Brünnert, Sallust und Dictys Cretensis, Progr. des Gymn. zu Erfurt, 1883.

Pratje, Quæstiones Sallustianæ, Göttingen, 1874.

See Dares.

Lodovico Dolce, L' Achille e l' Ennea, Venice, 1571–72.

Dunger, Die Sage vom Trojanischen Kriege in den Bearbeitungen des Mittelalters und ihre Antiken Quellen, Leipzig, 1869.

Egger, Mémoires de Littérature Ancienne, Paris, 1862.

Eneas, ed. Salverda de Grave, Halle, 1891.

Heyse, Romanische Inedita, Berlin, 1856.

Hild, La Légende d'Énée, Revue de l'Histoire des Religions, VI.

Pey, Essai sur li Romans d'Eneas, Paris, 1856.

Parodi, I Rifacimenti e la Traduzioni Italiane dell' Eneide di Virgilio prima del Rinascimento, Studi di Filol. Romanza, II.

Fabricius, Biblioth. Lat. Med. et Inf. Ætat., Florence, 1858.

Florentinus Turonensis, De Destructione Constantinopolitanæ sive De Ultione Trojanorum contra Græcos, Paris, 1496.

Fornaciari, Studi su Dante Editi e Inediti, Milan, 1883.

Fréret, De l'Origine des Français et de leur Établissement dans les Gaules, Œuvres, ed. 1796, Vols. 5 and 6.

Fuchs, De Varietate Fabularum Troicarum.

Gaspary, Geschichte der Ital. Literatur, Strassburg, 1885–88.

Gervinus, Geschichte der Poetischen National-Literatur der Deutschen, Leipzig, 1871–74.

Gest Hystoriale of the Destruction of Troye, ed. Panton and Donaldson, E. E. T. S., Nos. 39 and 56, 1869–74.

Brandes, Die Mittelenglische Destruction of Troy und ihre Quelle, Eng. Stud., VIII, 389.

Bock, Zur Destruction of Troy, Halle, 1883.

Gidel, Études sur la Littérature Grecque Moderne, Paris, 1866.

Ginguené, Histoire Littéraire d'Italie, Paris, 1811–35, 9 vols.; 2d ed., 1824–35, 14 vols.

Gorra, Testi Inediti di Storia Trojana, Turin, 1887.

Graesse, Die Grossen Sagenkreise des Mittelalters, Dresden and Leipzig, 1842.

Graf, Roma nella Memoria e nelle Immaginazioni del Medio Evo; Turin, 1882–83.

Greif, Die Mittelalterlichen Bearbeitungen der Trojanersage, Marburg, 1886.

W. Grimm, Ueber die Sage von der Trojanischen Abkunft der Franken, Kleinische Schriften, I, 204. Cf. Greif, sec. 2.

Gröber, Grundriss der Romanischen Philologie, Strassburg, 1888–97.

Guido delle Colonne, Historia Destructionis Trojæ. "Guido's Historia was first printed at Louvain (?), 1475; then at Cologne, 1477, in quarto; and at Strassburg in 1486, 1489, and 1494, in folio."—Sommer.

    Barth, Guido de Columna, Leipzig, 1877.

    Douce, Illustrations of Shakespeare and of Old Manners, London, 1807.

    Dunlop, History of Fiction, ed. Wilson, London, 1888.

    Gaspary, Die Sicilianische Dichterschule des 13 Jahrhunderts, Berlin, 1878.

    Mussafia, Über die Spanischen Versionen der Historia Trojana, Vienna, 1871; Sulle Versioni Italiane della Storia Trojana, Sitzungberichte der Wiener-Academie, Phil.-Hist. Classe, 1870–71.

    Nyerup, Almindelig Morskabsläsning i Danmark og Norge, 1816.

    Morel-Fatio, Romania, IV, 83.

Hector romances, see Joly, Benoît de Sainte-More, p. 853, note; Gorra, p. 265.

Heeger, Über die Trojanersage der Britten, Munich, 1886.

Heinrich von Braunschweig, excerpts in Dederich's Dictys and Dares.

    Hagen and Büsching, Literar. Grundriss zur Geschichte der Deutschen Poesie, Berlin, 1812.

Herbert von Fritslâr, Liet von Troye, ed. Fromman, Bibl. der Gesammt. Nat.-Lit., V, Quedlinburg and Leipzig, 1837.

Heywood, Life and Death of Hector, 1614 (modernization of Lydgate's Troy Book); The Iron Age, London, 1632.

Hildebert of Tours, ascribed to: anonymous Fall of Troy, Migne's Patrologia, Lat. Series. (Passages in common with Bernhardus.) Cf. Simon Capra Aurea.

Histoire Littéraire de la France, par des Religieux Bénédictins de la
    Congrégation de Saint-Maur, Paris, 1733–1888.
Ideler, Geschichte der Altfranzösischen National-Literatur, Berlin,
    1842.
L' Intelligenza, ed. Carbone, Firenze, 1868; Gellrich, Breslau, 1883.
    Borgognoni, Studi d' Erudizione e d' Arte, I, Bologna, 1877.
Joannes Antiochenus, 'Αρχαιολογία, pub. Müller, Fragmenta Histori-
    corum Græcorum, IV, V.
    Friederich, Zu Johannes von Antiochia, Neue Jahrb. für Philol.
        und Pädag., VI, 416.
    Köcher, De Joannis Antiocheni Ætate Fontibus Auctoritate, Bonn,
        1871.
    Wollenberg, Über Einige Curiose Druckfehler in der C. Müller-
        schen Recension der Excerpte des Joannes Antiochenus, Zeit.
        für Deutsches Gymnasialwesen, 1860; Excerpta ex Joanne
        Antiocheno, Berlin, 1861.
Joannes Malalas, Χρονογραφία, ed. Dindorf, Niebuhr's Corpus Script.
    Hist. Byz., Part VIII, Bonn, 1831; Cramer, Anecdota Græca
    e Codd. Mss. Bibl. Reg. Paris., II, 197.
    Frick, Zur Kritik des Joannes Malalas, Festgabe an Ernst Curtius,
        1884.
    Jeep, Die Lücken in der Chronik des Malalas, Rhein Mus., Neue
        Folge, XXXVI.
    Körting, De Vocibus Latinis quæ apud Joannem Malalam . . . Inve-
        niuntur, 1879.
Joannes Parisiensis, De Gallica Origine Regnorum, A. Du Chesne's
    Historiæ Francorum Scriptores Coætanei, Paris, 1636–49.
Josephus Iscanus, De Bello Trojano, ed. Dresemius, Frankfort, 1620;
    Valpy's Classics, II, London, 1819.
    Sarradin, De Josepho Iscani Belli Trojani . . . Poeta, Versailles,
        1878.
De Julleville, Histoire de la Langue et de la Littérature Française,
    Paris, 1890, I.
Kedrenos, Σύνοψις 'Ιστοριῶν, ed. Bekker, Niebuhr's Corpus Script. Hist.
    Byz.
Konrad von Würzburg, Der Trojanische Krieg, ed. von Keller, Biblio-
    thek des Literarischen Vereins zu Stuttgart, No. 44, 1858.
    Bartsch, Notes to Konrad, Bibl. des Lit. Vereins zu Stuttgart,
        No. 133, 1877.
    Jacobs and Ukert, Beiträgen für Ältere Literatur, I, 435.

Körting, Grundriss der Geschichte der Englischen Literatur, Münster, 1893, sect. 110, 155, 162; Encyklopædie und Methodologie der Romanischen Philologie, Heilbronn, 1884–86.

Krusch, Die Chronicæ des Sog. Fredogar, N. Archiv d. Gesellsch. für Ältere Deutsche Geschichts-Kunde, VII, 249, 423.

Lange, Untersuchungen über die Geschichte und das Verhältnis der Nordischen und Deutschen Heldensagen, Frankfurt-am-Main, 1832.

Raoul Lefèvre, Recueil des Histoires de Troie, Paris, 1532.
    See Caxton.

Loebell, Gregor von Tours und seine Zeit, Leipzig, 1839.

Lüthgen, Die Quellen und der Historische Werth der Fränkischen Trojasage, Bonn, 1875.

John Lydgate, Troy Book, printed 1513 and 1555.
    Warton, History of English Poetry, ed. Hazlitt, London, 1871.

Jacob van Maerlant, Istory van Troyen, ed. de Pauw and Gaillard, Ghent, 1889–91.
    Verdam, Episodes, uit Maerlant's Historie van Troyen, Bibliotheek van Middelnederlandsche Letterkunde, 1874.
    Blommaert, Oudvlaemshe Gedichten, I, 27, II, 73, 93 (fragments incorrectly attributed to Segher); Theophilus, Gedicht der XIVe Eeuw Gevolgd door Negen Andere Gedichten uit de Middeleeuwen, Ghent, 1858.

Konstantinos Manasses, Σύνοψις Χρονική, ed. Bekker, Niebuhr's Corpus Script. Hist. Byz.

Di Marzo, Di un Codice in Volgare della Guerra di Troja di Anonimo Siciliano del Secolo XIV, Palermo, 1863.

Du Méril, Poésies Populaires Latines Antérieures au Douzième Siècle, Paris, 1843.

P. Meyer, Les Premières Compilations Françaises d'Histoire Ancienne, Romania, XIV, 63.

Micali, Storia degli Antichi Popoli Italiani, Firenze, 1849.

Mongitore, Bibliotheca Sicula, Palermo, 1708–14.

Jacques Milet, L'Istoire de Troye la Grant, ed. Stengel, Marburg, 1883.
    Meybrinck, Die Auffassung der Antike bei Jacques Milet, Guido de Columna, und Benoit de Ste.-More, Marburg, 1886.
    Wunder, Über Jacques Milets Destruction de Troye la Grant, Leipzig, 1868.
    Bekker, Die Mysterien Le Siège d'Orléans und La Destruction de Troye la Grant, 1886.

Moët de la Forte-Maison, Les Francs, leur Origine et leur Histoire, Paris, 1868.

Mone, Ueber die Franken, Anz. für Kunde der Deutschen Vorzeit, IV.

Morf, Notes pour Servir à l'Histoire de la Légende de Troie en Italie et en Espagne, Romania, XXI, 18.

Muratori, Rer. Ital. Scriptores, 1723–51.

Nyrop, Storia dell' Epopea Francese nel Medio Evo, trans. Gorra, Firenze, 1886.

G. Paris, La Littérature Française au Moyen Âge, Paris, 1890.

P. Paris, Les Manuscrits François de la Bibliothèque du Roi, Paris, 1836–48.

Paul, Grundriss der Germanischen Philologie, Strassburg, 1893.

Passano, I Novellieri in Verso.

Petit, Bibliographie der Meddelnederlandsche Taal en Letterkunde, Leiden, 1888.

Flavius Philostratus, Heroicus, ed. Kayser, Leipzig, Bibl. Teubner.

Pierre de Beauveau, Troilus, ed. Moland and D'Héricault, Nouvelles Françoises du XIVe Siècle, Paris, 1858.

Mussafia, Zum Roman de Troilus des Pierre de Beauveau, Vienna, 1869.

Pindarus Thebanus, Iliad, Poetæ Latini Minores, VIII, Paris, 1824.

Bæhr, Storia della Letteratura Romana, ed. Pomba, I, sect. 94.

Wernsdorff, Epitome ac Summa Universæ Iliados Homeri Pindaro Thebano Auctore.

Isaac Porphyrogennetos, Περὶ τῶν καταλειφθέντων ὑπὸ τοῦ Ὁμήρου, ed. Hinck, Polemonis Declamationes quæ Exstant Duæ, Leipzig, 1873.

Preller, Römische Mythologie, 3d ed., Berlin, 1881.

Quadrio, Storia e Rag. d' Ogni Poesia, IV, Bologna, 1739.

Rajna, Le Origini delle Famiglie Padovane, Romania, IV, 161; Ricerche intorno ai Reali di Francia, Bologna, 1872.

Regpauischen Chronik, ed. Bernoulli, Germania, XXVIII, 34 (poem based on Konrad). Cf. Greif, sect. 129.

Roelof die Smit, Die Vergaderinge der Historien van Troyen, Harlem, 1485.

Roth, Die Trojasage der Franken, Germania, I, 34.

Rudolph von Ems, Die Zwei Recensionen der Weltchronik Rudolphs von Ems, ed. Vilmar, Marburg, 1839.

Rydberg, Undersökningar i Germanisk Mythologi, Stockholm, 1886–89; Eng. Trans., Anderson, London, 1889.

Hans Sachs, Die Zerstorung der Mechtigen Stat Troya, ed. von Keller.

Schaefer, Abriss der Quellenkunde der Griech. und Röm. Gesch., Leipzig, 1882-85.

Schwegler, Römische Geschichte, Tübingen, 2d ed., 1867-72.

Segher Dengotgaf, Dits 't prieel van Troyen, Dits 't paerlement van Troyen, Dits van den groten Strijt daer hem her Hector ende Achilles in onderspraken, Blommaert, Oudvlaemsche Gedichten der XIIe, XIIIe, en XIVe Eeuwen, Ghent, 1838, I.

Gallée, Een Fragment van Segher's Parlement van Troyen volgens een Utrechtsch Handschrift, Tijdschrift voor Nederlandsche Taal en Letterkunde, II, 2.

Seege of Troye, ed. Zietsch, Herrigs Archiv, LXXII, 11; Über Quelle und Sprache des Mittelenglischen Gedichtes Seege oder Batayle of Troye, Kassel, 1883.

Fick, Zur Mittelenglischen Romanze Seege of Troye, Breslau Diss.

Granz, Über die Quellengemeinschaft des Mittelenglischen Gedichtes Seege oder Batayle of Troye und des Mittelhochdeutschen Gedichtes vom Trojanischen Kriege des Konrad von Würzburg, Leipzig, 1888.

Simon Capra Aurea, Iliad, Book I, ascribed to Hildebert of Tours, Migne's Patrologia, Lat. Series, CLXXI, Paris, 1854; Leyser, Versus de Excidio Trojæ, Historia Poetarum . . . Medii Ævi, Halle, 17—.

Teuffel, Geschichte der Römischen Literatur, 1875.

Tiraboschi, Storia della Lett. Ital., Modena, 1772-78.

Togail Troi, The Destruction of Troy, Transcribed from the Facsimile of the Book of Leinster and Translated by Whitley Stokes, Calcutta, 1882. Seventy copies, privately printed.

Tὰ Τρωικά, anonymous, ed. Mai, Bibliotheca Uffenbachiana, Halle, 1720.

Trojanska pricha bugarski i latinski na svijet izdas, ed. Miklošich, Agram, 1871.

Trojumanna Saga, ed. Sigurdsson, Annaler for Nordisk Oldkyndighed, Copenhagen, 1848.

Keyser, Nordmaendenes Videnskabelighed og Literatur i Middelalderen.

Joannes Tzetzes, Ante-Homerica, Homerica, et Post-Homerica, ed. Jacobs, Leipzig, 1793; Bekker, Berlin, 1816.

Vallet de Viriville, Notice sur la Geste des Nobles Français Descendus du Roi Priam, Notices et Extraits des MSS. de la Bibliothèque Impériale, XIX, 2e partie.

Heinrich von Veldeke, Eneit, ed. Behagel, Heilbronn, 1882.
Pey, L'Énéide de Henri de Veldeke et li Roman d'Eneas.
See Eneas.
Vossius, De Historicis Latinis, II, III, Frankfurt-am-Main, 1677.
Ward, Catalogue of Romances in the Department of MSS. in the
British Museum, I, London, 1883.
Wattenbach, Deutschlands Geschichtsquellen im Mittelalter, Berlin,
1877–78.
Welcker, Der Epische Cyclus oder die Homerischen Dichter, Bonn,
1835.
Wesselofsky, Matériaux et Récherches pour Servir à l'Histoire du
Roman et de la Nouvelle, Petersburg, 1889.
Wormstall, Die Herkunft der Franken von Troja, Münster, 1869.
Zarncke, Ueber die Sogenannte "Trojanersage der Franken," Berichte
über die Verhandlungen der Königl. Sächs. Gesellsch. der
Wissensch., Leipzig, 1866, XVIII, 257.
Zimmer, Nennius Vindicatus, Über Enstehung, Geschichte, und Quel-
len der "Historia Britonum," Berlin, 1883.

9 780469 396357